PROPAGANDA AND INFORMATION IN EASTERN INDIA 1939–45

Centre of South Asian Studies,
School of Oriental and African Studies,
University of London

LONDON STUDIES ON SOUTH ASIA

1. Caste and Christianity
   D.B. Forrester
2. British Policy Towards the Indian States
   S.R. Ashton
3. The Assamese
   A.C. Cantlie
4. Dacca
   S.U. Ahmed
5. Crime, Justice and Society in Colonial Sri Lanka
   J.W. Rogers
6. Hindu and Christian in South-East India
   G.A. Oddie
7. Muslims and Missionaries in Pre-Mutiny India
   A.A. Powell
8. A Place for Our Gods
   M. Nye
9. Khizr Tiwana, the Punjab Unionist Party and the Partition of India
   I. Talbot
10. John Bullion's Empire
    G. Balachandran
11. Landlord Power and Rural Indebtedness in Colonial Sind
    D. Cheeseman
12. Krsna's Round Dance Reconsidered
    H.R.M. Pauwels
13. Ancient Rights and Future Comfort
    P. Robb
14. Tibet and the British Raj
    A. McKay
15. Caste, Protest and Identity in Colonial India
    S. Bandyopadhyay
16. James Long of Bengal
    G.A. Oddie
17. Caste, Class and Catholicism in India 1789–1914
    K. Ballhatchet
18. The Great Indian Education Debate
    Lynn Zastoupil and Martin Moir
19. The Poetics of Devotion
    Rachel Dwyer
20. Propaganda and Information in Eastern India
    Sanjoy Bhattacharya

PROPAGANDA AND INFORMATION IN EASTERN INDIA 1939–45

A Necessary Weapon of War

Sanjoy Bhattacharya

NEW YORK AND LONDON

For Dada, Didi and Sangeeta

First published by Lawrence Erlbaum Associates, Inc., Publishers

Published 2009 by Routledge

Routledge
Taylor & Francis Group
711 Third Avenue,
New York, NY 10017

Routledge
Taylor & Francis Group
2 Park Square,
Milton Park, Abingdon,
Oxfordshire OX14 4RN

First issued in paperback 2016

Routledge is an imprint of the Taylor and Francis Group, an informa business

All rights reserved. No part of this book may be reprinted or reproduced or utilised in any form or by any electronic, mechanical, or other means, now known or hereafter invented, including photocopying and recording, or in any information storage or retrieval system, without permission in writing from the publishers.

British Library Cataloguing in Publication Data
A catalogue record of this book is available from the British Library

Library of Congress Cataloguing in Publication Data
A catalogue record for this book has been requested

ISBN 13: 978-1-138-98396-0 (pbk)
ISBN 13: 978-0-7007-1406-3 (hbk)

Contents

Acknowledgements	vi
Abbreviations	viii
Glossary	xi
List of tables	xiv

Introduction		1
Chapter One	The Second World War, Indian Nationalism and the Challenges of State Mobilisation in Eastern India: A Survey	17
Chapter Two	State Propaganda and Civilian Audiences in Eastern India 1939–45: Forms, Applications and Scope	65
Chapter Three	An Ancillary to Propaganda: State Censorship and the Civilian Population in Eastern India 1939–45	122
Chapter Four	The Colonial State, 'Neutrals' and the Propaganda Campaign against the Indian National Congress 1939–1944	150
Chapter Five	Propaganda, Censorship and the British Indian Army: Eastern India 1942–45	173
Conclusion		202
Bibliography		225
Index		238

Acknowledgements

I have accumulated a great number of debts during the preparation of this book. The first of these is to the many outstanding teachers I have had as a student: Muhammad Amin, Sumit Guha, Shiv Shankar Menon and Tanika Sarkar as an undergraduate; Neeladri Bhattacharya, Sabyasachi Bhattacharya, Bipan Chandra, Dipankar Gupta and Madhavan Palat as a postgraduate, and Peter Robb and David Arnold as a doctoral candidate.

I should also like to thank many other friends and colleagues for their help. I am grateful to Alfred Gell, Alex McKay, Andrew Wines, Anil Kumar, Anupama Roy, Basudev Chatterji, Biswamoy Pati, Bob Anderson, Chris Bayly, Chris Pinney, Clive Dewey, David Taylor, Frank Spooner, Gordon Johnson, Gurusharan Singh, Hal Dixon, Indrani Sen, Joya Chatterji, Jyoti Kumar, Kumkum Roy, Lionel Carter, Mark Harrison, Michael Worboys, Nariaki Nakazato, Niels Brimnes, Norbert Peabody, Manjiri Kamat, Partha Sarathi Gupta, Paul Greenough, Peter Cain, Philip Woods, Ramachandra Guha, Sarah Glynn, Simeran Gell, Shahid Amin, Sudipto Kaviraj, Tan Tai Yong, Tony Cox, Ujjwal Kumar Singh and Walter Hauser for their suggestions. A number of good people provided help consistently during the completion of the manuscript: Selwyn, Sangeeta, Biswamoy, Indrani (Sen) and Mick were great sources of support during a period of great pressure.

Mention must also be made of archival officers who helped me access a wide range of sources. Ram Iqbalji was, undoubtedly, the most memorable of archivists I encountered during the project. The trip to the Bihar State Archives in Patna might have been a complete waste but for his help: his knowledge regarding the location of sources in an otherwise disorganised repository provided the necessary incentive to continue work in a rather difficult research environment.

ACKNOWLEDGEMENTS

Indeed, the War Series Files, which provide the main backbone for many of my arguments, might never have been unearthed except for Iqbalji's initiative. To him, I remain truly grateful.

Valuable assistance was also provided in the Bihar State Archives by Rajiv Ranjan Prasad and Tara Saran Sinha, who was the Director in 1993. Rajib Sahoo and Jagmohan Singh at the National Archives of India, Mondal Da at the Nehru Memorial Museum and Library and Rekha Trivedi, Director of the Uttar Pradesh State Archives, also provided much assistance.

I am, of course, grateful to the Felix Scholarships Trust for funding the doctoral project that has led to this monograph. Extra monies for research were made also available by the School of Oriental and African Studies and the University of London's Central Research Fund during an extended stint of fieldwork in India. But, mention also needs to be made of the generous assistance provided by the Scouloudi Foundation, London, the Wellcome Trust, London, and Sheffield Hallam University, Sheffield. This provided the resources necessary to complete the research needed to convert my doctoral dissertation into a monograph.

However, my greatest debts lie with my extended family, which has provided me unstinting support and encouragement. Indeed, this book would probably not have been possible without Dada, Didi, Sangeeta, Papa, Mummy, Mashy, Ajit Mama, Bachchu Mama, Mimi, Florence, Faith, Gordon, Bipan, Pati Da, Indrani Di, Didibhai, Jyoti, Guru, Kavita and Chiara. To them, I remain grateful.

Abbreviations

AHQ	Allied Headquarters, India.
AICC	All India Congress Committee
AIR	All-India Radio
AITM	All India Training Manuals, General Headquarters, India
ALFSEA	Allied Land Forces in South East Asia
API	Associated Press of India
BBC	British Broadcasting Corporation
BSA	Bihar State Archives, Patna, India
CBI	Central Bureau of Information
CID	Central Intelligence Department
CIO	Central Intelligence Officer
CMP	Civilian Medical Practitioner
CSASA	Centre of South Asian Studies Archives, Cambridge, U.K.
CSFR(1)	Provincial Chief Secretary's confidential fortnightly reports for the first half of the month
CSFR(2)	Provincial Chief Secretary's confidential fortnightly reports for the second half of the month
CP	Central Provinces
CPI	Communist Party of India
CSP	Congress Socialist Party
DCC	District Congress Committee
DGIMS	Director General of Indian Medical Services
DIGP	Deputy Inspector General of Police
DMI	Director of Military Intelligence, General Headquarters, India.
DMS	Director of Medical Services
DSB	District Soldiers' Boards

ABBREVIATIONS

DSP	Deputy Superintendent of Police
DUA	Dundee University Archives, Scotland, U.K.
EHLDF	Education, Health and Lands Department Files, Government of India.
GHQ	General Headquarters, India.
GOA	Government of Assam
GOB	Government of Bihar
GOBe	Government of Bengal
GOBr	Government of Britain
GOI	Government of India
GOO	Government of Orissa
GOUP	Government of the United Provinces
HPF	Home Political Files, Government of India
HPF(I)	Home Political (Internal) Files, Government of India
HPubF	Home Public Files, Government of India
IAMC	Indian Army Medical Corps
IAR	Indian Annual Register
IB	Intelligence Bureau, Home Department, Government of India
ICS	Indian Civil Services
IESHR	Indian Economic and Social History Review
IFI	Information Films of India
IGP	Inspector General of Police
IMD	Indian Medical Department
IMS	Indian Medical Services
INC	Indian National Congress
INP	Indian News Parade
IPTA	Indian People's Theatre Association
JAS	Journal of Asian Studies
L	Generic designation for a department, India Office Records
MAS	Modern Asian Studies
MDF	Medical Department File, Government of United Provinces
MDF(I)	Medical Department File, Government of India
MOI	Ministry of Information, Government of Britain
NAI	National Archives of India, New Delhi, India
NMML	Nehru Memorial Museum and Library, New Delhi, India
NWFP	North West Frontier Province
OIOC	Oriental and India Office Collections, British Library, London

OSS	Office of Strategic Services
OWI	Office of War Information, Government of the United States of America
PCC	Provincial Congress Committee
PDGF	Political Department (Special Section) General Files, Government of Bihar
PF	Police Files, Government of India
PHDF	Public Health Department Files, Government of India
PPAF	Provincial Press Adviser Series Files, Government of Bihar
PRO	Public Record Office, Kew, Surrey, U.K.
PS	Police Station
QMG	Quartermaster General, India
RAF	Royal Air Force
RDP	Radical Democratic Party
Rs.	Rupees
SAR	South Asia Research
SEAC	South East Asia Command
SSI	Secretary of State for India, India Office, Government of Britain
TDMR	Thomas Duff & Co.'s Managers' reports for Directors
TOP	Transfer of Power volumes
UP	United Provinces
UPSA	Uttar Pradesh State Archives, Lucknow, India
USA	United States of America
USAF	United States Air Forces
VEC	Viceroy's Executive Council
WIS (II)	Weekly Intelligence Summaries (India Internal), GHQ, India
WO	War Office
WSF	War Series Files, Government of Bihar

Glossary

Ahimsa	Doctrine of non-violence.
Aman	Rice grown on low wet ground, sown July–August and reaped in December; winter rice, the main crop.
Anna	A denomination of currency, 1/16th of a rupee.
Ashram	Hermitage.
Badmash	'Bad character'; hoodlum.
Bai/Ben	Sister, title of affection and respect.
Bajra	The bulrush millet, a common food-grain.
Bania	Merchant, shop-keeper; money-lender.
Bazaar	Market.
Bhadralok	Literally 'respectable' but used in historical discourse as an analytical category to imply a status group in Bengal who came from the upper castes; were economically dependent on landed rents and professional and clerical employment and kept a distance from the masses.
Bigha	A measure of land, 1/3rd of an acre.
Busti/Basti	A collection of huts; slum; sometimes, locality.
Chaukidar	Watchman.
Crore	100 *lakhs* or 10 million.
Dal/Dhal	Lentils.
Dacoities	Robberies.
Daroga	Police official in charge of a police station.
Goonda	Hooligan; ruffian.
Gur	Raw cane sugar or date jaggery.
Gurudwara	Sikh place of worship.
Halal	The killing of a goat (or other animals) by the slitting of their throats and their gradual bleeding.
Hartal	Stoppage of work; strike

Hat/Haat	Rural or urban market
Jatra	Play performed in the open
Jawar/Jowar	A type of millet
Jhatka	Literally a vigorous push, but used here in the context of the beheading of a goat with a single stroke of a blade.
Katha	Religious meeting.
Kisan Sabhas	Peasant Associations
Kharif	Autumn harvest
Lakh	One hundred thousand.
Lathi	Stick.
Madrassi/Madrasi	Native of Madras Presidency; generically used for speakers of any of the South Indian languages.
Mahajan	Merchant, dealer, banker, creditor, money-changer.
Marwari	Strictly, a native of Marwar in Rajputana; often settled elsewhere in India; usually a banker or merchant.
Masjid	Mosque.
Maulana	Muslim theologian.
Maulavi/Moulvi	A term used for a Muslim doctor of law or a Muslim learned man; also applies to a Muslim gentleman.
Maund	A measure of weight varying in different localities; the standard maund is 82.28 lbs.
Mofussil	Countryside as distinct from town; rest of district/province as distinct from its headquarters/capital.
Mohalla/Muhalla	Locality.
Palla	A musical, often performed in the open.
Pallawallah	Theatrical troupe.
Panchayat	Village council.
Pie/pice/paisa/paise	Unit of money of the value of 1/12 th of an *anna*.
Rabi	Spring harvest; crop sown after the rains and reaped in the first 3 or 4 months of the year.
Raiyat/Ryot	Peasant; cultivator.
Raj	British rule.
Santhal	A tribe of the Chota Nagpur area of Bihar, Bengal and Orissa.
Sanyasi	Hindu ascetic; travelling mendicant.
Satyagraha	A term used to denote the non-violent resistance movement launched by Gandhi against the British *Raj*.

GLOSSARY

Seer	2.057 lbs; 40 *seers* equals 1 maund.
Swaraj	Self rule; political independence.
Tahsildar	Officer in charge of a subdivision of a district; officer in charge of revenue collection in a zamindar's estate.
Talukdar	Landlord/tenure holder, usually collector of rent from *raiyats*.
Thana	Police station.
Zamindar	Landlord.
Zindabad	Long live! Long life to!

List of Tables

1.1 The progressive rise in the budget of the Engineering
    Department, GOI, 1939–44   20
1.2 Strength of the regular army (including British troops)
    in India between July 1939 and September 1943   24
1.3 Electorate for the provincial legislative assemblies in
    Eastern India during the elections of 1937   39
1.4 Strength of armed and unarmed police in the province of
    Eastern India as on 1 January 1943   42
2.1 Range of transmissions from A.I.R. stations in India   66
2.2 The distribution within India of a consignment of wireless
    sets sent from America in April 1943   70
2.3 The Government of India's total expenditure on film
    publicity between 1940 and 1945 (in rupees)   72
2.4 The number of copies of the Information Films of India and
    the Indian News Parade released every week between 1943–45   73
2.5 The Government of India's expenditure (in rupees) on
    printing, 1939–43   77
2.6 Average daily number of workers employed in factories
    (covered by the Factories Act of 1934) between 1939
    and 1945   85
3.1 A comparison of the circulation figures of the British and
    the Indian owned newspapers published in English in 1939   126
3.2 Circulation figures of vernacular newspapers (entirely
    owned by Indian firms) in 1939   136
5.1 Battle and Non-battle casualties (hospital admissions) for
    the British Indian Army based in the Indo-Burma Front,
    Burma and SEAC (excluding Ceylon), 1942–45   175
5.2 Wartime shortages of nursing staff in the military medical
    establishment in India   177

Introduction

This monograph represents an attempt to study the British colonial state in South Asia during the Second World War (1939–45) through an analysis of its policies of propaganda and information control. The primary regional focus of the book is the eastern part of the sub-continent: the area covered by colonial Assam, Bengal, Bihar, Orissa and eastern United Provinces, which was widely considered to be open to the threat of a Japanese invasion after December 1941. The region was, as a result, converted into the primary staging point for a massive Allied army in South Asia, which helped provision nationalist China till the end of the war, fight back the anticipated Japanese attacks and, then, lead a successful counter-attack against Axis forces in Burma and South-East Asia. The relative rarity of detailed studies delving into the impact of the Second World War on South Asia, despite the conflict's undoubted significance to the region's society, economy and polity, is therefore striking.[1] We have available only two empirically rich, but somewhat dated, studies of the wartime economy;[2] and one detailed examination of wartime political and military high-policy.[3] Moreover, the existing studies dealing with the last decade of British rule in India tend to treat, almost without exception, the wartime period as a passing phase between the twin historical landmarks of provincial autonomy and sub-continental partition.[4]

This deficiency in existing historiography has been exacerbated further by the continuing tendency amongst social scientists dealing with South Asia to study disparate episodes occurring during the wartime period in isolation, usually with minimal reference to the effects of the war on colonial economy and society.[5] This bias can be clearly seen in examinations of the 'Quit India' upsurge (the movement started in August 1942 after the arrest of Indian National

Congress members),[6] the Bengal Famine of 1943-44,[7] the creation and activities of the Indian National Army in South East Asia,[8] and the principal battles in North-Eastern India between 1944 and1945.[9] This study, on the other hand, is an attempt to bring the Second World War to the centre-stage, which is sought to be studied by using a more nuanced understanding of the British colonial state in South Asia and its wartime polices of propaganda and information.[10]

I. The British Colonial State in South Asia

There is a widespread tendency to treat the colonial state in South Asia as a monolithic entity. This has taken many forms. Some historians disclose such an understanding of the state by taking the central government's capacity to ensure the absolute implementation of its policies in the provinces for granted. Others, while recognising the role of Indian officials in weakening or slowing official initiatives, especially at the district and sub-divisional levels of administration, have never accorded them a formal role within the structure of the state, referring to them, instead, as Indian politicians, village administrators, rural magnates or even informants. These studies have been broadly united by an attempt to highlight the distinction between 'Indian' local self-government versus a well-defined 'British' structure of central and provincial government. And ironically, works with a distinctly different bias have often strengthened this view, by clubbing the Indian administrators, especially its subordinate ranks, into other simplistic categories. Many nationalist histories, leaning left-ward or otherwise, have tended to refer to Indian officials either as 'collaborators' or 'nationalists', based on a very specific understanding of their role in 'strengthening' or 'weakening' the colonial state's interests. In all these cases, therefore, the state is seen as being an essentially British edifice, with a sprinkling of senior and – typically powerless and paper pushing – senior Indian officials, which was propped up by a diverse set of crucial collaborative networks, dominated by Indian 'elites', 'magnates', 'politicians', 'loyalists' and 'informants'.

But, the administrative circumstances of colonial rule had always been much more complex. While policy-making powers within the military, a critically significant segment of the state apparatus, remained a closely monitored preserve of a British-dominated command structure right till 1947, the regular experiments with civilian government during the late nineteenth and the twentieth centuries brought in a number of Indians into positions of administrative power. Indeed, it is well recognised that an important, but possibly underscored, aim of the ever-broadening scope of local self-government was to tie the interests that dominated the new bodies more closely to imperial needs, while allowing a degree of autonomy in local administrative matters.

Nevertheless, studies examining the colonial state and its policies have tended to ignore, or at least, severely downplay, the fact that the individuals dominating the municipal boards, Indian or European, considered themselves to be a part of the larger administrative edifice established by the Raj and were necessarily required to deal with a range of other state officials of various services and ranks, a vast majority of whom were Indians, on a day to day basis. A detailed analysis of these interactions has been largely ignored in the historiography dealing with colonial South Asia, as has an assessment of the attitudes of the subordinate ranks of the central and provincial services to changes in administrative practise, political developments and, in the specific context of this study, to the events accompanying the Second World War.

Moreover, it has never really been acknowledged by those involved in examining state policy in colonial South Asia that the nature of interaction between the various grades of bureaucrats and services, and their activities within their respective spheres of influence, could never be completely determined by senior officials in charge of the central and provincial administrations. This is despite the fact that a great bulk of the existing archival material detailing the official correspondence between the centre and provinces during the twentieth century consistently highlights an inclination within, and the ability of, the district administration to adapt and modify orders in response to a variety of pressures emanating from within their respective localities. Local social and political relations, the infrastructural capabilities and constraints of a certain administrative set-up, and culturally informed opposition to particular Government of India policies could, and did, determine the extent of their implementation by local officials throughout the period of British rule in India.[11]

It is in this particular context that this work differs greatly from both the existing studies of the impact of the Second World War on the colonial state and its dealings with Indian nationalism. The conscious effort to study and compare policy and its effects at the different levels of administration – centre, province, district and sub-division – makes this monograph different from Johannes Voigt's valuable examination of military and civilian high-policy.[12] At the same time, the very superficial similarities between the terminologies used in this study and those present in an as yet-unpublished doctoral thesis, by Indivar Kamtekar, should not be allowed to detract from the fundamental methodological distinctions in the two works. Kamtekar's work has relied almost completely on the concept of an autonomous state, whose officials – of various administrative ranks, of social classes, and perhaps, even of races – seem to be united and driven by a set of policy concerns determined in civil and military high commands. These state functionaries, both military and civil, despite differences in their ranks and/or specific administrative contexts, are, thus, considered to be largely separated from the needs and influences of civil society.[13] This work, on the other hand, downplays the notion of state autonomy and does not confuse one's identification of being a part of a particular administrative structure with an unquestioning willingness to implement orders from higher authorities. Indeed, by highlighting the concerns evoked by – and strategies created during – war, the colonial state is seen here as a multi-layered administrative edifice, where officials were given – or sometimes took – the autonomy to interpret policy within their particular localities.

Therefore, the centralisation of wartime policy – or the 'militarisation' of the state, as it is often referred to – is not assumed to be either a smooth or simple process, which could be simply ensured by the mere passage of comprehensive legislative measures.[14] In underlining the great difference in passing special wartime laws, and having the capacity to implement them, an effort is made in this study to describe the difficulties encountered by the central government and General Headquarters (India) in ensuring the implementation of their vision of the mobilisation of a region totally unprepared for war. This study, therefore, examines the complexity of official relations between – and within – the Government of India, the provincial governments and the district administration on the civilian side; and the General Headquarters (India), the Eastern and South East Asia Command HQs and the local formations based in the region on the military side.

II. Propaganda, Information and 'Hegemony'

Historical works dealing with the uses of propaganda in colonial South Asia have unfortunately been greatly influenced by definitions predominating the historiography dealing with the uses of information in Europe.[15] There has, therefore, been a common tendency to employ the term to denote the conscious distribution of fallacious information. Whereas these pejorative associations have been most visible in politically-inspired polemics, where the term has been utilised to describe the supposed evils of certain organisations or individuals,[16] it has also been noticeable in more serious academic studies. The ambiguities of the meanings of, and the ideological baggage that has been attached to, propaganda has, for instance, been highlighted by Gyanendra Pandey, who has referred to the term in inverted commas in a piece dealing with Congress activism in the United Provinces.[17] Indeed, the sinister connotations linked to propaganda have been remarkably persistent in a wide range of academic writing dealing with the colonial period.[18]

But, such an approach is unnecessarily limiting for the historian dealing with British India; its rigidity disallowing one to unravel the great complexity accorded to propaganda policies in colonial administrative practise. For instance, while the Indian National Congress was often attacked through the use of what was recognised to be incorrect 'propaganda' (or news that was blown of out of proportion and context), the term 'propaganda' was also used to denote the description of welfare projects and schemes in operation.[19] Senior government officials, especially those at the level of the Government of India and provincial headquarters, would, of course, expect such initiatives to fortify support for the Raj, but developmental initiatives were also considered by many civil and military bureaucrats – especially in the districts and sub-divisions – as a contribution towards the requirements of a specific locality, or at the very least, sections of its population considered important.[20]

These complexities are clearly visible with regards to the nature and deployment of state propaganda during the Second World War. Official policies of information could consist, for instance, of what has been referred to, albeit in a related context, as a combination of 'facts, fiction, argument or suggestion', where the type of propaganda was determined by the intent behind its employment.[21] However, many officials in India, both military and civilian, would regularly use the term propaganda to describe general information about state policy, all of which, significantly, *did not* necessarily have to be flattering in tone. And perhaps more consequentially, propaganda was never solely equated with information, but also referred to a wide range of material benefits, which, in the context of a damaging war, covered a wide variety of items. Subsidised food, clothes and cooking media, as well medicines and medical aid were all seen as important propaganda items between 1942 and 1945, and the information released along with these benefits usually tended to describe little more than their mode, time and terms of distribution.

That the distribution of material resources were sometimes an integral part of larger public relations projects cannot, of course, be denied.[22] However, in other instances, and this is striking, material propaganda was sought to be released in order to counter the effects of acute economic and social problems, bereft of political messages, usually to maintain the law and order situation. Even though certain military and civilian officers could, and did, attribute strategic goals to such policies, bureaucrats based in the locality and employees of district boards were often informed by a sense of local accountability and, not infrequently, self-preservation. There were, very obviously, differing views about how to fight and mobilise the Indian Empire in support of the war, which is nowhere so clearly represented as in the definition, nature and deployment of the official policies towards propaganda and information between 1939 and 1945.

It is well worth re-stating here that the official efforts at mobilising the support of indigenous audiences for the colonial government and its policies through the distribution of print, oral and material propaganda, while suppressing views inimical to its own, were as old as the Raj itself. In fact, quite a few studies of the British experience in India have in recent years described how the generation and the control of information was important for the purposes of 'conquest, trade and government'.[23] But, the developments in the twentieth century, especially those during and after the First World War, and the growth of nationalist influence, presented the state with vastly increased challenges in the related fields of propaganda deployment and information management.[24] The mobilisation of troops apart,[25] a growing nervousness in official circles about the damage incurred by the spread of nationalist activism into rural India brought about a re-organisation of the policies of propaganda and information.[26] In creating such a new system, great importance was unsurprisingly given to catering to the needs of the Punjab – the army's primary recruiting area – which saw the establishment of District Soldier's Boards that were 'used as centres for disseminating counter propaganda against Congress and other anti-government organisations'.[27]

However, the scope of the new structures of propaganda and information control was expanded to cover the other provinces as well, and this was demonstrated, amongst other things, by the creation of a new Central Bureau of Information, which was formally established on 1 June 1919.[28] Aside from the production of a variety of propaganda material, the Bureau also assisted the central and provincial government departments, and semi-official organisations to develop special publicity agencies to highlight administrative improvements and rural development schemes, especially during periods of Congress-sponsored agitations. For instance, bodies called *Aman Sabhas* were established in all the 48 districts of the United Provinces during the Non-Cooperation movement of 1920–21.[29] Similarly, a 'network of propagandism' consisting of district, *tehsil*, *pargana* and village leagues was put into place during the Civil Disobedience movements of the 1930s. The efforts of their 'non-official' members were complemented by those of the District Magistrates, Commissioners, Sub-Divisional Officers and District Publicity Officers, who held a series of *durbars* and lecture tours,[30] and maintained during the upsurge of 1932.[31] Though the Civil Disobedience movement of 1932 was withdrawn two years later, the Government of India persisted with attempts to contradict Congress criticisms of the Raj and of the nature of the constitutional reforms.[32]

The policy of attacking the Indian National Congress's leadership's viewpoint in official propaganda continued till 1937, when the preparations for the provincial elections caused the authorities to decide to adopt a neutral attitude towards the event and its participants: Reginald Maxwell, then Deputy Secretary to the Government of India's Home Department, mentioned that the idea of organising a propaganda campaign against the All India Congress Committee had been dropped since it would place the official agencies 'on doubtful ground'.[33] The subsequent formation of 'popular' ministries meant that the overt publicity attacks against the Congress were suspended at all levels of the administration, and this policy was only reversed after the souring of relations immediately after the outbreak of the Second World War.[34] Indeed, the ministry period witnessed an uneasy truce, especially in the Congress-controlled provinces, where the alliance was characterised by the concerted monitoring – and denunciation – of the restive, and usually left-wing, elements within or without government. There were, nevertheless, other arenas, where the temporary rapprochement between the bureaucrats attached to the state and the ministerial functionaries were much less well defined. The Congress ministries's efforts to re-shape provincial government, especially in their dealings with local administration, were usually viewed with a degree of suspicion. In the context of this study, it is more relevant that influential elements in both camps shared a common, albeit occasionally simplistic, belief about the capacity of all welfare initiatives to popularise regimes.[35]

This, in turn, causes one to query the usefulness of applying the notion, and interpretations, of 'hegemony' in this analysis of propaganda policy and information control during the Second World War. Recent research has, of course, highlighted the dangers of using exaggerated forms of Gramscian notion of 'cultural hegemony', which is treated as an instrument allowing the 'British' state, or an undifferentiated 'British ruling class', comprehensive political and ideological control.[36] A comparatively more fruitful approach has been to locate the 'ways in which colonial ideology served the ruling class by helping to make their rule appear natural and legitimate'.[37] But, the debates regarding the uses and limits of colonial hegemony once again raise questions about the structure of the colonial state. When Douglas Haynes points out that colonial hegemony was both *negotiated* and *limited*, as 'indigenous figures were constantly reshaping the meaning of appropriated concepts', disallowing the Raj 'to penetrate many areas of indigenous culture', he, like many others, seems to be denying Indian officials a formal role within the state structure and administration of policy.[38] Similarly, Partho Chatterjee, in his reference to the creation of structural alliances between the Raj and 'traditional elites' on the basis of mutual self-interest, seems to downplay the fact that the colonial authorities, or at the very least elements of it, did indeed seek to strengthen their administrative capabilities by deploying increasing numbers of Indians in the formal structures of the state.[39]

This study, which seeks to study the attitudes of Indian officials working within the formal structures of the wartime state, thus, finds it easier to accommodate the argument that not all attempts by the colonial state to manufacture consent amongst the subject population constitute 'hegemony'.[40] Indeed, this work describes a situation wherein a difficult strategic crisis forced the colonial officers, both British and Indian, to deploy an array of strategies to ensure the effective mobilisation of the Second World War. In other words, the concept of 'hegemony' detracts from the approach utilised here because of its inclination to overestimate the solidarity of the colonial regime, which, at the risk of repetition, is a premise this study seeks to avoid studiously, as it negates the possibility of analysing the roles played by local administrative necessities in determining the ultimate form of implementation of policies designed by the Government of India.

Therefore, while the roles played by some of the Raj's institutions in moulding the attitudes and self-perceptions of at least certain sections of Indian society is not discounted, this work concentrates on examining the role played by the public relations structures developed especially to deal with the situation arising during the Second World War. Their activities were, needless to say, often integrated with the activities of the pre-existing publicity organs, but by and large, the scope of the new structures of propaganda and information control – like the challenges they were intended to tackle – were completely new. In other words, the attempts to manufacture consent between 1939 and 1945 were usually only marginally linked to older hegemonic 'projects', as unexpected strategic challenges forced the Government of India to come up with a variety of new measures that were intended to gain the support of some groups, while scaring others into political inaction.

An effort is also made in this work to underline the capacity of audiences to inform the shape of official propaganda and information policies. The unwillingness to recognise the importance of delineating the target audiences has often prevented historians from making empirical distinctions between policy deployment at different levels of government. Gerald Barrier provides a useful instance of this trend. His work on censorship does not define the target audience, and seeks to describe the state's stance towards the press and the publishing industry on the basis of descriptions provided by a few British central government employees, even though he notices that officials based at the different levels of the colonial state had varying attitudes towards the issue of proscription.[41] Milton Israel, similarly, fails to identify the groups targeted by the state's publicity networks and uses rather indeterminate categories, like 'the elite' and 'considerable sections of the population', to describe the audience. The results are plain to see. Israel, who examines the period between 1920 and 1947, views official wartime propaganda as merely constituting an intensive application of pre-existing publicity schemes, and fails to detail the structures specifically created, especially between 1942 and 1945, to cater to a much broader cross-section of Indian society.[42] The aim of the chapters that follow, by contrast, is to study official policies of propaganda and information control in Eastern India, at the different levels of colonial administration, during the Second World War. Based on archival material collected from a range of repositories, some hitherto unused, this work operates with the notion that the working of each administrative level was informed by the perspectives of, as well as the material and technological constraints facing, its employees. It, therefore, emphasises the existence of mutable official strategies at every level of the state apparatus, where bureaucrats sought to influence specific audiences and were, in turn, affected by them.

Notes

1 The only real exception is a recently released collection of essays, with an excellent article by Dr. Srimanjiri on wartime Bengal. The piece delineates the complexities of the Indian National Congress's – and the state's – political mobilisation in the province during a period of extreme food shortages. See, Srimanjiri, 'Denial, Dissent and Hunger: War-time Bengal, 1942–44', in B. Pati (ed), *Turbulent Times: India, 1940–44*, Mumbai, 1998, pp. 39–66.
2 See H. Knight, *Food Administration in India, 1939–47*, Stanford, 1954, and N.C. Sinha and P.N. Khera, *Indian War Economy [Supply, Industry and Finance]*, New Delhi 1962.
3 J.H. Voigt, *India in the Second World War*, New Delhi, 1987.
4 See, for example, K.K. Aziz, *The Making of Pakistan: A Study in Nationalism*, London, 1967; S. Sen, *Muslim Politics in Bengal 1937–47*, New Delhi, 1976; U. Kaura, *Muslims and Indian Nationalism: The Emergence of the Demand for India's Partition, 1928–40*, New Delhi, 1977, and A.I. Singh, *The Origins of the Partition of India, 1936–1947*, Delhi, 1987. A special issue of the journal *South Asia*, dealing with the Partition and colonial North India has, despite containing a series of extremely good essays on a range of new themes, done significantly little to highlight the significance of the war in accelerating the trends leading to the independence and division of the British Indian Empire. See, D.A. Low (ed), *South Asia, North India: Partition and independence*, Special Issue, Vol. XVIII, 1995.
5 The only possible exception to this is I. Kamtekar, 'The End of the Colonial State in India, 1942–47', Unpublished Ph.D. thesis, University of Cambridge, 1989.
6 See, for example, F.G. Hutchins, *Spontaneous Revolution The Quit India Movement* Delhi, 1971; A.C. Bhuyan, *The Quit India Movement, the Second World War and Indian Nationalism*, New Delhi, 1975; P.N. Chopra (ed), *Quit India Movement: British Secret Report*, Faridabad, 1976; G. Pandey (ed), *The Indian Nation in 1942*, Calcutta, 1988; P.R. Greenough, 'Political Mobilization and the Underground Literature of the Quit India Movement, 1942–44', *MAS*, 17,3, 1983; B. Chakrabarty, 'Political Mobilization in the Localities: The 1942 Quit India Movement in Midnapur', *MAS*, 26,4, 1992, and most recently, J. Masselos, 'Bombay, August 1942: Re-readings in a Nationalist Text', in Pati (ed), *Turbulent Times*, pp. 67–108.

7 See, for example, M.S. Venkataramani, *The Bengal Famine of 1943:The American Response*, Delhi, 1973; P.R. Greenough, 'Indian Famines and Peasant Victims: the case of Bengal in 1943–44', *MAS*, 14, 2, 1980; P.R. Greenough, *Prosperity and misery in modern Bengal: the famine, 1943–44*, New York, 1982; A.K. Sen, *Poverty and famines: An essay on entitlement and deprivation*, Oxford, 1981; A.K. Ghose, 'Food Supply and Starvation: A Study of Famines with reference to the Indian Sub-Continent', *Oxford Economic Papers*, 34, 2, 1982; O. Goswami, 'The Bengal Famine of 1943: re-examining the data', *IESHR*, 27,4, 1990; T. Dyson and A. Maharatna, 'Excess mortality during the Bengal famine: A re-evaluation', *IESHR*, 28, 3, 1991, A. Maharatna, 'Malaria Ecology, Relief Provision and Regional Variation in Mortality During the Bengal Famine of 1943–44', *SAR*, Vol. 13, No. 1, 1993.

8 See, for example, K.K. Ghosh, *The Indian National Army: The Second Front of the Indian Independence Movement*, Meerut, 1969, and J. Lebra, *Jungle Alliance: Japan and the Indian National Army*, Singapore, 1971.

9 See, for example, S.W. Kirby, *The Decisive Battles*, London, 1961; C.E. Lucas-Phillips, *Springboard to Victory*, London, 1966; A. Swinson, *The Battle of Kohima*, New York, 1967, and L. Allen, *Burma: The Longest War, 1941–45*, London, 1984.

10 Although the significance of the administrative uses of wartime intelligence and information has been hinted at, no detailed study of this aspect of official policy exists as yet. For references to deployment of state policies of information during the Second World War, see Kamtekar, 'The End of the Colonial State'; N. Narain, 'Co-option and Control: The Role of the Colonial Army in India, 1918–1947', Unpublished Ph.D. thesis, University of Cambridge, 1993, and M. Israel, *Communications and power: Propaganda and the press in the Indian nationalist struggle, 1920–1947*, Cambridge, 1994.

11 For a good analysis of the impact of local power relations on colonial policing, see D. Arnold, *Police Power and Colonial Rule: Madras, 1859–1947*, Delhi, 1986.

12 Voigt, *India in the Second World War*.

13 Kamtekar's thesis is openly driven by a conceptualisation of the state used in the work of Theda Skocpol. See, T. Skocpol, *States and Social Revolutions: A comparative analysis of France, Russia and China*, Cambridge, 1979. While Skocpol's framework seems relatively useful for studying the French Revolution of 1787, the Russian Revolution of 1917, and the Chinese experience between 1911 and 1960, its imposition on the British Indian context of the 1940s is far less compelling. In fact, Skocpol's analysis gives great significance to the capacity of major political and economic crises to force changes in class relations and contribute to, what she calls, 'social-revolutionary transformations'. Kamtekar's study, however, seems to completely marginalize the effects of class tensions on wartime politics, state structure and society. See, I. Kamtekar, 'The End of the Colonial State in India'.

14 A good example of the inclination to equate the creation of wartime legislation with the capability to implement them is provided by Indivar Kamtekar's work. Ibid. The great dangers of such assumptions is

powerfully highlighted in a recent, but rather simple-minded, analysis of the colonial state and its relationship with Indian nationalism. See, B. Chakrabarty, *Local Politics and Indian Nationalism: Midnapur, 1919–1944*, New Delhi, 1997.

15 The 1957 edition of the Penguin *Dictionary of Politics* describes propaganda as being 'Statements of policy or facts, usually of a political nature, the real purpose of which is different from their apparent purpose'. The term is defined further as 'a statement by a government or political party which is believed to be insincere or untrue, and designed to impress the public at large rather than to reach the truth or bring about a genuine understanding between opposing governments or parties'. Quoted in J.C. Clews, *Communist Propaganda Techniques*, London, 1964, p. 4. The pejorative associations attached to the term were largely a result of the Nazi use of propaganda, even though Joseph Goebbels was not the first to utilise it. See D. Welch, *The Third Reich: Politics and Propaganda*, London, 1993, p. 3.

16 For instance, see S.R. Goel, *Netaji and the CPI*, Bombay, 1962.

17 See, G. Pandey, 'Mobilization in a Mass Movement: Congress 'Propaganda' in the United Provinces (India), 1930–34', *MAS*, 9, 2, 1975.

18 Bhagwan Josh, for example, employs it to describe the communists' exaggerated and unsubstantiated claims about their strength in the Punjab. See, B. Josh, *Communist Movement in Punjab, 1926–47*, Delhi, 1979, p. 205. Bidyut Chakrabarty, like many others, uses the term to allude to the lack of authenticity of the content of particular pamphlets and documents. Chakrabarty, 'Political Mobilization in the Localities', p. 807.

19 The complexity of the situation is well-represented by the statement made by Lt Gen Thomas Hutton, the Secretary of the Reconstruction Committee of the VEC, in 1943, that 'We have yet to realise that a country can be very largely governed, as well as educated and reformed, by propaganda alone. The success of government, as of individuals, depends more on what people think of their achievements than on what they have actually done.' T. Hutton, Reconstruction Committee of Council, to G. Laithwaite, Secretary to Viceroy of India, 27 and 28 April 1943, document 672 in N. Mansergh and E.W.R. Lumby (eds), *India: The Transfer of Power*, iii, London, 1971. Hutton's statement is important precisely because it hints at the existence of a group of officials who hoped to be able to introduce a 'development' policy for India. However, the debates regarding the issue of post-war reconstruction reveals how such bureaucrats were isolated within the highest echelons of power by those preparing to negotiate for British withdrawal from empire. This issue is studied in greater detail in S. Bhattacharya and B. Zachariah, "A Great Destiny': The British Colonial State and the advertisement of post-war reconstruction in India, 1942–45', *SAR*, 19, 1, 1999.

20 Public relations apart, a range of British 'improvement' schemes of various kinds had been in existence for some time, especially in the traditional concerns of colonial economics: agriculture, agrarian debt and irrigation, and consequently village uplift. See, for instance, M.L. Darling, *The Punjab Peasant in Prosperity and Debt*, Oxford, 1925. Also see, C. Dewey,

Anglo-Indian Attitudes: The Mind of the Indian Civil Service, London, 1993.
21 P.M. Taylor, *Projection of Britain: British overseas publicity and propaganda*, Cambridge, 1981, p. 5.
22 While the allotment of a variety of benefits by the colonial administration, or the Congress, to selected audiences has been touched upon in a number of studies, their authors have not identified these as being integral components of larger propaganda policies. For example, while T.Y. Tan's description of the working of the District Soldiers' Boards in the Punjab refers to the distribution of a variety of economic benefits by the state apparatus within the colonial army's recruiting areas, he does not perceive these as having constituted a potent propaganda tool. T.Y. Tan, 'The Military and the State in Colonial India, 1900–1939', Unpublished Ph.D. thesis, University of Cambridge, 1992. Also see, T.Y. Tan, 'Maintaining the Military Districts: Civil-Military Integration and District Soldiers' Boards in the Punjab, 1919–1939, *MAS*, 28, 4, 1994. Srimanjiri points out that an outlawed 'Congress' organisation was able to increase its popularity and legitimise its standing in Midnapur (Bengal) through, amongst other things, relief measures organised after the devastating cyclone of October 1942. See, Srimanjiri, 'Denial, Dissent and Hunger', pp. 55–58.
23 C.A. Bayly, 'Knowing the Country: Empire and Information in India', *MAS*, 27, 1, 1993, p. 42. Also see, C.A. Bayly, *Empire & Information: Intelligence gathering and social communication in India, 1780–1870*, Cambridge, 1996; A. Farooqui, *Smuggling As Subversion: Colonialism, Indian Merchants and the Politics of Opium*, New Delhi, 1998, and P.G. Robb, *The Evolution of British Policy towards Indian Politics, 1880–1920: Essays on Colonial Attitudes, Imperial Strategies and Bihar*, New Delhi, 1992, p. 293.
24 Describing the effects the First World War, Sumit Sarkar declares that '... the War affected Indian life through massive recruitment, heavy taxes and war loans, and a very sharp rise in prices, and may be directly related to the two-fold extension of the national movement – towards considerable sections of the peasantry and towards business groups – which manifested itself immediately afterwards under Gandhi. In both cases – as well as with industrial labour which, also made a spectacular entry onto the national stage in the immediate post-war years – what is repeatedly evident is a combination of multiplying grievances with new moods of strength or hope: the classic historical formula for a potentially revolutionary situation'. S. Sarkar, *Modern India, 1885–1947*, Delhi, 1983, pp. 168–169.
25 The pressures imposed by India's participation in the First World War caused the colonial authorities to develop new networks of propaganda in the primary recruiting centres for the army and its ancillary services, as well as the other provinces. M. Israel, *Communications and power*, p. 29. In all 1,161,489 soldiers were recruited in India between August 1914 and November 1918 to fight in all the major strategic theatres of the First World War. In addition, the Government of India made a 'gift' of 100 million pounds to the British war-effort at the outbreak of the war

(followed by a further contribution of 45 million pounds in 1918). See A.L. Levkovsky, *Capitalism in India: Basic Trends in its Development*, Bombay, 1966, p. 96.

26 Israel has described how, 'A priority for the immediate post-war years was the establishment of an information system that would allow it to compete with other users, particularly with the developing communications network of the nationalist movement.... Public opinion, whatever its perceived quality had become important to the Government of India and it was determined to influence it.' See, Israel, *Communications and power*, pp. 29–30. New networks were continually developed and deployed between 1914 and 1937, primarily to counter or to collect information about the effects of the Congress on indigenous opinion. The Joint Select Committee, while considering the 1918 Government of India Act in 1920, betrayed many of the fears plaguing colonial administrators located at the various levels of administration. The Committee was concerned about the fact that the case of those hostile to the authorities was 'becoming every day more widely disseminated by means of the vernacular press' and encouraged the mounting of a 'counter-propaganda' campaign. *Ibid.*, p. 31. These fears, and a belief in the use of official propaganda, remained unshaken a decade later. A note prepared in 1929 by J. Coatman, then the Government of India's Director of Public Information, declared that, 'Day by day, an enormous volume of this poisonous rubbish [anti-government propaganda] is broadcast, and it must be remembered that the number of Indian newspapers which are doing the daily broadcasting runs into some hundreds.... The vernacular press deserves something more than a passing mention, for, to my mind, there can be very little doubt that its influence is far greater than that of the English part of the press... the majority of them are anti-Government, [and] we thus have a regular spate of hostile criticism, and more or less violent abuse every day. The other case is but rarely presented to the masses, and the accumulated effect of the noxious matter which they tend to imbibe from the newspapers every day must be very great. The document concluded by suggesting the mobilisation of various schemes of 'counter-propaganda', notably by encouraging landowners and 'big business' to organise the publication of pro-government newspapers. Quoted in private demi-official letters from the Viceroy to the Governors of Madras, Bengal, Bombay, Agra and Oudh, Punjab, Bihar and Orissa, Central Provinces, and Assam, 23 March 1929, L/PO/3/3A, OIOC. Similar arguments were put forth in the Simon Commission report as well, which complained that, It is not fair... to the large body of citizens who are being invited to assume wider responsibilities and who are passing through a period of training and political education to leave them ignorant of all but one side of the case.... The need for a fair representation of policy and facts is not confined to India. The misleading effect on public opinion throughout the world is no less important to be kept in mind. We have already described the astonishing lengths to which a certain section of the Indian Press has gone in vilifying the Administration and attacking its servants...'. Quoted in confidential report on propaganda and publicity [by the Bengal Publicity Board], January 1932 to March 1933, p. 1, L/I/1/424, File 171/4, OIOC.

27 Tan, 'The Military and the State in Colonial India', p. 131. Tan has described how, 'Conferences and assemblies of retired soldiers and pensioned officers were regularly organised by the DSBs in military villages ... to remind them that their continued eligibility for land grants, jagirs, assignments of land revenues, special pensions, and other rewards depended not only upon their passive loyal behaviour, but more importantly, on their willingness to come out in open support of the state in times of trouble or disorder. If they failed to take an active part in helping government suppress sedition in their respective villages, they would be liable to have their pensions forfeited.' Ibid.
28 Memorandum on [official] publicity work in India, Home Department, GOI, 29 July 1920, L/PJ/6/1581, OIOC. For a detailed description of the activities of the Central Board of Information see retrenchment file, CBI, 12 July 1922, HPF(I) 857/1922, NAI.
29 M. Israel, *Communications and power*, pp. 41–42. Also see, note on publicity in UP, c.1932, L/PO/3/3A, OIOC. A good description of the deployment of the *Aman Sabhas* in different political contexts is also provided in P. Reeves, *Landlords And Governments in Uttar Pradesh: A study of their relations under Zamindari abolition*, Bombay, 1991.
30 Note on publicity in UP, c.1932, L/PO/3/3A, OIOC. Also see letter from W.S. Hopkyns, Chief Secretary, GOBe to all Divisional Commissioners and District Officers, 23 December 1931, L/I/1/424, File No. 171/4, OIOC.
31 Letters sent by the Government of India to the provincial authorities in 1932 declared that the 'Government of India desire to invite the attention of local Governments to the great importance of propaganda and publicity in combating the civil disobedience movement and to express the hope that it will be possible for them to revive and, if practicable, to extend the organizations and methods which proved successful during the similar campaign of 1930'. Confidential letter from the Secretary, Home Department, GOI to all local governments and administrators, 14 January 1932, L/PO/3/3A, OIOC. Also see Note on publicity in UP, c.1932, ibid.
32 M. Israel, *Communications and power*, p. 90.
33 Departmental note by R.M. Maxwell, Deputy Secretary, Home Department, GOI, HPF(I) 4/4/37, NAI.
34 See, Israel, *Communications and power*, pp. 93–98.
35 Schemes of 'development' and 'welfare' were often re-adapted in response to less than positive local reactions. For instance, certain preventive public health measures, like vaccination programmes, despite their potentially advantageous aim of eradicating disease, were regularly opposed due to a combination of secular and cultural reasons. See, S. Bhattacharya, 'Re-devising Jennerian vaccines?: European technologies, Indian innovation and the control of smallpox in South Asia, 1850–1950', *Social Scientist*, 26, 11–12, Nov.-Dec. 1998. Therefore, the effectiveness of these policies in allowing the spread of 'British' control – or 'hegemony' – have to be necessarily questioned, as attempts to apply such policies forcibly often had quite the contrary effect of increasing levels of opposition to the colonial administrative network.
36 A good example of this is provided by the more recent works of Bhagwan

Josh and Shashi Joshi. See, B. Josh, *The Colonial State, the Left and the National Movement, Volume II: 1934–41*, New Delhi, 1992.
37 D. Engels and S. Marks (eds), *Contesting Colonial Hegemony: State and Society in Africa and India*, London, 1994, p. 3.
38 D.E. Haynes, *Rhetoric and Ritual in Colonial India: The shaping of a Public Culture in Surat City, 1852–1928*, Berkeley, 1991, pp. 14–15.
39 P. Chatterjee, 'Was there a hegemonic project of the colonial state?', in Engels and Marks (eds), *Contesting Colonial Hegemony*, pp. 79–84.
40 T. Raychaudhuri, 'Dominance, hegemony and the colonial state: the Indian and African experiences' in Engels and Marks (eds), *Contesting Colonial Hegemony*, p. 268.
41 N.G. Barrier, *Banned: Controversial Literature and Political Control in British India, 1907–1947*, Columbia, 1974. This bias originates, in large measure, from a number of factors: the primacy given to examining the 'content', and the credentials of the 'producers', of propaganda material, as well as an unwillingness – or perhaps an source-driven inability – to analyse the material and technological capacities of the distributive networks available to the various publicity organisations. See, for instance, S. Narwekar, *A History of the Indian Documentary Film*, Delhi, 1994, and P.S. Gupta, *Radio and the Raj, 1921–47*, Calcutta, 1995.
42 Israel declares at the beginning of his work that it '... emphasises the significance of the All-India stage and its elite players in the media'. Israel, *Communications and power*, p. 21.

Chapter One

The Second World War, Indian Nationalism and the Challenges of State Mobilisation in Eastern India: A Survey

The immediate consequences of the decision by Lord Linlithgow (who served as Viceroy between 1936–1943) and the British government to declare its Indian empire at war against Germany in September 1939 without consulting any of the country's political parties has already been very well documented. Unhappy with this potent reminder of the limits of political devolution, the Working Committee of the Indian National Congress instructed its provincial ministries to withdraw from office and committed the party to opposing the British war-effort within the country. Less well documented, however, are the difficulties faced in ensuring this egress from office, and their effects on wartime politics. The withdrawal of the ministries, like their formation, was not a smooth process. It has to be remembered that factional manoeuvrings apart, there had always been recurring disagreements between those who wanted a Congress ministry and those who were keen to rid themselves of the constraints it placed on agitational politics. Indeed, these tensions were never really resolved, which resulted in certain wings of the party persisting with their agitations throughout 1937 and 1939, and then providing vociferous support for Gandhi's call for the resignation of Congress governments. But, the events after September 1939 also brought to prominence a group of politicians in Eastern India who seemed keen to continue partaking in the activities of provincial legislative assemblies, although they were often forced to indulge their craving for formal politics in a very round about way.[1]

Seen in this light, the six years of war (September 1939–August 1945) in India presented a situation where there was a significant expansion in the number and the ideological complexity of political opponents ranged against the colonial authorities. However, the scale of opposition to the war-effort was initially rather unspectacular, and this can be largely attributed to the relatively-settled material conditions between September 1939 and November 1941 (the European phase of the war), which tended to have a dampening effect on most local agitations.[2] Notably, this was also the case during the national *satyagraha* initiated by Gandhi in 1940, which turned out to be quite a tame affair to the undisguised relief of the central and provincial authorities.[3] Even the effects of the news about the Allied reverses in Western Europe, in the form of the fluctuating food prices and withdrawals of bank savings in urban centres, remained transient.[4] The political situation in Eastern India witnessed a sea-change with the Japanese entry into the war in December 1941. The strategic reverses that followed in South East Asia, especially the fall of Singapore and Burma to Japanese forces, ushered in acute shortages of all manner of essential commodities and forced the mobilisation of a large Allied army in the region, allowing a range of political opponents to tap into difficulties that at times proved to be completely incurable.

Thus, while diverse groups of Congress activists sought to rally support for a series 'national issues' elucidated by the party Working Committee, especially the demand for independence, their operations against the authorities tended to remain firmly rooted in the utilisation of problems significant within their respective localities and constituencies, which sometimes caused unexpected political alliances to develop. It was, of course, not uncommon for links to exist between the cadres operating at the various strata of the colonial administration, or indeed those active amongst specific sections of the civilian populace at a particular level of the state. But their preoccupation with the concerns of specific localities, and with disparate ideologies, imparted a considerable degree of independence to their activities. This frequently manifested itself, for instance, in the utilisation of strikingly dissimilar symbols and themes during attempts to popularise, or criticise, particular issues.[5] This variety in the nature of political activity was, not unsurprisingly, replicated in the actions of the Congress's 'underground', which was composed of a melange of organisations that sprouted up throughout the country in response to the official attempts to crush or weaken the party's organisational framework in the aftermath of the 'Quit India' agitation of August 1942.[6]

This chapter outlines the range of issues that were used to criticise the colonial administration in wartime, which, in turn, played a great role in determining the shape, the deployment and the concerns of the official policies of propaganda and information.

I. The Trials of Wartime Mobilisation

The Japanese entry into the war wrought dramatic changes in the strategic, economic and political situation of India in general, and the eastern parts of the country in particular. The region was, by all accounts, totally unprepared for a major war. The armed forces were pathetically under-equipped and in the first half of 1942, there was no air defence worth speaking of. There were virtually no anti-aircraft guns, air-raid floodlights or radar sets, and the Royal Indian Air Force could only deploy 8 'serviceable Mohawks' to defend Calcutta, which, being the hub of the British war-effort in Eastern India, was open to attacks from carrier-based Japanese planes.[7] These weaknesses were mirrored in other areas as well. For example, no Royal Air Force airfield in India was suitable for use by modern heavy aircraft in 1941, and even as late as mid-1942 Calcutta was the only urban centre in the area with an airport capable of serving military aircraft. The Japanese threat from the east, and the need to facilitate the arrival of the American Air Force in India, resulted in an 'urgent demand' for 200 airfields.[8]

The result, inevitably, was the launching of a great range of defence works. By November 1942, for instance, there were 5 aerodromes 'complete in all respects', 83 aerodromes containing one all-weather runway and 60 aerodromes with 'fair weather strips'.[9] Similarly, an expansion of the road communication networks in Southern and Eastern India, which did not receive much attention till the outbreak of the war in the Far East, was also begun. Road building was given tremendous significance for a variety of reasons. Firstly, the Japanese mastery over the Bay of Bengal forced a closure of the ports on India's eastern seaboard, which impeded the transfer of both men and material.[10] Secondly, an extension of the rail network, which could have compensated for the loss of shipping routes, could not be pursued due to the extreme shortage of rolling stock.[11] Thus, the construction of a new road was started in October 1942 with a view to link Dumri, Deogarh, Hansdina, Purnea, Siliguri, Cooch-Behar and Dhubri, while improvements were begun on two other important highways in the region: the Raipur-Vishakapatnam road and the Assam Access road.[12] These activities involved a considerable mobilisation of resources (the enormity of the task undertaken is reflected in the central Engineering Department's burgeoning budget between 1941 and 1944, indicated in Table 1.1), and forced the

Table 1.1 The progressive rise in the budget of the Engineering Department, GOI, 1939–1944

Years	Amount (in millions of Rs.)
1939–40	40
1940–41	200
1941–42	450
1942–43	1000
1943–44	1000

Source: War Department History: Engineer Matters (September 1939–August 1945), p. 3, L/R/5/282, OIOC.

requisitioning of vast amounts of land and other private property for military use.[13]

All these building activities proved very disruptive to local economies and societies in Eastern India as the creation of the new military installations often forced the evacuation of entire villages, which increased the existing work load of the civilian authorities busy assisting the military.[14] The fact that the compensation offered for requisitioned property proved insufficient in a period of rapid inflation did not help matters and engendered much disaffection in the localities.[15] Moreover, the problems were exacerbated by the fact that the affected civilians, many of whom were dispossessed cultivators, were not engaged in military construction sites. Use was made instead of specialised 'labour battalions' that were composed primarily of the members of the 'aboriginal tribes' of Bengal, Bihar and Orissa.[16]

The Congress cadres, many of whom were only loosely attached to the party, and the members of the other political organisations, some ostensibly 'allied' to the colonial state, responded to such problems by criticising them through newspapers, books, pamphlets, leaflets, posters, public meetings, processions, door-to-door campaigning, and 'relief schemes'. One official report mentioned, for instance, that 'Congress propaganda is conducted in the country through the medium of young students who travel from village to village and who talk to the people, particularly on bazaar days, and assist in village work'.[17] In keeping with the party's varied membership, which sought to develop the support of a range of audiences, the Congress deployed activists not only among those dispossessed of their lands but also among the labourers employed at the building sites. Party members based in the affected localities were encouraged to report on all 'negative reactions' to requisitioning and, whenever possible, busy themselves in organising protests around them,[18] and certain party notables were assigned to visit the eastern provinces and encourage the mobilisation of agitations challenging enforced evacuations and the unsuitability of compensation. Mira Ben, a European member of Gandhi's entourage, for example, visited aerodrome sites in Orissa and exhorted villagers to demand more money for the lands taken away from them.[19] In Bengal, Satish Das Gupta, the president of the Calcutta office of the *Khadi Pratisthan* (a Congress subsidiary), shifted to the organisation's branch in Munsirhat where evacuees from the areas around Feni sub-division (Noakhali district) were encamped, and, as well as conducting 'relief work' among them, assisted in the formulation of petitions against the authorities. Das Gupta later set up a *Ujhar Sahajya Office* [Evacuee Relief Office] at Feni and organised an agitation among the 300-odd families who had been asked to evacuate the villages surrounding the local aerodrome.[20] Similar activities were also organised by Rajendra Prasad and other provincial Congress Committee members in Bihar,[21] and by R.K.L. Nandkeolyar in Assam.[22]

Activists attached to a variety of parties, not least the Congress and CPI, also remained keen to organise, or participate in, protests against the implementation of the 'denial' policy in Eastern India in 1942. Although the authorities had decided to avoid the utilisation of the Soviet practice of burning all the resources in areas about to be conquered by the enemy,[23] their 'limited denial policy' involved the destruction, or the removal, of various means of transport from particular threatened areas in the region.[24] In addition, widespread, and very public, preparations were made to destroy the oil fields, and the refineries, in Digboi (in Assam) and the ports in Chittagong and Calcutta, while large amounts of paddy and rice were actually removed from parts of the eastern provinces.[25] In May 1942, for instance, about 50,000 *maunds* of rice were transported from Orissa to Bihar '... mainly to assist the Denial Policy scheme under which large surpluses of rice [we]re to be removed from the coastal areas'.[26] Bihar and the United Provinces were relatively less affected by the measures, though large-scale preparations were made in the former province to initiate 'denial' in case of an emergency and all its senior district officers were informed in April 1942 that they needed to arrange the removal of all means of transport from the districts of

Singhbum, Manbhum, Ranchi, the Santal Parganas and Hazaribagh as soon as they were informed of a Japanese invasion of India.[27]

While the bureaucrats in the localities recognised the unpopularity of the 'denial' policy, their enduring fear of a Japanese invasion and the existence of considerable pressure from the local military authorities, whose decisions were invariably supported by senior officials attached to the Government of India and the provincial headquarters, ensured that the local civil administrations carried the measures through.[28] The Eastern Army Headquarters even applied pressure on senior officials based in the provincial capitals to ensure that their civilian officials in the district co-operated in the implementation of the policy.[29]

The issue of destroying private property so as to deny its use to advancing Japanese forces became a potent political symbol in the hands of those challenging the authorities in Eastern India, even though large sections of the region remained more or less untouched by the policy. One military intelligence summary noted in April 1942, for instance, that there was 'much ill informed defeatist criticism in nationalist Hindu circles' about the 'supposed intention of the Central Government to enforce a total application of the 'scorched earth' policy'.[30] The Provincial Congress Committees' response to the 'denial' policy was to form 'People's Volunteer Brigades', which traversed the eastern provinces and supported demonstrations against the application of the measures and thereby tried to enlist support for the party future.[31] Such activity was particularly marked in Orissa and Bengal, where party members, who were often joined by communist activists, busied themselves in campaigning against the removal of rice from the province.[32] An official report from Bengal declared that:

> Measures for the denial of transport continue in certain coastal areas but difficulties are reported from most districts.... In Contai and Tamluk the Congress, whose collaboration in implementing Government's policy was promised when the Minister for Civil Defence Co-ordination recently visited the area, is now reported to *be misrepresenting the denial policy and causing difficulties*....[33]

The negative political impact of the 'denial policy' was so marked at all the levels of society that even parties ostensibly supportive of the British war-effort were forced to refuse support for the measures, especially if their constituencies were affected by the implementation of the policy.[34] The Governor of Bengal complained, for instance, that the interests of Fazlul Huq, Chief Minister in 1942:

... l[ay] among the peasants, and he like Gandhi has been fed with stories of hardships resulting from [the] enforced evacuation and the operation of the denial policy. His principal concern at the moment therefore seems to be to obviate causes of complaint rather than to denounce the Congress proposals as injudicious and fifth columnist.[35]

Herbert, in an earlier letter, had underlined his 'increasing disappointment' at the failure of the other members of the elected ministry to take 'any active interest' in the prosecution of the war effort,[36] despite the fact that he had requested them to tour their particular districts and encourage their constituencies to co-operate with the authorities during the implementation of the 'denial policy'.[37] Similarly, the communist cadres based in the affected localities of Eastern Bengal were found to be organising rallies and 'strong' propaganda against the 'denial' measures, even though the Communist Party of India's politbureau had acknowledged the necessity of the policy. The Government of Bengal dealt with this particular problem by arming its district administrators with comprehensive powers to ban their activities.[38]

Apart from contending with criticism about the 'denial policy', the colonial authorities in Eastern India were also forced to deal with a series of problems arising from the presence of an enormous Allied army in the region, an issue which was used by activists attached to most parties to mobilise opposition against the authorities. Nonetheless, the difficult strategic situation in South East Asia caused the size of the British army based in India to be increased noticeably between 1942 and 1945 (see Table 1.2) and their personnel were supported throughout this period by a large number of African,[39] American[40] and Chinese troops.[41]

Although the Government of India and the provincial governments tried to limit the friction between the Indian army and civilians by making the task of requisitioning of goods needed by the military solely a civilian function, the clashes between civilians and troops remained frequent, and at times extremely serious in nature.[42] The misdemeanours on the part of the military personnel ranged from murder, rape, arson, robbery to petty theft, and caused additional administrative burdens to be placed on the already overworked bureaucracies in the localities of the eastern provinces.[43]

The civilian administrators' attempts to investigate such cases, frequently to assuage local opinion, were often rendered ineffective by the intransigence of the local military authorities. The problems faced by them were powerfully highlighted in a set of instructions circulated

Table 1.2 Strength of the regular army (including British troops) in India between July 1939 and September 1943

Period	Number of troops
1 July 1939	225,172
1 January 1940	223,457
1 January 1941	343,763
1 January 1942	605,446
1 January 1943	1,382,048
[1] October 1943	1,689,988

Source: Secret War Department History – Expansion of the Armed Forces in India, L/R/5/273, p. 42, OIOC.

among all British and Indian units based in the region. This stated that:

> There is a feeling among the civil police that in some units of this army there is a lack of co-operation and liaison, and a desire to shield military offenders, which is displayed in incivility towards officers of the civil police and a lack of desire to assist them in tracing offenders in unit lines. It cannot be too strongly emphasised that in so doing the police are performing their duty as citizens and officers of civil power. All ranks must realise that they are firstly citizens and that their status as members of the military forces of the Crown in no way absolves them from their duty as such. When a police is so engaged he will be given all the assistance possible by the Commanding Officer and all ranks and be treated with that courtesy to which his position entitles him.[44]

While this missive reportedly made the tasks of investigating officers more pleasant, the 'incidents' between troops attached to Indian army detachments and civilians continued unimpaired throughout 1942–45.[45]

The resulting administrative difficulties were increased by the trouble created by certain members of the American and Chinese detachments located in Eastern India. Many in the higher echelons of power in India, and Britain, had seemed predisposed to dislike the Chinese presence in the sub-continent due to a variety of reasons: they were considered by many in the Indian army to be 'mere rabble' and thus militarily ineffective,[46] powerful bureaucrats feared that they might assist a Congress-led uprising,[47] and senior military strategists in Britain were concerned that they might assist in increasing 'American influence' in the region.[48] But nonetheless it was decided that a Chinese military presence in the eastern provinces would have to be tolerated so as not to annoy the Government of the United States, on whose support the Allied military effort in South Asia and the Far-East was greatly dependant.[49] In practice, however, the conduct of American troops proved to be a much greater irritant to the colonial authorities, and violent incidents, especially murders and rapes, in which U.S. servicemen were involved remained quite common between 1942 and 1945. Reports of 'affrays' between them and the local populace were a common feature, especially in Bengal and Assam, throughout this period.[50] Unfortunately for the local bureaucracies in Eastern India, the provisions of the Allied Forces [United States of America] Ordinance of 1942 precluded them from prosecuting the guilty personnel, who could only be tried by American military courts. This ordinance, which had been passed in October 1942, declared that '... no criminal proceedings shall, subject as hereinafter provided, be prosecuted in British India before any Court of British India against a member of the military and naval forces of the United States of America'.[51]

The situation with regards to the American troops was made even more galling for the Indian bureaucrats by the leniency of the sentences passed and the difficulties faced in acquiring information regarding the nature of the punishments meted out,[52] despite the American authorities' promises to the contrary.[53] An analysis prepared by the Government of India's Home Department on the basis of reports received from the provinces declared that:

> While the relations between the American forces and civilians are reported to be satisfactory by most of the Provinces, the reports of Bengal and Assam are far from positive in this respect. The reason may be two fold:- Some of the serious offences were concerning women and trespass into private homes for immoral purposes. This form of crime, of course, arouses widespread public indignation. Secondly, the results of some of the trials gave the impression that the American Courts Martial had not done justice in those cases. The fact remains that in parts of Bengal and Assam the relations between the civilian population and American troops have not been entirely satisfactory owing to the behaviour of those troops.[54]

Three cases in particular received considerable attention, possibly because they took place in major cities in the region. The first involved a soldier who was acquitted despite having stabbed a taxi driver to death. A spokesman for the Government of Bengal found his trial 'unsatisfactory suggesting that the American authorities should be asked to ensure that more responsible officers [we]re appointed to the military court in these cases'.[55] The second involved the death of an Anglo-Indian boy, who was shot by American soldiers while trying to steal their jeep. These troops were acquitted by a military tribunal and this angered officials within the Government of Bengal, one of whom declared that, '... it is clear that the whole incident was from the point of view of this Government and the general public very unfortunate and that the circumstances under which the boy... met his death were most deplorable and contrary to the ideas of British justice'.[56] The third concerned the case of a young Assamese girl in Jorhat, who died after being raped by an American soldier. Although he was found guilty, the defendant was sentenced to only two months' 'rigorous imprisonment and some forfeiture of pay'. This punishment was considered by the provincial authorities to be 'totally inadequate'.[57]

Not surprisingly, tales, real or contrived, of Allied troops misbehaving with Indians, especially women, were utilised by political activists opposing the war-effort. Military intelligence reports pointed out in 1942 that a 'campaign' had been started by political opponents to 'vilify' the military personnel based in Eastern India.[58] Referring to one example of such activity, a Government of India official wrote to Gandhi that:

> Reports have been circulated throughout the country that the film star, Miss Leela Chitnis, was raped by soldiers in Bombay. The lady herself has repudiated the whole story and pointed out that she was in Gwalior at the time of the alleged outrage and not in Bombay. I have now heard at least four different film stars named as the victim of this outrage and been told of all of them that they died of their injuries. So far as I know and have been able to find out, no film star has been in any way molested.[59]

In similar fashion, the Chief Press Adviser reported that a spate of 'malicious rumours and reports' against the armed forces was being circulated by political activists and that these were receiving 'widespread publicity' in the national and local newspapers. He added that this situation was made all the more unacceptable by the fact that many of the allegations turned out to be incorrect when investigated, and asked the provincial administrations to follow the Government of India's example in making it clear in their official communiqués that, 'whenever an allegation [against members of the Allied army] is found to be unsubstantiated, false or grossly exaggerated, immediate action will be taken wherever possible ... to prosecute its originator and those who has given publicity to it.'[60]

Nevertheless, the dissemination of information regarding the misconduct of troops with women continued unimpaired throughout 1942–45, especially in the localities, through 'underground' print publicity, lectures given by squads of travelling activists, and impromptu public meetings. For instance, one of the many books published and distributed secretly in Eastern India described in great detail how some of the European soldiers who had been sent to suppress the 'Quit India' movement in the village of Chimur (Chanda district, Central Provinces) had raped thirteen Indian women and 'molested' four others, and it also contained 'true copies' of 'statement [sic] by [the] victims of rape'.[61] In a similar vein, an edition of the 'Congress Samachar', a mimeographed Hindi magazine brought out in Bihar by a group of party members who had gone into hiding in August 1942, accused British soldiers of looting and assaulting women in the Banka Subdivision.[62] Public protests, albeit usually temporary, were also organised between 1943 and 1945 in localities of Bengal to condemn incidents arising from the 'sexual enthusiasm' of serving Allied personnel,[63] and the local vernacular press would sometimes level criticisms against the immoral 'white soldiers'.[64]

Due to the official censors' insistence that the misdemeanours of troops should not be publicised in the national press, the issue was rarely discussed by the bigger papers sympathetic to the Congress's goals. However, references to the topic in such broadsheets became more frequent in 1945, with the gradual relaxation of censorship measures,[65] and interestingly, complaints regarding the issue were by no means solely a Congress preserve. An article in an edition of *Dawn*, the mouthpiece of the Muslim League, stated that:

> What is sheer wanton butchery in India, they call it fun in the United States [sic].... American military authorities cannot plead ignorance of the facts which [the] Calcutta papers are now reporting with greater frequency.... In the Central Assembly, Mr. Trivedi, War Secretary, stated that there appeared to have been 71 cases of assaults on women by military personnel in Bengal and Assam. The figure must be considered an understatement, when none will dispute that for every case reported there must be several more that are suppressed, mostly by the victims themselves.... But the American soldier in India is not the

only criminal. In the Bengal Assembly on February 21, Sir Nazimuddin, the Premier, referred to eight cases of unauthorised entry into houses by foreign and Indian military personnel, of which one was being tried by court martial while the others were under investigation.... It is for the Army authorities to prevent what soldiers may term fun, but what is tragedy for India.[66]

Articles in the Communist Party of India's paper, the *People's War*, and its vernacular editions, remained similarly critical of the official inability to prevent, or punish, such 'outrages' by troops based in the sub-continent.[67]

It was also a common practice for Congress and CPI cadres in Eastern India to attribute other problems afflicting the localities to the presence of foreign troops.[68] For example, it became standard in 1943 for political activists to blame the high prices and the shortages of food products on 'government purchases for military purposes'.[69] Some Congress members referred to the threat that these armies constituted. In one incident, an activist caused a stir by expressing the 'fear that these troops might be used to burn down mills and factories in pursuance of the 'scorched earth' policy'.[70] In another context, activists operating in Assam were reported to be stoking hostility against American detachments by claiming that their personnel would be utilised by the Government of the United States to take over the control of the Indian sub-continent after the expected British departure after the war.[71] And military intelligence noted in 1943 that leaflets were being disseminated with the purpose of 'exacerbating Hindu feelings' against the civilian and army authorities by accusing them of slaughtering 30,000 cattle daily, including 'even pregnant cows and cows with milk', for feeding foreign soldiers.[72]

Accusations about the misbehaviour of troops fitted in well with economic worries, and the authorities were consistently attacked for the crisis afflicting Eastern India. The Allied reverses throughout South-East Asia and Burma in 1942, and the defensive measures that were consequently initiated by the administrators in charge of the eastern provinces, had an almost immediate negative impact on the region's supply of food items (especially rice, oils and salt), cooking and lighting fuels (coal and kerosene), cloth, and medicines.[73] The loss of cheap Burma rice, which had fed the poorer sections of society immediately pushed up price of the commodity. Other local economies in Eastern India adversely hit for other reasons. Many people in the district of Gorakhpur in the United Provinces depended on remittances sent from Hong Kong, Bangkok, Singapore and Rangoon, and the loss of these earnings, which in one sub-division was estimated to be equal to the land revenue extracted from the area, engendered enormous financial difficulties within the locality.[74] Similar trends were also noticeable in the villages in the Nilpahari sub-division of the district of Rangpur in Bengal, which had subsisted for decades on the cultivation of tobacco for export to Burmese markets.[75]

The resultant economic climate encouraged the hoarding of food, especially rice, by individual families as well as by Indian mercantile groups. This pushed food prices in Eastern India further,[76] and caused the administrations of Assam, Bihar, Bengal and Orissa to police the export of rice, or paddy, to Bengal so as to combat the rampant smuggling of these commodities from Assam, Bihar and Orissa to Bengal.[77] However, the onset of famine conditions in parts of Bengal by mid-1943 caused the Government of India to use the Defence of India Rules to reverse the other provinces' decision to regulate the export of rice, even though the Government of India Act of 1935 had made trade and commerce a provincial prerogative.[78] Despite provincial reservations, this 'free-trade' policy remained in force between May and July 1943, the measures were enforced often under military supervision, and 1,648,627 *maunds* of rice and 229,956 *maunds* of paddy were sent to Bengal.[79]

The 'free-trade' policy allowed mercantile local groups, who sold rice for a profit to purchasers from Bengal, to deplete local supplies of rice in Assam, Bihar and Orissa, and this caused a steep rise in the prices of food grains in these three provinces.[80] It also had the unfortunate effect of extending famine conditions to previously unaffected areas.[81] A vivid description of the outcome of the 'free-trade' policy in Orissa goes thus:

> For a time there were virtually famine conditions. It was not that supplies of food were short, but the prices soared, and attempts to control them were little more than palliatives. This was particularly the case when the Government of India, in a desperate effort to get food to the war factories in Bengal, established a free trade area in rice between Bengal and the adjoining provinces, where prices at once sky-rocketed to the Bengal level.[82]

The food shortages in the region continued into 1944, and the shortfall that year was considered so severe, that the military authorities volunteered to forgo 10 per cent of the wheat allotted to them by the central government's Food Department.[83] The suffering within the provinces of Eastern India were increased further by the shortage of medicines necessary to combat the epidemics that broke out in the aftermath of the famine.[84]

All parties sought to make political capital out of these difficulties. Public meetings in which the expense and the shortages of food were blamed squarely on the administration remained common throughout 1942–45,[85] and 'Congress underground' literature advertised similar messages. The suggestion in one such pamphlet that local problems, especially those of an economic nature, needed be utilised to mobilise support for the 'Quit India' movement represents how certain elements within the party sought to discredit the authorities. The relevant sections of the document ran thus:

> The movement will not conform to a uniform pattern.... Its outward manifestation will exhibit as great a variety as local problems.... This infinite diversity of expression should be welcome. It is bewildering to the enemy and should be encouraged by working up and bringing to a head the particular local grievance which is most acute in any area.... Each such problem is the focal point for the initiation of the movement in that area. The general plan will direct the search for such force; point out why our festering economic sores will be the most suitable starting points for local agitation, being the most deeply felt and the quickest, most natural and the most unifying inciting agents for the local people; explain how these issues can never be solved within the framework of the existing system.... There are many battle fronts in this war as there are classes and sections and individuals waging it, and action on all fronts is simultaneous. But the most extensive and significant field of work lies in the country-side [sic], where our peasantry offers the biggest reserve of man-power and where the village economy is threatened with imminent breakdown. Let peasant representatives in the villages be approached by our central agents.... Let them select the initial targets for assault in each village or group of villages. Let the rising and simmering discontent against these immediate grievances be churned up into an angry ferment....[86]

The activities of all the Congress groups may not have conformed wholly with this exhortation, but that some such efforts occurred cannot be doubted. Local officials frequently voiced their dissatisfaction regarding the dissemination of 'contorted propaganda' regarding the food situation, and reported how the Congress was encouraging its agents in small towns and villages to win over the support of the local populace by playing upon economic grievances.[87] Similar complaints were, of course, made about other parties as well.[88]

The distress arising from the famine, and the epidemics that followed, provided the political activists ranged against the *Raj* with more ammunition against the authorities. The topics dwelt upon in nationalist propaganda included graphic, and sometimes exaggerated, descriptions of starvation deaths in the countryside, the break-up of families during the exodus from the affected localities, and the lack of facilities accorded to the destitute within the various official camps.[89] Emphasis was given to cases where the migration of starving refugees, from the *mofussils* of Bengal to Calcutta or to other provinces (notably Assam and Bombay), was forcibly halted by the provincial police, sometimes with military assistance.[90] In addition, schemes like the 'Hindustan Relief Fund', started by the proprietors of the *Hindustan Times*, sought to underline the official inactivity during the famine.[91] And, literature disseminated by the members of Congress underground organisations regularly encouraged people to stop the 'movement of crops' from their localities to the cities of Bengal, and one pamphlet advised its audience that 'In the towns and cities the edge of the people's hunger should be turned through propaganda and personal contact against the British Government which [wa]s responsible for starving the people.'[92] Describing the tone, and the mode of transmission, of such propaganda, a civil servant who had been based in Bengal, stated that:

> ... the reports of the Famine in the press made excellent propaganda against the Government.... Any story that could cause alarm, however unjustified, was given maximum publicity.... Early in the summer [of 1943] a report appeared in the Calcutta press that in Malda, a man had slain his wife, because he had not the means to support her, and could not bear to see her slowly starve to death. It was an effective and heart-rending story, but it was only the plea concocted by the lawyer for the defence in a very sordid murder case.... Probably the most alarming stories about the famine were spread by word of mouth or by letter, and not by the press.[93]

Significantly, the widespread distress resulting in Eastern India due to the famine of 1943 even caused certain loyalist establishments to criticise the colonial administration. The most notable instance of a hitherto pro-government institution launching a tirade against the lack of official initiatives to combat the crisis, was that of *The Statesman*, a British-owned paper. Apart from continuously challenging the veracity of the official communiqués regarding the issue, the paper kept printing what came to be known, in official circles, as 'starvation photographs' to the bureaucracy's chagrin.[94] The tone of the rest of the provincial press, English and vernacular, remained equally, if not more, hostile.[95] This predicament persisted in 1944 and caused Wavell, who gave up the position of Commander in Chief of the Indian armed forces to take over the post of Viceroy in October 1943,[96] to report that the Bengal Governor's efforts to publicise the official efforts aimed at improving the economic situation were being nullified by the antipathy of the local papers.[97] The crisis resulting from the famine caused the Government of India to lose other allies as well. In Orissa, the famine led to the ultimate split of the coalition ministry that had been formed on 24 November 1942, since it caused many of its members to attack the Chief Minister, the Maharaja of Parlakhimedi, for defending the Government of India's 'free-trade' policy in 1943.[98] An official report, which described the proceedings of the 'food debate' in the Indian Legislative Assembly in November 1943 mentioned, with some trepidation, that 'even' the European group had remained critical of the nature of the state's economic policies in 1943.[99]

The other major political parties in the region, the Muslim League and the Communist Party of India, remained similarly critical of the colonial administration, despite their 'pro-war' stances. The League's publicists made in abundantly clear that the Government of India, and not its ministry in Bengal, were responsible for the famine.[100] The CPI's cadres based in Eastern India kept up a multi-pronged campaign against the authorities' handling of the food crisis, and the epidemics that followed, throughout 1943–44.[101] Articles in the party politbureau's mouthpiece, the *People's War*, provided graphic descriptions of deaths caused by starvation and disease;[102] a melange of communist organisations highlighted the official inefficiency during the crisis while advertising the party's own relief measures;[103] and a medley of publications and plays, performed by theatrical groups in the cities and travelling troupes in the countryside sponsored by the party, attributed the catastrophe to the an 'alien' colonial administration.[104] A party pamphlet released in the first half of 1945, repeated the common CPI claim that three and a half million people had died in Bengal between 1943 and 1944, thereby challenging official efforts to put the mortality figure of one and a half million casualties.[105]

Another abiding feature of all nationalist activity was the attempt to advertise all varieties of official 'atrocities'. This theme had, of course, been used to criticise the Raj throughout the inter-war years, but references to it became more common as the use of force was sharpened during the wartime period.[106] The extreme measures used to combat the 'Quit India' movement, and the localised uprisings that followed, provided the INC, the CSP and even the CPI with a much-enlarged pantheon of martyrs. One of the many 'public statements' denouncing the official crackdown stated that:

> We cannot help feeling extremely concerned with the events that have occurred in the country since the arrest of Mahatma Gandhi and other Congress leaders.... We ... wish to enter our emphatic protest against [the] uncivilised measures which the Provincial Governments have employed in their attempt to suppress popular demonstrations. All over the country the police and military authorities have fired indiscriminately on unarmed crowds of men and women, dispersed them by tear gas attacks or lathi charges resulting in bloodshed and acute physical suffering and thereby filled every Indian heart with deep resentment. Such repression has resulted in an outburst of public wrath, causing public destruction of property....[107]

The issue was also advertised by Congress and its sympathisers during the 'celebration' of 'National Weeks'.[108] Moreover, articles in pro-Congress papers, like the *Hindustan Times*, would quite frequently criticise the government for the 'hardships suffered by the political prisoners in India'.[109] Reporting on the papers' activities, a note from the Calcutta Police's Special Branch reported how:

> According to Mrinal Kanti Bose of the Amrita Bazar Patrika in pursuance of the request of Mr. Dev Das Gandhi, Editor, Hindustan Times ... and President of the All India Newspaper's Conference, he is now collecting material regarding Government repression in Bengal since the August movement of 1942 and the unwarranted interference [sic] with the Press.[110]

The literature released by the Congress diverse 'underground', completely unconstrained by official restrictions, was able to adopt a much more stringent tone compared to the national press while advertising cases of 'repression'.[111] Other 'underground' publications labelled the suppression of the 'Quit India' movement as representing 'ruthless repression and fascist tyranny',[112] and described the 'inhuman tortures' perpetrated by the 'British administration'.[113] Many of these pamphlets were consciously directed at state employees, especially policemen and soldiers, based in the localities.[114] Describing a sample of the 'underground' literature distributed in the localities of the United Provinces after August 1942, a civil servant mentions how:

> a Hindi pamphlet came into ... [his] hands, describing the 'brutal suppression' of the freedom fighters. Crude illustrations showed [Micky] Nethersole [an I.C.S Commissioner] and Marsh Smith [Deputy Inspector General of Police] gloating over naked Indian women hanging from their heels in trees and being lashed with whips.[115]

Though such leaflets, usually mimeographed or hand-written, were widespread in the localities of Eastern India throughout the wartime period, their presence was most marked between 1942 and 1945.[116] Official intelligence reviews also reported in 1944 that Congress activists, ostensibly 'busy with ... distressed [sic] activities', were touring areas like Ballia, in Eastern United Provinces, in order to 'stir up bitterness arising out of the repression necessitated in that area in 1942 by the rebellion'.[117]

The official 'atrocities' perpetrated against Congress members were also advertised by other Indian political parties. Conspicuous in this regard were the activities of the CPI, which launched a series of agitations demanding the release of Gandhi and the imprisoned Congress cadres. To the displeasure of the senior central government officials who had been instrumental in removing the ban on the Communist Party, its propaganda consistently refuted the Government of India's attempts between 1942 and 1944 to label the Congress as a pro-Japanese organisation.[118] In similar fashion, other prominent political figures ostensibly supportive of the war, like Swami Sahajanand Saraswati, the influential *bhumihar kisan* leader, also spoke up against the violent suppression of the 'Quit India' movement and the 'suffering' endured by Congress members.[119]

The political parties also sought to increase their support base through a variety of welfare organisations and networks. In the case of the Congress, these so-called 'constructive departments' took the form of spinning centres or village defence committees, and their members would not only busy themselves in disseminating print and oral propaganda, but also serve the people in times of distress by distributing essentials like food and homespun cloth amongst villagers.[120] Needless to say, the banning of the Congress in August 1942 forced shifts in strategy. The party's version of events and its efforts to organise – or link up with – local agitations were kept up by a number of front organisations. Congress members and sympathisers located in Eastern India, were often forced to operate through bodies which had no ostensible links to the party. A number of such organisations was set up after the suppression of the 'Quit India' movement so as to provide financial assistance to the families of political activists who were in jail or who had died 'as a result of police action'. An apt example was the Sufferers' Relief Committee – which was formed in Bengal in September 1942 but whose employees were also active in Assam, Bihar and Orissa – whose aim was to give 'relief to deserving survivors and relatives of firing during the August 1942 disturbances'. The Orissa Relief Committee played a similar role and also provided sustenance to released political prisoners who had lost their 'previous sources of income as a result of imprisonment'. The Allahabad Legal Aid Committee was formed to provide 'proper legal aid' to people being tried for 'sabotage, arson and criminal conspiracies' in the United Provinces during August 1942. A plethora of cognate organisations also sprung up during the famine of 1943. The All Bengal Food and Famine Relief Committee initiated a scheme of helping 'spinners and weavers' by the distribution of food, during which the '*Charkha* ....an emblem of the Congress ... [wa]s given prominence'. And the National Relief Committee, formed in Calcutta in September 1943, concentrated on distributing food in the *mofussils* and, worryingly for the authorities, employed 'ex-political prisoners for the purpose'.[121]

II. The Audiences and Goals of the Official Policies of Propaganda and Information

It is usually ignored that the official public relations campaigns between 1939 and 1945, which were intended to counter opposition to the war-effort and generally fortify 'Indian morale',[122] gave more prominence to some audiences than others. This determination of the targets of propaganda and information schemes was, of course, crucial as it usually decided the type of message transmitted, the scale of official activity and the media used.[123]

But whereas the deteriorating relations with the Congress, in the context of the Second World War, shaped the direction and scope of many of the official public relations schemes,[124] other concerns played a role as well. Notable in this regard were continuing fears about the impact of the formation of Congress ministries on the attitude of Indian bureaucrats, especially the subordinate services. The question caused great nervousness amongst the European element within all branches of the civil services, who responded by directing publicity and welfare schemes at the indigenous employees of the state in the hope of retaining their support for the war-effort.[125] The European unease about the body of Indian officials was by no means misplaced. The Congress's acceptance of office in 1937 had made Indian bureaucrats based at all administrative levels more guarded in their loyalty towards British rule, and this political renegotiation had caused even senior Indian officials to try and forge ties with the Congress, the Muslim League, or other significant organisations like the Krishak Praja Party in Bengal and the Momin Conference in Bihar.[126] What worried many within the Government of India was that these attitudes were often carried over into the war, and this was seen to be highlighted by the tendency of many bureaucrats to 'go soft' on the political activists within their respective spheres of authority. Khitish Chandra Ganguly, the Deputy Magistrate of Rangpur (Bengal) between 1942 and 1944, would, for instance, often secretly warn local politicians in advance that they were going to be arrested, so that they could leave the town before the event. He also regularly handed out what were considered, by his provincial superiors, to be insufficiently harsh sentences.[127] Though such activities remained almost impossible to detect, and thereby difficult to report, references to similar cases in other localities of Eastern India were made intermittently in military intelligence.[128] One Indian official has referred to these activities as representing the effects of the 'mental adjustments' brought about by the developments 'on the political front',[129] and another said that 'some senior civil servants ... did their best to further the national cause' while in service.[130] However, the most telling account of the legacy of the Congress ministries is described thus:

> The popular ministries in the provinces had already resigned on the outbreak of the war, in response to a mandate from the Congress High Command.... At first sight, this was merely a return to the form of government that had prevailed before provincial autonomy was accepted by the Congress. But the reality was quite different. Before the popular ministry took over in 1937, it was the done thing to revere the Raj and parade one's loyalty like a banner.... Two years of Congress rule quickly established a new set of norms. It was the done thing now to parade one's patriotism and, if possible, a third cousin twice removed who had been in jail in the civil disobedience movement.... By the time the Congress went and the Governor returned to the saddle, everyone had realized that the British were not a permanent fixture.[131]

An awareness of these developments is powerfully illustrated by the widespread nervousness among senior British officials about the possible fickleness of Indian ICS officers during a Congress-led agitation.[132] One senior British official, who had been in a position to observe changes in two provinces declared that, 'at the back of every Hindu officer is the anticipation, and possibly the hope, that a Congress Ministry will return to power'.[133] These fears also affected the British officials posted in the districts and the sub-divisions, where pragmatic concerns bred other more powerful anxieties. There was a widespread anxiety amongst them to gauge, and repair, the damage done to the 'morale' and the 'loyalty' of the subordinate services, especially the police forces, during the ministry period. They recognised that these personnel would have to be relied upon to maintain order in times of trouble, during which officials might become the target of violent crowds, and remained keen to lessen, if not remove altogether, all 'subversion' within their administrations. This was very often sought to be achieved, amongst other things, through the judicious distribution of all forms of propaganda material.[134]

In addition, the strategic implications arising from the progress of the Second World War had a marked effect in determining the direction of official public relations efforts. The approach of the war to the India's eastern frontiers in the first half of 1942 caused great disquiet amongst almost all sections of the civilian population, and this was sought to be generally countered. The Government of India remained especially worried about the impact of 'rumours' on morale, and the Deputy-Secretary of its Information and Broadcasting Department wrote:

> I am directed to invite the Provincial Government's attention to the problem of...preventing the spread of baseless rumours in the bazaars ... Autochthonous rumours, which have local origin, spring simply from imagination and are propagated from mouth to mouth. Even in ordinary times these rumours can be quite disturbing, but in times of panic they not only begin to breed like flies, but their potency in ravaging public morale is greatly increased. In view of the approach of the war to India, it has become more than ever necessary to see that the repetition of unconfirmed reports and the spread of false rumours are reduced as much as possible.[135]

But, the colonial authorities in the much reduced British empire were now being increasingly forced to reappraise their administrative priorities in order to be able to contribute materially to the flagging Allied military effort world-wide. In India this reassessment of official exigencies took the form of the central government giving absolute primacy to wartime mobilisation. This, in turn, involved the military command being given unprecedented powers to determine strategic policies in the provinces of Assam, Bengal, Bihar, Orissa and United Provinces, as well as all the princely states in this region, all of which were treated as a 'threatened area' and an unified administrative bloc for military purposes. Correspondingly, great importance was now given to South Asian army personnel based in Eastern India as they were seen as the state's first line of defence against internal disorder,[136] in a situation where India was considered, after August 1942, to be 'an occupied and hostile country'.[137] So, the civilian authorities in this region, themselves an important target of special schemes of propaganda and information, were ordered to devote their attention to the needs of the Eastern Army Command and the South East Asia Command. This involved them being forced to concentrate the material and manpower resources available to them towards the creation of amenities for the troops.[138]

An immediate, and striking, effect of these policies was the administrative tendency to prioritise Indian social groups in terms of their strategic 'worth', and their subsequent division into so-called 'priority' and 'non-priority' classes. While economic, print and oral propaganda were sought to be targeted at Indian society as a whole, the increasing paucity of official resources meant that the various 'priority' classes became the primary targets of official wartime welfare initiatives. These trends are particularly noticeable when one examines the official publicity efforts directed at the civilian population in India. In the first two years of the war the state's primary targets were the politically active, and vocal, 'educated middle-classes', a general term used by senior central and provincial government employees to refer to those conversant in the English language.[139] This section of society was considered significant, even though many senior British officials recognised that many of them supported the demand for Indian independence,[140] since their reactions to the war tended to receive frequent press coverage in Britain and America; as they were seen as being able to contribute to the plethora of war-funds that had been set up, and a majority of them had the right to vote in the provincial elections and were, therefore, expected to play an important part in determining the choice of the inevitably momentous post-war constitutional settlement.[141]

Table 1.3   Electorate for the provincial legislative assemblies in Eastern India during the elections of 1937

Province	Total electorate
Assam	815,341
Bengal	6,695,483
Bihar	2,412,229
Orissa	520,225
United Provinces	5,335,309

Source: *Returns showing the results of elections in India, 1937*, London, 1937, p. 5, L/I/1/607, OIOC.

However, the civilian audiences began to be more carefully defined after December 1941. Whereas the English-educated sections were still targeted, greater attention began to be given to the 'poorer middle classes' subsisting on fixed salaries, who were adversely affected by the wartime inflation and articulated their discontent in vernacular newspapers, which were considered significant because of their capacity to foment trouble in the localities.[142]

In addition, concerted efforts were made to reach particular 'occupational groups' considered, for varying reasons, to be especially significant to the war-effort. Since the colonial authorities' expectations from each of these groups differed (and indeed, the inverse was true as well), the war effort was often marketed amongst them in strikingly dissimilar forms. A good example is a comparison of the aims of the publicity blitz targeted at two civilian 'occupational groups' given primacy by both the Government of India and the military authorities: the big business interests and the labour employed in the so-called 'war industries' and 'war works'.

For the Government of India, the significance of business interests lay in the fact that much of wartime production was left to concerns owned by them. But as the war wore on, the ever-increasing profitability of industries caused them to be seen as invaluable sources of tax receipts in a period of rapidly rising administrative and defence costs. Indeed, various official schemes were initiated with the purpose of skimming away some of the profits being made by Indian business from the onset of the war. A good example of this were two wartime 'insurance' schemes. The first was the 'War Risks (Goods) Insurance Ordinance', which was legislated on 1 October 1940 and whose 'compulsory provisions' came into force the following month. Following the onset of the war in the Pacific theatre in December 1941, a 'War Risks (Factories) Insurance Ordinance' was promulgated on 8 April 1942. The declared 'object of the scheme was mainly to create and maintain the necessary confidence in industry and to ensure increasing industrial production, the bulk of which was devoted to the war effort.'[143] Both schemes – which owners of industries, mines, gas-supply undertakings and electricity companies located *throughout* India were forced by law to subscribe to – were run at a healthy profit by the Government of India: the total premia collected amounted to 42 *crores*, while the expenditure incurred by the authorities in administering the schemes did not exceed Rs. 50 *lakhs*.[144]

Later projects – such as the 'Excess Profits Tax', which was imposed in 1942, and a new sub-section of the Defence of India rules which sought to plug a legal loophole, whereby costs incurred during the setting up of ancillary industries were deducted from the taxable profits used by Indian industrialists to avoid the payment of this levy – had similar motives. At the same time these forms of official intrusion were also an attempt to counter the inflationary trends created by the way in which the war was financed: production for the war effort in India under the principles of 'Lend Lease' was on a system of credit whereby the Government of India paid private producers in India for goods produced on behalf of the Government of Britain, in rupees which were rolled out of the printing presses at a huge rate.[145] Although certain 'priority classes' – like urban labour and certain sections of the government service – were provided with dearness allowances to combat the effects of the consequent inflation,[146] this proved an inadequate solution, and in many cases certain daily necessities were provided in kind as it was no longer viable to provide dearness allowances at a high enough rate to enable people to buy the ordinary necessities of life.[147] But it was also obvious that inflation had to be fought at a more effective level by taking larger amounts of money out of circulation,[148] and the imposition of the Excess Profits Tax was seen as an adequate way of tackling the problem.[149]

To the Government of India's anxiety to rally business interests was added a concern for another 'priority class': the workers attached to 'strategically' significant industries and military installations. These included the workers in 'war-industries' (factories producing munitions and other commodities of use to army personnel as well as certain mining concerns),[150] unskilled labour involved in the construction of military installations and strategic roads in the operational areas of

Eastern India,[151] and the transport workers (railway and port labour).[152] The significance of the rationale for this – the stabilising of factory production in India, which despite being important to Britain's strategic imperatives from 1939 took on an added significance for the Allied war-effort in the Far-East from December 1941 onwards, and the smooth running of the Allied war machine – is obvious. The operation of 'war-industries', like the railway system and the ports, was dubbed an 'essential public-service' from February 1941 onwards and this allowed the colonial authorities to 'legally' deploy coercive measures with a view to preventing 'mass migrations ... as a result of panic' from industrial areas.[153] In fact, the Essential Services (Maintenance) Ordinance of 1941, which affected labour, declared that the legislation authorised an:

> ... officer ... to prohibit any person engaged in any employment covered by the ordinance to depart, without the consent of government ... out of any such area or areas as may be specified. The ordinance makes it an offence punishable with imprisonment for a term which may extend to one year and with fine, for any person to abandon such employment or absent himself without reasonable excuse. The fact that a person apprehends that by continuing in his employment he will be exposed to increased physical danger does not constitute a reasonable excuse.[154]

However, it was recognised by civil servants within the Government of India's Defence Co-ordination Department that attempts to impose severe penalties could be rendered ineffective by the sheer magnitude of the task and the shortage of official personnel, and so the use of 'advance propaganda' was recommended.[155] Between 1942 and mid-1945, this primarily took the form of a wide range of material benefits.[156]

In addition, the strategic, social and economic difficulties in Eastern India sometimes caused the colonial administration to target propaganda schemes amongst the affected, but 'non-productive', rural masses so as to encourage them to 'stay put', not block the major roads or impede strategic manoeuvres in the region.[157] Significantly, and this has been continually ignored in the existing studies of the Second World War, these efforts were very often *also* a product of the nervousness arising amongst local bureaucrats, both European and Indian, from the possibility of a Japanese invasion,[158] from an awareness of the discontent among the populace due to the wartime economic difficulties and the political capital being made of this situation by activists,[159] and from a recognition of the persistent insufficiency of policemen (see Table 1.4 for a description of the strength of the provincial police forces in 1942) and other personnel in the localities throughout the conflict.[160]

The nature of the anxieties among European civil servants in India after the fall of Rangoon is perhaps best represented by the description provided by the wife of an IPS officer. According to her, British families began to:

> ... think up wild plans of what we should do if India were over-run. Could we stain the children's faces with walnut juice and let the *ayahs* take them back to their villages? Any sort of blitz one felt one could face among one's own people, rather than face the Japs and their atrocities on foreign soil, among people who far from being one's own, might well turn hostile to save one's own skins [sic] if for no other reason....[161]

Feelings of dread were stoked further by frequent advice from the Government of India's Civil Defence Department about how to deal with attacks by 'enemy parachutists',[162] and formal instructions or informal hints from the provincial headquarters that senior officials in the localities evacuate their families. One such circular distributed in Bihar, a province considerably removed from the hostilities, declared that:

> It has been suggested to [the] Government that they might issue instructions to their officers serving in areas which lie within the danger zone of air raids, in regard to the removal of their families. Government have given this question their most anxious consideration and they are of the opinion that the time for the issue of any instructions has not yet

Table 1.4 Strength of armed and unarmed police in the provinces of Eastern India as on 1 January 1943

Province	Police	Armed personnel	Unarmed personnel
Assam	5,226	2,074	3,152
Bengal	38,981	17,962	21,019
Bihar	15,946	5,527	10,419
Orissa	4,236	1,829	2,407
United Provinces	38,606	20,375	18,231

Source: Statement [on strength of provincial police forces] from quarter ending 31 December 1942, PF 21/16/42, NAI.

arrived. Their officers are in the same position as other citizens and are free to use their discretion in this matter of the evacuation of their families. All that Government consider it necessary to say at present is that if any officer even now removes his family from his place of duty, his action will not be interpreted by Government as anything improper.[163]

Likewise, disturbances in which the rural poor were involved preyed on the minds of the provincial officialdom, even though these were very often localised affairs. Events like the disorders which followed the launch of the 'Quit India' movement of August 1942, the 'Eram incident' in Orissa in September 1942,[164] and the food riots of 1943 had the effect of increasing the officials' fear that the 'masses' could be rallied against the administration. Apart from afflicting the civil servants who had witnessed these incidents, it also affected those in charge of undisturbed localities, whose views were informed by regular reports describing the outbreaks of violence and the measures employed to combat them. The distribution lists attached to the Chief Commissioners' fortnightly reports describe how widely these documents were issued within the local bureaucracies – copies were sent to all senior District and Sub-Divisional officers – apart from being sent to the Government of India and other provincial headquarters. During certain periods, such as December 1941 or August–September 1942, fortnightly reports from a particular province were copied and widely distributed in the localities of others.

Moreover, correspondence between the Government of India and the provincial governments describe how senior officials based within the localities were sent a variety of reports about the measures taken to tackle crises of various denominations by the authorities in charge of other localities, in the belief that these would prepare them to cope with all eventualities within their respective spheres of authority. The topics dealt with in these reviews ranged from descriptions of the problems faced by the British administrations in South-East Asia before during the Japanese invasion, to incidents of violence that had taken place within India.[165] This caused a situation where isolated incidents of deliberate vandalism in the *mofussils* were often granted undue importance by local administrators. In January 1943, for instance, the bureaucrats all over Bihar were reported to be terrified about the fact that the Congress 'underground' might resume widespread disturbances after they read about 'the excessive sabotage of telegraph and telephone lines' within Shahabad district in December 1942.[166]

Not unexpectedly, the persistence of such fears among local officials based in Eastern India caused them to react vigorously, throughout 1942–45, against central government policies considered by them to be capable of exacerbating the disturbed economic, or law and order, conditions within their spheres of authority. In 1942, the presence of the American and Chinese units, was frowned upon in the localities because of their frequent clashes with the local populace, the officials' lack of any powers to prosecute them and because these units could not be called into assist the administration to crush any uprisings.[167] Similarly, the Government of India's imposition of the 'free-trade' policy between May and June 1943 caused antagonistic reactions in the provinces. For instance, the Governor of Bihar reported in June 1943 that his district officers 'were rebellious' over the 'law and order aspect' of implementing the policy, and that one British officer had asked to be relieved if it were continued.[168] These apprehensions were noted in a military intelligence report in July 1943, which stated that the shortages of food had caused civil servants in the localities of the eastern provinces to fear that '... there [wa]s an increasing risk that the feeling of unrest engendered by the economic situation m[ight] develop into a serious menace to law and order'.[169] The civilian officials' trepidation was underlined in yet another Eastern Army review which stated that the district administrators feared that the 'smouldering discontent engendered by severe economic conditions' might 'be fired' by local acts of violence either 'fortuitously or deliberately'.[170] This widespread fear of rebellions caused officials to continually endeavour to curb the outbreak of trouble through the distribution of material and information propaganda material amongst the rural populace in general, and its poorer sections in particular. The nature and effects of these public relations programmes, as well as those targeted at the 'priority classes', is assessed in greater detail in the following chapter.

Notes

1 It is often forgotten, for instance, that Congress members continued to participate in the proceedings of provincial legislative assemblies even after the withdrawal of the party ministries. For a good description of such Congress activity during the Second World War, see K.M. Patra, *Orissa State Legislature And Freedom Struggle 1912–47*, New Delhi, 1979.
2 S. Sarkar, *Modern India*, Delhi, 1983, p. 383.

3 Reports on the political situation in India by the Central Intelligence Officers touring the provinces, c.1941, HPF(I) 241/41, NAI. Describing the situation in the spring of 1941, a civil servant who had been based in the United Provinces declared that, 'The Congress were now campaigning openly against the British regime. They held meetings advocating opposition to the war-effort, an offence under the Defence of India Act. The effect on recruitment to the armed forces was slight but, if only to maintain self-respect, the authorities were bound to prosecute'. Recollections of E.A. Midgley, ICS, MSS EUR F. 180/78, OIOC.

4 R. Hunt and J. Harrison, *The District Officer in India, 1930–1947*, London, 1980, p. 206.

5 The use of varied political symbols against the colonial administration during the war has been recently discussed by Srimanjiri, 'Denial, Dissent and Hunger: War-time Bengal, 1942–44', in B. Pati (ed), *Turbulent Times: India, 1940–44*, Mumbai, 1998.

6 Official reports would often point out how the Congress cadres operating in the localities would reproduce circulars released by the party's Working Committee or the Provincial Committees in the vernaculars, and their dialects, and frequently alter them by incorporating discussions of parochial issues so as to increase their popularity amongst the members of their constituencies. See, for instance, *Report on the Disturbances 1942–43, Supplementary Secret Evidence*, New Delhi, 1944, pp. 24–34, R/3/1/352, OIOC.

7 A massive effort was made to modernise and enlarge the Indian Air Force from April-May 1942 and by December that year there were 29 fully operational squadrons in the country. War Department History – Modernisation and Mechanisation of the Armed Forces of India (September 1939 to February 1944), pp. 23–70, L/R/5/275, OIOC. For more information on the gradual growth and sophistication of the RAF, see Secret War Department History – Expansion of the Armed Forces in India, p. 66, L/R/5/273, OIOC.

8 Secret War Department History: The Defence of India, 6 May 1944, pp. 35–36, L/R/5/274, OIOC. Also see, War Department History: Engineer Matters (September 1939–August 1945), pp. 16–27, L/R/5/282, OIOC.

9 War Department History – Modernisation and Mechanisation of the Armed Forces of India (September 1939 to February 1944), pp. 65–66, L/R/5/275, OIOC.

10 In March 1942 the Ministry of War Transport and the Admiralty instructed their representatives in Calcutta to reduce the tonnage proceeding north of Vizagapatnam to the 'absolute minimum'. Subsequently, faced with inadequate air-defences the navy removed number of ships from Calcutta, Vizagapatnam and Madras to the ports in the west coast and in accordance to this policy 55 ships sailed southwards between 27 March and 5 April 1942 (of these only 36 reached their destination safely. The 19 ships intercepted and sunk by the Japanese navy represented a loss of 92,215 tons). On the 6 April all sailings from Calcutta were discontinued. Note on shipping losses in the Bay of Bengal, c.1942, L/WS/1/1287, OIOC.

11 The services run by the railway authorities in Bengal and Assam remained unsatisfactory throughout 1942–43. Secret War Department History – Transportation and Movements (September 1939-December 1944), 1945, pp. 1–7, L/R/5/280, OIOC.
12 Before 1942, road building activities had been dictated by the war in Europe, the Middle East and the India's North Western frontiers. See, War Department History – Supply and Transport (September 1939 to August 1940), pp. 1–3, L/R/5/284, OIOC. *History of the War Transport Department, July 1942 to October 1945*, New Delhi, 1946, p. 50, L/R/5/297, OIOC.
13 The powers of officials attached to the Central Public Works Department were increased substantially for the duration of the war. Powers were delegated, for instance, to Superintending Engineers posted in the Eastern, Western and Southern 'aviation circles' under the Defence of India Rules, and they were empowered to requisition stocks of any material required for 'urgent' defence works. Memorandum on steps taken to facilitate and expedite the execution of increased demand for public works for the duration of the war, n.d, War History of the Department of Works, Mines and Power, L/R/5/298, OIOC. The Defence of India Rules contained a number of provisions conferring comprehensive powers to the authorities to requisition property of any description, movable or immovable. Secret review of war legislation in the courts, n.d, pp. 15–16, L/R/5/292, OIOC.
14 See, for instance, recollections of G.M. Ray, ICS, p. 6, MSS EUR F.180/23, OIOC.
15 Reports on the 'grievances' which were subject of the [Congress] Working Committee's resolution of 10 July [1942], n.d, L/PJ/8/596, OIOC.
16 *Report on the Revenue Administration of the United Provinces for the year ended 30th September 1942*, Allahabad, 1944, pp. 2–3, V/24/2445, OIOC.
17 Intelligence reports through commercial and other channels, April–June 1942, L/I/1/1015, OIOC.
18 Secret express letter from R. Tottenham, Additional Secretary, Home Department, GOI to the Chief Secretaries, GOA, GOBe and GOB, 5 June 1942, HPF(I) 4/4//42, NAI. Also see File No. G–31 on Refugees and Evacuees, 1942, AICC collections, NMML.
19 Extract from the GOO fortnightly report dated 5 June 1942, HPF(I) 4/4/42, NAI. Also see confidential telegram from GOA to Home Department, GOI, 12 June 1942, ibid.
20 Satish Das Gupta was served an externment order on 19 July 1942, with which he refused to comply. He was arrested the next day and charged with sedition (he was sentenced to two years' rigorous imprisonment). HPF(I) 4/20/42, NAI. The Bengal Provincial Congress Committee also posted prominent party members to the other affected localities. For instance, Dr. J.R. Dhar was sent to Jessore; Dr. Sachi Mohan Chowdhuri to Chittagong, and Kamini Kumar Datta to Comilla (in Tippera district). See File No. G–31 on Refugees and Evacuees, 1942, AICC collections, NMML.
21 Secret departmental note, Home Department, c.May 1942, L/PJ/8/596, OIOC.

22 Letter from H.G. Dennehy, Chief Secretary, GOA to R. Tottenham, Additional Secretary, Home Department, GOI, 6 July 1942, HPF(I) 4/4/42, NAI.
23 The decision to avoid the implementation of a Soviet style 'scorched earth' policy in India was taken due to a variety of practical reasons: the enormity of the threatened areas; the lack of skilled, and reliable, personnel for supervising a comprehensive policy of denying resources to the enemy; the realisation that any large scale measures could not be kept 'entirely secret' from the civilian population, and a fear that it would create 'millions' of refugees in Eastern India (a situation which the provincial governments were not equipped to handle). Secret telegram from the Defence Department, GOI to L. Amery, SSI, GOBr, 31 March 1942, L/WS/1/1242, OIOC. Also see, most secret summary of case for the decision of H.E, the VEC, c.April 1942, HPF(I) 230/42, NAI.
24 P.D. Martyn, an ICS officer in Bengal, mentions how he was responsible for, '... the movement to North Bengal of elephants from the Chittagong area and the sinking, or trans-shipment, out of the danger area, of much of the riverine craft of the Sunderbans'. Recollections of P.D. Martyn, ICS, p. 21, MSS EUR F. 180/13, OIOC. In addition, bicycles and all forms of motor transport were also removed from the threatened areas. Comparable schemes were undertaken in parts of Assam and Orissa. See reports on the 'grievances' which were subject of the [Congress] Working Committee's resolution of 10 July [1942], nd, L/PJ/8/596, OIOC.
25 It was underlined that while '... wholesale destruction ... [was] not contemplated ... it [wa]s undesirable that the enemy ... be enabled to increase his penetration on account of the assistance he w[ould] gain from stocks of essential commodities in the area. It follow[ed], therefore, that all power stations ... [were to] be destroyed, as their destruction w[ould] cause factories to cease work. Oil installations, including the Refinery at Digboi, w[ould] also be destroyed'. Secret note on demolition policy, GOI, c.1942, L/WS/1/1242, OIOC.
26 Confidential memorandum from J.W. Houlton, Secretary, Civil Defence Department, GOB to the Headquarters, Eastern Army Command, 17 May 1942, WSF 50(iv)/1942, BSA. Grain was also removed from the coastal delta region of East Bengal. Recollections of W.H.J. Christie, ICS, p. 14, MSS EUR F. 180/96, OIOC.
27 Most secret letter from J.W. Houlton, Secretary, Civil Defence Department, GOB to all Commissioners of Divisions, District Magistrates, Additional Deputy Commissioners and Superintendents of Police, 8 April 1942, WSF 50(v)/1942, BSA. Also see most secret letter from Y.A. Godbole, Chief Secretary, GOB to all Commissioners of Divisions, District Magistrates, Additional Deputy Commissioners and Superintendents of Police, 26 April 1942, KW to WSF 50/42, BSA.
28 A good description of the pressures on the civilian administrators in this regard is provided by F.O. Bell, who was the District Magistrate of Bakarganj in 1942. He states in his unpublished memoirs that, 'The impact of war on Bakarganj was really felt when at military request, boats and cycles were first registered, and then made subject to movement control. The army command were convinced that if there was a Japanese invasion,

or some sort of infiltration, the enemy would move more swiftly if they could commandeer local means of transport. Cycles were not numerous in this riverine district, but boats there were by the thousands, and they were the life blood of the community.... Boat owners were required to remove their boats from the 'prohibited area'. A boat receiving station was set up at Palang, in the Faridpur district.... Thousands of boats were received at Palang.' Recollections of F.O. Bell, ICS, MSS EUR F. 180/8, OIOC. Also see, memoirs of O.M. Martin, ICS, p. 233, Martin papers, CSASA.

29 Describing his position to Linlithgow, the Viceroy of India, Herbert, the Governor of Bengal, wrote that, 'We have now been advised by the Military that the phase of this programme [of denial] has been reached in which all boats in coastal districts are to be removed 20 miles from the coast. The task will not be easy, for in some areas in Eastern Bengal boats are essential for marketing purposes, and their removal may involve considerable economic dislocation. Nevertheless, the work will be done. We are helping District Officers by sending them all the additional staff that can be spared ...'. Letter from J.H. Herbert, Governor, GOBe to Linlithgow, Viceroy, 8 April 1942, MSS EUR F. 125/42, OIOC.

30 *Monthly Intelligence Summary (GHQ and AHQ.), No. 4, 4 April 1942,* Simla, 1942, p. 6, L/WS/1/317, OIOC.

31 Rajendra Prasad, Prafulla Chandra Ghosh, Vallabhbhai Patel and Shankarrao Deo were asked to '... preach the new gospel [regarding the scorched earth policy] in their respective provinces'. Secret departmental note, Home Department, GOI, c.May 1942, L/PJ/8/596, OIOC.

32 AICC Inspectors' notes, Utkal [Orissa], c.1942, F.No. P–22 (Part II)/1942, AICC collections, NMML.

33 Extract from the Bengal fortnightly report [Chief Secretary's] for the second half of May, 1942, HPF(I) 164/42, NAI [emphasis original].

34 A report from Bengal described how the members of the Fazlul Huq ministry had been faced with 'considerable pressure' from their 'followers' in the localities and that these ministers feared that the economic hardships engendered by the 'denial policy' would cause them to lose popularity among their respective constituencies. Letter from J.A Herbert, GOBe, to Linlithgow, Viceroy, 8 May 1942, MSS EUR F. 125/42, OIOC.

35 Letter from J.A. Herbert, GOBe, to Linlithgow, Viceroy, 28 July 1942, L/PJ/8/651, Part 2, OIOC. Mr. A.K. Fazlul Huq was forced to resign from the Chief Minister's chair by Herbert on 28 March 1943, and was replaced by Sir Nazimuddin from 24 April 1943.

36 Herbert was nevertheless careful to absolve one particular minister – Khan Bahadur Hashem Ali Khan (of Bakarganj) – of all blame. He did point out, however, that Khan had been greeted by 'black flag' demonstrations organised by the Muslim League during his official tour of Bakarganj, the purpose of which had been to explain the necessity of the 'denial' policy. Letter from J.A. Herbert, Governor, GOBe. to the Viceroy, 21 April 1942, MSS EUR F. 125/42, OIOC. The Muslim League had been active organising opposition to F. Huq's ministry in Eastern Bengal with the objective of gaining a foothold among the Krishak Praja Party's constituencies. Confidential letter from J.A. Herbert, GOBe, to Linlithgow, Viceroy, 10 January 1942, ibid.

37 Letter from J.A. Herbert, GOBe, to Linlithgow, Viceroy, 8 April 1942, MSS EUR F. 125/42, OIOC.
38 Letter from J.A. Herbert, GOBe, to Linlithgow, the Viceroy, 7 July 1942, MSS EUR F. 125/42, OIOC.
39 African troops were considered invaluable for operations in Burma: West African troops were considered particularly useful for jungle missions and protecting porter transport, while soldiers from the eastern part of the African continent were used to bolster the infantry and mechanised artillery divisions in India. Most secret telegram from the A. Wavell, Commander in Chief, India, to the War Office, GOBr, 9 December 1942, L/WS/1/963, OIOC.
40 The American army was divided into three separate groups in India, each with its own headquarters and commanding general. The first, comprising of land forces, was led by Lieutenant-General J.W. Stillwell; the second, the 10th US Army Air Force, was commanded by Major-General L.H. Brereton, and the third, consisting of the service and supply departments, was under the charge of Major-General R.A. Wheeler. Most secret note on the 'Order of Battle: U.S. Forces in India', enclosure to most secret letter from R.C. McCay, India Office, London to H.W. Dinwiddie, War Office, GOBr, 8 July 1942, L/WS/1/1292, OIOC. American army stations were set up in Agra (UP), Allahabad (UP), Asansol (Bengal), Calcutta (Bengal), Dibrugarh (Assam), Dinajpur (Bengal), Fyzabad (UP), Gaya (Bihar), Guskhara (Bengal), Jhansi (UP), Lucknow (UP), Mohanbari (Assam), Nimita (Bengal), Ramgarh (Bihar) and Tezpore (Assam). Secret station list of US Army forces in India, 1 July 1942, ibid.
41 The first Chinese divisions arrived in India from Northern Burma after the Japanese conquest of that country in May 1942. These troops, of the 22nd and the 38th divisions, and those who arrived from China subsequently, were based in Ledo (Assam) and Ramgarh (Bihar). Official correspondence noted that there were 23,700 Chinese personnel at Ramgarh (who were being trained by about 160 American officers), 10,664 in the 'Ledo area' and 10,000 (the 30th Division) were due to arrive 'soon' in June 1943. Confidential note by General Staff Branch (Intelligence Section), GHQ, on the training of Chinese troops by Americans in India, c.June 1943, L/WS/1/1292, OIOC. By the end of June, the strength of the Chinese army in India was increased to 42,000 men. See secret memorandum by L. Amery, SSI, GOBr, c.June 1943, L/WS/1/1362, OIOC. Its strength increased to 57,000 in July 1943. See most secret telegram from Commander-in-Chief, India to Chiefs of Staff Committee, War Cabinet, GOBr, 26 July 1943, ibid. By mid-1944 the number of Chinese soldiers in India had almost doubled to 102,000, a figure which remained largely constant till the end of the hostilities in the Far East. See secret telegram from the War Department, GOI to the Secretary of State for India, GOBr, 24 May 1944, ibid.
42 Recollections of A.H. Kemp, ICS, p. 13, MSS EUR F. 180/18, OIOC.
43 Like many other district officials, H.F.G. Burbridge, a police officer in Assam, recalled how his district was stricken with 'troubles' after he was forced to comply with 'endless demands' for buildings, land and vehicles by the military authorities. A note titled 'The war in Assam 1939–45, from the

view of a district police officer', n.d., by H.F.G. Burbridge, IPS, MSS EUR F. 161/32, OIOC. There were also cases of troops entering bazaars and assaulting shopkeepers. See, for instance, PF 196/43, NAI. Regular investigations about the behaviour of Indian army personnel were carried out and appended to reports forwarded to the Government of India. See, reports on the grievances which were subject of the [Congress] Working Committee's resolution of 10 July [1942], n.d., L/PJ/8/596, OIOC. Also see, recollections of V.G. Matthews, ICS, p. 19, MSS EUR F. 180/44, OIOC.

44 Eastern Army Instructions No. 26060/13/A–2, 10 July 1942, PF 7/9/45, NAI.

45 'European members' of the Royal Air Force would often come looking for prostitutes in the bazaar of Subhapur *mofussil* (in Feni), which would cause friction with the local inhabitants. Note by G.H. Gordon, Sub-Divisional Officer, Feni, c.1943, PF 7/9/43, NAI. Similarly, some West African troops, who had been based in Tripura state, were driven away, and one soldier was 'severely assaulted', by the members of Haripur village (Police station Kotwali) after having gone there in an attempt to procure women. Confidential memorandum from the District Magistrate, Tippera to the Additional Secretary, GOBe, 23 February 1944, PF 7/26/44, NAI. Comparable cases were reported from other localities as well. See letter from M.R. Sarkar, Sub-Divisional Officer, Gaibandha to the District Magistrate, Rangpur, 23 April 1944, PF 7/36/44, NAI. Also see, report entitled 'Certain allegations against the Military Personnel at Ghoshpur, PS Boalmari [Faridpur]' by D.K. Ghosh, Additional District Magistrate, Faridpur, Bengal, 28 February 1945, PF 7/17/45, NAI.

46 A telegram describing Chinese troops arriving in India in 1942, on the basis of reports sent by senior Indian army officers, declared that, 'Stillwell following on same route ... and with [him] part of Chinese Army. Binns reports Army [sic] mere rabble.... On his advice military authorities at Manipur asked to disarm and control Chinese if possible as otherwise will ... become embroiled with hillmen whose loyalty will be seriously shaken if they are looted by our Allies'. Secret telegram from Linlithgow, Viceroy to L. Amery, SSI, GOBr, 15 May 1942, L/PS/12/714, OIOC.

47 Linlithgow, the Viceroy, and Amery, the SSI, both aired their misgivings about Stilwell's (the Supreme Commander of U.S. forces in India) plans in mid-1943 to increase the strength of the Chinese forces in India from 42,000 to 100,000. The latter declared that, 'The presence of [more] Chinese troops may cause the Chinese Government to raise a claim in certain eventualities to meddle in India politics.... The larger the force which they maintain in India the greater this risk becomes. There might even be [a] danger of Chinese troops assisting the Congress Party, either overtly or surreptitiously, in the event of really serious civil disorders breaking out in India, particularly if the situation got temporarily out of ... our military control'. See secret memorandum by L. Amery, SSI, GOBr, c.June 1943, L/WS/1/1362, OIOC.

48 Apart from the fear that it would be difficult to dislodge large bodies of Chinese soldiers from Burma after the country was re-conquered from the Japanese, the British Chiefs of Staff Committee declared that, 'There is the further point that an increase of Chinese troops in India would

undoubtedly mean an increase of American influence and of American claims to run [the] campaign from Assam. We therefore recommend from a military point of view that no more Chinese troops should be accepted in India ...'. Secret report by the Chiefs of Staff Committee, War Cabinet, GOBr, 23 June 1943, L/WS/1/1362, OIOC.

49 Officials were worried that the rejection of the Chinese proposal of sending more troops to strengthen the Allied detachments in Eastern India would, 'have an unfortunate effect on ... relations not only with China, but also the United States. It would be misrepresented as a further refusal of Chinese military assistance and the resulting propaganda put out by the Chinese in the United States might have serious consequences'. Telegram from War Office, GOBr to Commander-in-Chief, India, c.October 1942, L/WS/1/1362, OIOC.

50 See, for instance, list of cases involving assaults [by American personnel] upon Indian civilians between 1 January 1944 and 30 August 1944, PF 7/9/45, NAI. Upper Assam and the districts of Rajshahi and Dacca in Bengal witnessed the largest number of clashes between U.S. troops and the local populace. Departmental note, Home Department, GOI, c.1945, PF 7/11/45, NAI. Also see report by Rai Bahadur J.P. Ray, District Magistrate, Burdwan, 17 April 1944, PF 7/41/44, N.A.I, and letter from M.A. Haque, DSP, Jorhat to DIGP, GOA, c.1944, PF 7/48/45, NAI. Sometimes more serious incidents occurred in the localities. One such incident involved the 'wrongful action of American authorities at Chakulia airfield, Bihar, in carrying out searches in neighbouring villages and detaining a number of villagers'. See, PF 7/65/44, NAI.

51 See, M/3/1197, OIOC.

52 Letter from Adjutant General's Branch, GHQ to the Allied Liaison Office, General Staff Branch, GHQ, 31 August 1944, PF 7/9/45, NAI.

53 The US army authorities had agreed to the British request that the Government of India be informed about what action was taken by them in cases where their personnel had committed 'serious civil offences' and had been handed over to them for trial by court martial. According to an Indian army report, 'In view of the difficulties which might be experienced by the US Forces in notifying the correct District Magistrate or Police authorities, we [the Adjutant General's office] suggested that the necessary information should be passed to this Section in the first instance in order that it may be forwarded by us to the Provincial Government concerned through [the] War Department [Government of India]'. Secret departmental note, Adjutant General's Branch, GHQ, 19 November 1943, PF 7/9/45, NAI. However, the information provided by American authorities remained spasmodic and sketchy throughout 1942–45. See departmental note by R. Tottenham, Additional Secretary, Home Department, GOI, 22 March 1945, HPF(I) 33/12/45, OIOC.

54 Departmental note, Home Department, GOI, c.1945, PF 7/11/45, NAI.

55 See departmental note, External Affairs Department, GOI, 28 October 1944, PF 7/70/44, NAI.

56 Letter from P.D. Martyn, Additional Secretary, GOBe, to R. Tottenham, Additional Secretary, Home Department, GOI, 26 May 1945, PF 7/84/44, NAI.

57 Letter from M.A. Haque, DSP, Jorhat to DIGP, GOA, c.1944, PF 7/48/45, NAI.
58 *Monthly Intelligence Summary (GHQ and AHQ), No. 4, 4 April 1942*, Simla, 1942, p. 1, L/WS/1/317, OIOC.
59 Letter from D. Young, Public Relations Directorate, GOI to M.K. Gandhi, 6 April 1942, L/PJ/8/596, OIOC.
60 Kirchner explained further that all attempts 'to bring into hatred or contempt ... the armed forces [w]ere 'prejudicial acts' within the meaning of [the] Defence of India Rules, but in order to draw attention to the fact and remove any ambiguity, an explanatory amendment ... [was] made in the Defence of India [legislation]'. See express letter from J. Kirchner, Chief Press Adviser, GOI to all provincial governments, 12 June 1942, HPF(I) 21/16/42, NAI.
61 India Ravaged, 1943, n.d., pp. 12–30.
62 Quoted in CSFR(2), Bihar, April 1943, HPF(I) 18/4/43, NAI.
63 Recollections of G.P. Woodford, ICS, p. 18, MSS EUR F. 180/16, O.I.O.C
64 A notable, and representative, instance of nationalist attempts to use racial categories in order to instil hostility against the armed forces was that of the *Yogi*, a Hindi daily published from Bihar, which was 'warned' by the Provincial Press Adviser's office on 24 January 1942 for printing an editorial entitled 'Terror of White Soldiers'. See CSFR(2), Bihar, January 1942, HPF(I) 18/1/42, NAI.
65 For example, an article in the *Indian Express*, a pro-Congress paper, which described an incident in Calcutta where three 'well-to-do' women travelling in a taxi had been carried away and raped by American troops, declared that, 'American military authorities must take prompt measures to prevent outrages of this kind. A country is judged abroad by the behaviour of its nationals. The better type of American has been able to give a good account of himself and make friends in the neighbourhoods where his duty has been cast. But his good offices by way of promoting goodwill can make no impression if evil actions of the kind reported from Calcutta are not dealt with sternly. Unless the weight of cultured American opinion is exerted fully against the misdeeds of their lower breeds who have been disgracing themselves scandalously, the whole atmosphere on Indo-American relations is apt to be embittered and poisoned irretrievably. Once this happens, all American talk of making a better world after the war will only engender withering scorn in India.' *Indian Express*, 13 March 1945.
66 *Dawn*, 15 March 1945.
67 Departmental note by F.G. Cracknell, Home Department, GOI, 15 March 1943, HPF(I) 33/12/45, NAI. Also see, *People's War*, 11 March 1945.
68 See departmental memoranda, Home Department, c.1942, HPF(I) 21/16/42, NAI.
69 See for instance, CSFR(1), Bihar, March 1943, HPF(I) 18/3/43, NAI. Also see, CSFR(1), Assam, May 1943, HPF(I) 18/5/43, NAI.
70 CSFR(2), Bihar, June 1942, HPF(I) 18/6/42, OIOC.
71 Chief Censor's Information Summaries, May–August 1942, HPF(I) 20/26/42, NAI. Also see, letter from G.S. Bozman, Information and Broadcasting Department, GOI to J. Hennessy, Information Officer with the Agent General for India in USA, 2 May 1944, L/I/1/1133, OIOC.

72 Most secret WIS(II), 12 February 1943, L/WS/1/1433, OIOC.
73 The Governor of Bengal reported in June 1942, for instance, that the 'denial' policy had 'seriously interfered with the economic life of the areas concerned. It is difficult to dispose of paddy and rice in coastal areas, and the reverse trade in kerosene, mustard oil, &c., has virtually ceased, many fishermen have lost their livelihood altogether at a time of year when they normally expect to make their annual profit from the hilsa season; it is impossible to ferry cattle and bagardars to carry on cultivation in the char areas.' Letter from J.A. Herbert, Governor, GOBe, to Linlithgow, Viceroy, 19 June 1942, MSS EUR F. 125/42, OIOC.
74 *Report on the Revenue Administration of the United Provinces for the year ended 30th September 1942*, Allahabad, 1944, p. 3, V/24/2445, OIOC.
75 Recollections of D. Macpherson, ICS, p. 41, MSS EUR F. 180/12, OIOC.
76 Secret telegram from A. Wavell, Commander-in-Chief, India to War Office, GOBr, 11 December 1942, L/WS/1/1247, Part 1, OIOC. Also see secret telegrams from A. Wavell, Commander-in-Chief, India to War Office, GOBr, 25 December 1942, 9 January 1943 and 14 April 1943, ibid.
77 Rice was regularly being smuggled out from Bihar into Bengal in boats down the Ganges. CSFR(2), Bihar, March 1943, HPF(I) 18/3/43, NAI. Also see CSFR(1), Bihar, April 1943, HPF(I) 18/4/43, NAI. Similar problems were faced by the authorities in Assam as well. It was reported in May 1943 that the total seizures from smugglers in Goalpara district stood at 85,234 *maunds* of paddy and 1,484 *maunds* of rice. Enormous amounts of these commodities were also being smuggled out of Sylhet district. CSFR(1), Assam, May 1943, HPF(I) 18/5/43, NAI.
78 *The Famine Enquiry Commission, Final Report*, Madras, 1945, p. 65, V/26/830/11, OIOC.
79 See table attached to letter from T. Rutherford, GOBe, to the Viceroy, 2 October 1943, R/3/2/49, File No. 2, Coll. ix, OIOC.
80 For a description of the price rises in Bihar, see CSFR(1), Bihar, May 1943, HPF(I) 18/5/43, NAI. The impact of the policy of 'free-trade' on Assam is described in CSFR(2), Assam, May 1943, ibid. The provincial governments were only able to 'regain control' over the situation after the prices of grains fell following the abandonment of the 'free-trade' policy. *The Famine Enquiry Commission, Final Report*, Madras, 1945, pp. 4–37, V/26/830/11, OIOC.
81 A report from Assam mentioned that the 'free-trade' policy caused a 'phenomenally high' rise in the prices of food and how '... the result [wa]s virtually a quasi famine condition among poorer classes'. CSFR(2), Assam, May 1943, HPF(I) 18/5/43, NAI. A similar situation arose in Bihar. See autobiographical note, D.W. Stanton-Ife, p. 7, Stanton-Ife papers, CSASA.
82 Recollections of R.S. Swann, ICS, p. 4, MSS EUR F. 180/25, OIOC. For a good description of the disruptive influence of the 'free-trade' policy on the economies of the localities of Orissa and its contribution to accentuating famine conditions in the province, see Patra, *Orissa State Legislature And Freedom Struggle*, pp. 202–213.

83 Secret telegram A. Wavell, Viceroy, India, to L. Amery, SSI, GOBr, 4 March 1944, L/I/1/1110, OIOC.
84 A report from Auchinleck mentioned in 1944 that Eastern India was plagued by endemic 'food difficulties' and an 'acute' shortage of quinine, and that Bengal and Bihar were stricken by a malaria epidemic. Secret telegram from C.J.E. Auchinleck, Commander-in-Chief, India to War Office, GOBr, 15 August 1944, L/WS/1/1248, OIOC. The severity of the malaria epidemic was reduced in 1944–45, with the onset of the cold weather. Secret telegram from C.J.E. Auchinleck, Commander-in-Chief, India to War Office, GOBr, 30 January 1945, ibid. In addition, large parts of Eastern India were also afflicted with 'devastating [smallpox and cholera] epidemics' after the 'Bengal tragedy' of 1943. Once again, the paucity of vaccines in India, most of which were being supplied to the military authorities, intensified the pandemics. Memorandum on Public Health activities during the War by C.A. Bozman, Commissioner, Public Health, GOI, 20 August 1945. See War History of the Public Health Department, L/R/5/294, OIOC.
85 For instance, see CSFR(2), Bihar, December 1941, HPF(I) 18/12/41, NAI.
86 Pamphlet entitled 'The Freedom Struggle Front', attached to departmental note, Home Department, GOI, 11 December 1942, HPF(I) 3/8/42, NAI.
87 Extracts of notes made by an officer at the 'Commissioner's Conference' held at Calcutta on 14 December 1942, attached to secret note on the 'Congress Movement', General Staff Branch, GOI, 22 December 1942, HPF(I) 3/8/42, NAI.
88 See, for instance, extracts from secret reports by District Magistrates in Bihar, Eastern United Provinces and Assam, c.1943, WSF 63/iii/43, BSA.
89 See, for instance, *Hindustan Times*, 5 July 1943. Also see article entitled 'A Second and Worse Famine Threatens Bengal: Causes of Last Catastrophe Coming Again' in *Amrita Bazar Patrika*, 18 January 1944. Officials bemoaned the existence of such hostility. One report criticised the 'invention' of 'astronomical figures' of casualties in the mofussils and declared that 'One calculator has killed a quarter of Bengal's population'. Secret telegram from the External Affairs Department, GOI to L. Amery, SSI, GOBr, 25 November 1943, L/WS/1/1247, Part 1, OIOC. Also see letter from H. Tufnell-Barrett, Additional Secretary, GOBe, to R. Tottenham, Additional Secretary, Home Department, GOI, 28 January 1944, HPF(I) 33/37/43, NAI.
90 Secret telegram from the External Affairs Department, GOI to L. Amery, SSI, GOBr, 25 November 1943, L/WS/1/1247, Part 1, OIOC. Also see note on the migration of destitutes from Bengal to other provinces, c.1943, HPF(I) 90/43, NAI.
91 Secret report on the activities of the various Relief committees and Legal Aid committees organised by Congressmen, c.1943, HPF(I) 4/1/1944, NAI.
92 *Inquilab*, No. 4, 10 October 1943. Annexure to note by E.J. Burbridge, Assistant Director, IB, GOA, 22 March 1944, HPF(I) 3/13/44, NAI. Another, distributed widely in the localities of Bengal on behalf of the province's Provincial Congress Committee, prescribed the following slogans for the celebration of the 'Independence Day' in 1944: 'Long live

revolution; Bande Mataram; Quit India, Englishmen; Carry on vigorously, drive away the English; Either victory or death; Present famine is the creation of the Imperialist English; Sacrifice your life but do not part with paddy.' Translation of a cyclostyled bulletin in Bengali entitled 'Independence Day Programme' attached to a memorandum by the IB, Home Department, GOI, 21 January 1944, HPF(I) 3/2/44, NAI.
93 Recollections of D. Macpherson, ICS, pp. 43–44, MSS EUR F.180/12, OIOC.
94 *The Statesman's* stance disturbed officials within the Government of India's Home Department, who complained that the paper seemed to be suffering from a 'left nationalist deviation'. Secret Home Department review, c.September 1943, HPF(I) 33/37/43, NAI.
95 One report mentioned how the press all over the country was 'in full cry ... after official scapegoats' and exploiting the issue for 'political purposes'. Secret telegram from the Information and Broadcasting Department, GOI to L. Amery, SSI, GOBr, 2 September 1943, L/WS/1/1247 Part 1, OIOC. Another official review underlined how the Indian owned press was using the adverse food situation to discredit the central government and the 'British generally'. Secret telegram from the Information and Broadcasting Department, GOI to L. Amery, SSI, GOBr, 23 September 1943, ibid.
96 General Sir Archibald Wavell, the Commander-in-Chief of British forces based in India in 1942, was appointed Field Marshal from 1 January 1943 and replaced the Marquess of Linlithgow as Viceroy from 20 October 1943 (General Sir Claude Auchinleck assumed charge of the Commander-in-Chief's office from 20 June 1943). Wavell remained in office till the arrival of Mountbatten in India on 22 March 1947.
97 Secret telegram from A. Wavell, Viceroy, to L. Amery, SSI, GOBr, 12 March 1944, L/I/1/1110, OIOC.
98 Report from W.W. Lewis, GOO to A. Wavell, Viceroy, 1 February 1944, R/3/1/187, OIOC. Also see, text of Pandit Nilkanth Das's speech on the food situation in the Indian Legislative Assembly, 16 November 1943, MacDonald papers, MSS EUR F. 360/10, OIOC.
99 Confidential telegram from the Information and Broadcasting Department, GOI to L. Amery, SSI, GOBr, 22 November 1943, HPF(I) 51/6/44, NAI.
100 Ibid.
101 Secret telegram from A. Wavell, Commander-in-Chief, Indian army to War Office, GOBr, 14 April 1943, L/WS/1/1247 Part 1, OIOC. For further descriptions the activities of the communist cadres with regards to the food position see CSFR(1), Bihar, January 1943, HPF(I) 18/1/43, N.A.I and CSFR(2), Bihar, March 1943, HPF(I) 18/3/43, NAI. The communists' 'exploitation' of the economic situation was also reported from the United Provinces. See CSFR(2), UP, May 1943, HPF(I) 18/5/43, NAI.
102 For instance, see an article by Somnath Lahiri entitled 'Queues of Death' in the party's mouthpiece, which provided graphic descriptions of starvation deaths all over Bengal. *People's War*, 5 September 1943. Articles describing the effects of the epidemics and the shortage of the

required medicines, which was blamed on the colonial administration, remained common throughout 1944. See, for example, *People's War*, 27 February 1944; 16 April 1944; 28 May 1944; 30 July 1944; 27 August 1944; 10 September 1944; 15 October 1944; 19 November 1944 and 1 April 1945.

103 Cadres of the Communist Party of India formed more than a hundred *Jana Raksha* (People's Protection) associations in Bengal and a large number of 'food committees' throughout Eastern India. *People's War*, 18 April 1943. Also see CSFR(2), Bihar, February 1943, HPF(I) 18/2/43, NAI, and CSFR(2), Bihar, March 1943, HPF(I) 18/3/43, NAI. Military intelligence from Eastern India would also frequently report how communist cadres operating within the localities of the region were 'spreading alarmist forecasts' about the famine through a variety of publications and 'local food campaigns'. Such activity was most noticeable in East Bengal (particularly in the district of Chittagong). See, for instance, most secret WIS(II), 14 April 1944, L/WS/1/1433, OIOC.

104 The cultural fronts organised by the Communist Party of India often attracted prominent non-communists like the famous novelist Tarashankar Banerjee. The IPTA, which remained active throughout the war, drew well-known figures like Balraj Sahni, Khwaja Ahmad Abbas, Kaifi Azmi, Salil Chaudhuri, Sambhu Mitra, Debabrata Biswas, Suchitra Mukherjee and Sukanta Bhattacharji. Sarkar, *Modern India*, p. 413. The organisation's 'Independence Day' pledge for 1944 is a good example of Communist anti-government propaganda. It declared that, 'Independence Day this year comes at a time when utter extinction faces Bengal, the land which gave us our Renaissance and where was born our national movement. Five million Bengalis have already been wiped out by the famine, which started there over 6 months ago.... The bureaucracy out to hide the bankruptcy of its Indian policy from the world at large, has been saying for the last two months that the famine in Bengal is over. Just the opposite is the truth. Malaria, Small-pox, dropsy, typhoid, a host of epidemics have come in the wake of starvation.... In the towns and villages, an army of helpless women and children deserted by their destitute men folk is left. Mothers are selling their children and women are offering themselves up to prostitution, as the only way of getting a meal a day...'. Daily intelligence digest by DIB, GOI, 22 January 1944, KW to HPF(I) 7/5/44, NAI.

105 B. Sen, *Rural Bengal in Ruins*, Bombay, 1945, p. 1. Also see P.G. Bhaduri, *Aftermath of Bengal Famine: Problem of Rehabilitation And Our Task*, Calcutta, 1945.

106 Leslie Johnson, who had been district officer in the United Provinces, stated that '... [he] d[id] not remember any authenticated cases of sheer brutality [during the Raj].... outside occasions ... like ... in 1942, when everyone's blood was up. Dreadful things had been done on both sides. And reprisals are anything but bloody .... there were cases when brutalities were committed in the name of restoring peace and order all over the country'. Oral interview with L.J. Johnson, ICS, MSS EUR T. 37, OIOC.

107 Report on public statement released by certain ladies protesting against action taken by the Government in connection with the Congress Civil Disobedience Movement (1942), c.1943, HPF(I) 3/87/42, NAI.
108 This amounted to 'holding meetings and taking out processions without licence, flag hoisting ceremonies, the observance of Labour Day, Quit India Day, Fasting Day and Students' Day and finally of Martyr's Day in which speeches ... [were made] describing the so-called British atrocities.' CSFR(2), Bihar, March 1943, HPF(I) 18/3/43, NAI.
109 Daily Digest, IB, Home Department, GOI, 3 July 1943, HPF(I) 3/47/43, NAI.
110 Extract from Calcutta Police (Special Branch) Daily Notes, 2 September 1943, attached to note by E.J. Beveridge, Assistant Director, IB, Home Department, GOI, 9 September 1943, HPF(I) 3/47/43, NAI.
111 The preface of one such book, which was released in January 1943, declared that: 'This series is chiefly intended to give an unvarnished, objective picture of the frightfulness practised by the British Government in India under the guise of crushing the uprising which followed the arrest of Indian leaders on the 9th of August 1942. As far as possible it will only contain reports which are either already sufficiently authenticated or are generally known to be substantially true and are believed by all but that impersonal entity called 'the Government'. It is not denied that much of the horrors was [sic] possible because there were Indians to do the dirty job. But the Indian personnel of Government as a whole has been definitely lukewarm and unwilling, and in almost all cases the brutalities have been carried out under expert European management, whether the manager was a bloodthirsty Governor, a ferocious District Manager, or a self-satisfied, callous Viceroy.... As against about 70 lives lost on the Government side, the estimated number killed on the people's side either in course of encounters or wanton stray shooting at unwary or harmless individuals is 25,000. The official figure would probably be 2,000. But even officials, in their private capacity, believe that the truth is nearer the former figure.' India Ravaged, preface, no pp.
112 Inquilab, No. 4, 10 October 1943. Also see, annexure to note by E.J. Burbridge, Assistant Director, IB, GOA, 22 March 1944, HPF(I) 3/13/44, NAI.
113 CID Records, Bihar, No. 190 LLXXII; Account No. 655, NMML.
114 See pamphlet in Assamese titled 'A Message from the Congress and for the matter of that of Mahatma Gandhi to the police and the military', c.1942, KW 5 to HPF(I) 3/80/42, NAI. Similar views were also espoused in leaflets, written in Assamese, titled 'A direction from general public to all Government and semi-Government officers', 'A direction from All India Congress Committee' and 'All India Congress Committee'. Ibid.
115 Recollections of E.A. Midgley, ICS, p. 49, MSS EUR F. 180/78, OIOC.
116 *Report on the Disturbances 1942–43, Supplementary Secret Evidence*, New Delhi, 1944, pp. 24–34, R/3/1/352, OIOC.
117 Monthly intelligence report no. 141 C.L., June 1944, H.Q. Civil Liaison Organisation [UP & Western Area], 7 July 1944, HPF(I) 3/46/44, NAI.
118 Secret summary of communist activity for August and September 1942, IB, Home Department, GOI, HPF(I) 7/5/42, NAI. Also see S. Bhattacharya,

'The Colonial State and the Communist Party of India, 1942–45', *SAR*, Vol. 15, No. 1, 1995, pp. 71–72.
119 *Hunkar*, 10 January 1943 and 21 February 1943 This newspaper, which was published in Hindi, was the mouthpiece of the Kisan Sabha controlled by Swami Sahajanand. It had a significant readership in Bihar and the eastern parts of United Provinces.
120 AICC Inspectors' notes, Assam, Bihar, Bengal and Utkal, c.1942, File No. P–22 (Part II)/1942, AICC collections, NMML
121 Secret report on the activities of the various Relief committees and Legal Aid committees organised by Congressmen, c.1943, HPF(I) 4/1/1944, NAI.
122 See, for instance, the secret 'Draft Plan of Propaganda for India', by the Overseas Planning Committee, Paper No. 128, MOI, GOBr, 6 May 1942, INF 1/556, PRO.
123 Therefore, depending on the audience, the advertisement of the war-effort was often packaged is strikingly different ways. It is, therefore, useful to avoid dismissing all wartime propaganda material as an invention of the disseminator: a particular publicity item could represent the truth, be an absolute fabrication, or merely be the truth out of context, depending on the audience or the current strategic situation.
124 The Congress's opposition to Linlithgow's declaration of war ended this propaganda truce with the party. Efforts were made to win Congress support for the British war-aims, but the pre-eminence given to mobilising resources for the conflict increased the tensions between government and the Congress. Richard Tottenham, the Additional Secretary to the Government of India's Home Department, marked the resulting intolerance of dissent in a letter to the provinces in August 1940. It declared that 'the Government of India are responsible for ensuring that no circumstances come into existence which might in any way have the effect of impeding the efficient prosecution of the war, an object which must in present circumstances have precedence over all other considerations. It is obvious that any threat to the maintenance of law and order in India, or any action that might tend to disturb or upset the administration of the country, would have the effect referred to above. The possibilities are numerous – ranging as they do from an organized campaign of open defiance of constituted authority promoted by some political party, to less recognisable, but nonetheless dangerous, activities which may lead to the undermining of authority and the promotion of feelings of insecurity and thus eventually culminate in local or widespread outbreaks of disorder...'. Secret letter from R. Tottenham, Additional Secretary, Home Department, GOI to the Chief Secretaries of all provincial governments, 2 August 1940, PDGF 69/12, BSA.
125 It has to be kept in mind that Indians had a significant presence in the ICS, and predominated in the other wings of the central services and the provincial civil services by 1939. Moreover, the new wartime bureaucracy that was created to deal with the strategic crisis arising from the Japanese threat was almost completely Indian in composition.
126 See, for instance, A. Mitra, *Towards Independence 1940–47: Memoirs of an Indian Civil Servant*, Bombay, 1991, pp. 73–101. The formation of

the elected provincial ministries in 1937 ushered in a new wave of bureaucratic adaptation, which, apart from even affecting administrative practise in the 'military provinces' of India, increased the scope of re-adapting policies prescribed by the Government of India. The ballot box, despite a limited franchise, could bring Indian politicians to power, and this thoroughly re-shaped local bureaucratic relations. The new ministers were given the ability to determine bureaucratic fortunes, and although they could sign dismissal orders for civilian bureaucrats, they had the power to transfer them to unsavoury locations, which many officials, both European and Indian, considered tantamount to a demotion.

127 Ganguly's actions were not informed by nationalist zeal. Indeed, he considered Gandhi and many of the local Congress big-wigs to be 'bounders' who were disturbing the status quo. He was, however, acutely aware of their capacity to create trouble in his sphere of administration and thus found it expedient to cultivate good relations with them. Interview with I. Banerjee, 11 November 1993. The situation arising from the war in the Far-East between 1942 and 1943 provided increased employment opportunities for the educated middle-classes in Eastern India. In Bengal, the educated Hindus, who had been denied jobs between 1937–41 by the stern application of the communal reservation policies of the Fazlul Huq ministry, considered the government posts which were created by the presence of the Allied army to be an absolute godsend. However, Prakash Chandra Ganguly, who became a Civil Liaison Officer during this period, remained careful not to annoy the sensibilities of the prominent Congressmen, Krishak Party members and the Muslim Leaguers he encountered. Ibid.

128 An intelligence report (dated 3 September 1942) from Bihar mentioned how a military party which had gone to the village Dariagawan to arrest Jagannath Singh, the local Congress leader who also happened to be the son of the local rural magnate, found that he had escaped the previous night, since the news of his forthcoming capture had been 'leaked out' by local officials. Similar incidents were also reported from the villages Chatran and Barnia. Secret military (daily) intelligence summaries, 27 August 1942 to 8 September 1942, Stanton-Ife papers, CSASA.

129 Recollections of C.S. Venkatchar, ICS, p. 45, MSS EUR F. 180/85, OIOC.

130 Recollections of D. Vira, ICS, MSS EUR F. 180/84, OIOC.

131 R.P. Noronha, *A Tale Told By An Idiot*, New Delhi, 1976, pp. 2–3.

132 Recollections of J.D. Shukla, ICS, MSS EUR F. 180/81, OIOC.

133 Secret report from M. Hallett, Governor, GOUP to Linlithgow, Viceroy, 23 April 1941, HPF(I) 3/31/40, NAI. Hallett had previously held the Governorship of the province of Bihar.

134 See, for instance, extract of report by the provincial leader of the Bihar branch of the National War Front, c.1943, CSFR(2), Bihar, February 1943, HPF(I) 18/2/43, NAI.

135 Secret letter from P.N. Thapar, Deputy Secretary, Information and Broadcasting Department, GOI to the Chief Secretaries of all provincial governments, 24 December 1941, PPAF 4/1942, BSA.

136 The primary 'internal security' role of the colonial army consisted of 'duties in aid of civil power'. *AITM*, No. 2 (1940), L/MIL/17/5/2240,

OIOC. In 1939, of the 35 battalions available in India, 26 were allocated to 'internal security'. During the 'Quit India' movement, 57 and a half battalions (many from the field army) had to be employed to crush the Congress 'rebellion' and to protect the railway lines from sabotage. By mid-1943, only 12 battalions were allocated to internal security. Secret letter from India Office, GOBr, to T.E. Williams, War Office, GOBr, 6 July 1943, L/WS/1/1337, OIOC.

137 This decision was taken as the 'Quit India' movement had proved, according to the military authorities, that the police forces in India were inadequately staffed and provisioned. Most secret note from the GHQ, India to the War Office, GOBr, 15 January 1943, L/WS/1/1337, OIOC.

138 The onset of the war in the Far-East caused increased attention to be given to the distribution of all varieties of propaganda, especially material resources in the form of cash bonuses and subsidised food, among the state's employees with the aim of securing 'general contentment'. Secret express letter from R. Tottenham, Additional Secretary, Home Department, GOI to all provincial governments, 5 October 1942, HPF(I) 3/84/1942, NAI. The distribution of food by the colonial authorities amongst the personnel of the armed forces and the 'essential services' was maintained throughout the famine of 1943. Recollections of W.H.J. Christie, ICS, p. 14, MSS EUR F. 180/96, OIOC.

139 Describing the 'primary audience' targeted by the Government of India's Information and Broadcasting Department between 1939 and 1945, Frederick Puckle, who was its secretary throughout the period, declared that 'those who hear, read or see at first hand, what you put over, is that small section of the population which listens to foreign stations, reads foreign news and sees British films. This is educated India.' Secret War History of the Bureau of Public Information 1939–45, GOI, p. 4, L/R/5/295, OIOC. This view was reiterated by other senior figures within the central government. In a lecture given in April 1944 to a gathering of military and civil policy-makers, an official re-emphasised the importance of considering, and influencing, the attitudes of these 'educated few' who formed '5 per cent' of the country's total population. See appendix A to WIS(II), 5 May 1944, L/WS/1/1433, OIOC. The provincial authorities attempted to reach these sections of the civilian population as well: Casey, who was appointed the Governor of Bengal in 1944 and was active in expanding Bengal's publicity organisations, made implicit references to the importance given to English educated Indians during the production and dissemination of official propaganda. R.G. Casey, *An Australian In India*, London, 1947, pp. 28–29.

140 See, for instance, secret note by Major General N. Molesworth, GHQ (India), 1 September 1942, L/WS/1/1337, OIOC. Also see extract of report by the provincial leader of the Bihar branch of the National War Front, c.1943, in CSFR(2), Bihar, February 1943, HPF(I), NAI.

141 See, for instance, telegram from the Home Department, GOI to L. Amery, SSI, 7 June 1942, L/PJ/8/596, OIOC.

142 Indeed, increased nationalist criticism about the dislocation of the local economies caused district officers to lay increasing emphasis on the censorship of hostile political publicity. See S. Bhattacharya, 'Wartime

policies of State Censorship and the Civilian Population: Eastern India, 1939–45', *SAR*, Vol. 17, No. 2, 1997, pp. 166–172.
143 History of the War: 'The War Risks Insurance Scheme', p. 6, L/R/5/301, OIOC.
144 Ibid., pp. 7–25.
145 Dietmar Rothermund actually provides figures of the number of rupees printed during the war and shows how the increase in circulation of money corresponded with the period in which goods for civilian consumption were becoming scarce within the colonial economy. See, D. Rothermund, *An Economic History of India*, New York, 1986, pp. 119–120.
146 The Government of India's Railway Department, for instance, sanctioned to the temporary railway staff (whether employed on munitions or railway work) a bonus of one day's pay for each completed month of continuous employment. In the spring of 1941 the first dearness allowance was given to the workers with 'back effect from September 1940'. It was subsequently increased on the 1st of November 1941, on the 15th of June 1942 and yet again on the 1st of February 1943. Note on staff matters, undated, War History of Mechanical Department's (Railways) Activities, L/R/5/293, OIOC.
147 Even though the 'dearness allowances' sanctioned to the railway workers were steadily increased during the war, 'the danger of inflation necessitated a revision of the Government's attitude in regard to relief in cash' and forced the rapid expansion of the organisation of 'railway grainshops'. War History of Mechanical Department's (Railways) Activities, pp. 28–29, L/R/5/293, OIOC. Similar trends were also noticeable with regards to police personnel and civil servants attached to other departments. See, for instance, secret weekly intelligence reports from the Deputy Inspector General of Police, Government of Assam, for the weeks ending 3 June 1943 and 9 June 1943, PF 174/58/42 (C), NAI; Extract from the record of the proceedings of the National Defence Council, c.November 1942, HPF(I) 3/84/1942, NAI, and note by D. Pilditch, IB, Home Department, GOI, 10 December 1942, PF 174/58/42 (C), NAI. As a result of a substantial grant made by the central Home Department, the Government of Bihar announced an immediate increase in pay for its police forces. Constables were given an extra Rs 5 a month, armed police given an increase of Rs 3 a month and 'ordinary police' were given an additional Rs 2 a month. The province's 57,000 *chowkidars* were awarded a 'war bonus' of Rs. 2 per month. Letter from T. Rutherford, Governor, GOB to Linlithgow, Viceroy, 13 February 1943, R/3/1/23, OIOC. Also see, secret War History of the Home Department, pp. 25–28, L/R/5/289, OIOC.
148 It was also pointed out that given the fact that the war demand was a priority, there would be an absolute shortage of consumable goods for civilian consumption. As a result, unless productive power could be increased to meet both war and civilian demand, dearness allowances in cash would themselves add to inflationary tendencies. Confidential letter from the Dearness Allowance Sub-Committee to B.R. Ambedkar, Chairman of the Tripartite Labour Conference and Member for the

Department of Labour, VEC, 20 January 1944, Gregory Papers, MSS EUR.D.1163/8, OIOC.
149 See, for instance, 'Proceedings of the first meeting of the Reconstruction Committee (Trade, International Trade Policy and Agricultural Policy) held at New Delhi on the 22nd and 23rd May 1942'. Copy in Gregory papers, MSS.EUR.D. 1163/4, OIOC.
150 Two-thirds of Bengal's urban population lived in Greater Calcutta (which included the cities of Calcutta and Howrah, and 40 other municipal towns, most of which were industrial hamlets along the banks of the Hooghly river), which was considered to be one of the most important industrial areas in India since it had a large number of 'war factories'. The *Famine Enquiry Commission Report on Bengal*, Madras, 1945, pp. 4–5, V/26/830/10, OIOC. All the new arms and munitions factories to be set up in, and after, 1942 were located in Kanpur in the United Provinces. This included a rifle factory, two open hearth furnaces, gun forging presses, and anti-aircraft and field gun factories. The units producing optical instruments for military use was moved from Calcutta and relocated in Dehra Dun (Western United Provinces). Secret letter from the Supply Department, GOI to L. Amery, Secretary of State for India, GOBr, 10 April 1942, L/WS/1/1286, OIOC. The major mining concerns were located in Bihar (coal and mica) and Assam (petroleum and coal). War History of the Labour Department, L/R/5/291, OIOC.
151 The unskilled workers mobilised for the construction of strategic roads and other military sites were organised into 'labour battalions'. Though the first five units were formed in June 1940, the real expansion of the Indian Auxiliary Pioneer Corps (as they were called from 1941) occurred after the outbreak of the Pacific war. While this augmentation was initially made possible with the assistance of the Indian Tea Association, which agreed to close some tea-gardens in order to release 58,000 labourers and 220 European supervisors, recruitment into the services was regularised with the assistance of the provincial authorities and the recruitment of men from the tribal territories of Assam, the Darjeeling district of Bengal and the tribal districts of Bihar. By the end of September 1943 the strength of the corps was approximately 109,000 men. War History of the Labour Department, L/R/5/291, OIOC.
152 The importance of rail workers increased considerably after the shortage of coastal shipping in 1942 caused a diversion of goods, of both military and civilian use, from ships to railways. While the morale of port workers was considered to be of great consequence from the onset of the war, their importance in official eyes increased manifold from the second half of 1943 after the traffic to the ports of eastern India increased dramatically as a result of the preparations for the re-conquest of Burma. Secret War Department History: Transportation and Movements (September 1939–December 1944), 3 September 1945, pp. 1–17, L/R/5/280, OIOC.
153 See, for instance, most secret letter from the Defence Co-oridination Department, GOI to all Chief Secretaries and Chief Commissioners of provinces, 12 March 1941, HPF(I) 15/1/41, NAI.

154 Note on wartime legislation affecting labour, c.1941, HPF(I) 318/42, NAI.
155 See, for instance, most secret letter from the Defence Co-ordination Department, GOI to all Chief Secretaries and Chief Commissioners of provinces, 12 March 1941, HPF(I) 15/1/41, NAI.
156 See, for instance, note on coal mines welfare, n.d, War History of the Labour Department, L/R/5/291, OIOC.
157 Most secret letter from the Chief Secretary, GOA, to the Secretary, Defence Department, GOI, 22 April 1942, HPF(I) 230/42, NAI. Also see most secret letter from J.W Houlton, Secretary, Civil Defence Department, GOB to H.B.L Braund, High Co-ordinating Officer for Civil Population Movements, Eastern Army Area, 20 January 1943, WSF 29 (93)/1942, BSA.
158 John Eadie Bishop, an IPS officer, describes in his private papers how there was a widespread fear of a Japanese invasion, and victory, in Eastern India between December 1941 and May 1942 amongst all denominations of the colonial officialdom based in Eastern India. The situation was considered to have become so critical by the authorities, that he and six Indian policemen began to be trained during April and May 1942 in the use of wireless transmitters, and the identification of tanks, planes and army units. The object was for this team to be 'left behind' in the area east of the Chota Nagpur region of Bihar, which the military expected to be overrun by the Japanese, so that they could gather intelligence regarding the Axis troop positions and transmit this to the British headquarters in Western India. Note by J.E. Bishop, IPS, Bishop papers, MSS EUR D. 1241, OIOC.
159 The Chief Secretaries' reports from Assam, Bengal, Bihar, Orissa and the United Provinces for 1942 were full of references to the anxieties among local officials about the strategic situation, its impact on the economic conditions in the region and the resultant discontent amongst the local civilian populace. See HPF(I) 18/1–12/42, NAI.
160 The shortcomings of the local 'repressive apparatus' in Eastern India during the Second World War was obvious to all District Officers. Provinces like Orissa did not even have a sufficient number of senior bureaucrats. According to a civil servant who had been posted in Orissa, it had '... the bare minimum of staff from [the] Imperial Services'. Recollections of R.S. Swann, ICS, p. 2, MSS EUR F. 180/25, OIOC. Samuel Solomon, another ICS official based in Orissa, mentions in his recollections how he would often wonder after the fall of Singapore whether he would be taken prisoner the next day, since he was aware that the province had no coastal defences. He adds '... we in Orissa did make serious plans to withdraw to Sambhalpur, in the interior of the Province, should the Japanese land, and our furniture and effects had already been dispatched there by rail, before the emergency passed'. Recollections of S. Solomon, ICS, MSS EUR F. 180/24, OIOC.
161 'One Woman's Raj', unpublished memoirs of Viola Bayley, pp. 71–72, Bayley papers, CSASA.
162 See, for instance, letter from A.W. Ibbotson, Secretary, War Department, GOI to all provincial governments and Chief Commissioners, 28 May 1942, PF 174/17/42, NAI.

163 Confidential circular from the Bihar Secretariat, GOB to all district officers, 13 April 1942, WSF 29(11)/1942, BSA. One senior civil servant's memory of the impact of the events of 1942 in Orissa were the 'instructions from the Government to take to one's heels with speed if the Japanese landed'. This caused him to keep his car filled with petrol and a keep a cache of Rs. 200 in coin handy for the purpose. Recollections of R.S. Swann, ICS, p. 3, MSS EUR F. 180/25, OIOC.

164 Secret and personal letter from H. Lewis, Governor, GOO to Linlithgow, Viceroy, India, 26 October 1942, MSS EUR F. 125/84, OIOC.

165 For instance, see, confidential letter from C.L. Bryson, Under Secretary, Home Department, GOI to all provincial governments and Chief Commissioners, 17 April 1942, HPF(I) 211/42, NAI. Also see, letter from F. Puckle, Secretary, Information and Broadcasting Department, GOI to E. Conran-Smith, Secretary, Home Department, GOI, 20 March 1942, HPF(I) 215/1942, NAI. Ashok Mitra, who had based in India during the war, mentions how his sources of information between 1942 and 1943 'had been practically limited' to provincial fortnightly reports, government circulars and his 'Congress acquaintances'. Mitra, *Towards Independence*, p. 101.

166 CSFR(1), Bihar, January 1943, HPF(I) 18/1/43, NAI.

167 The continual nationalist criticism about the law and order problems contributed by the presence of the American forces was made even more galling to officials in the localities of Eastern India by the fact that they could not call upon these soldiers in case of a crisis, a fact that has been ignored in the existing historiography on the subject. For instance, Sumit Sarkar, describing the Government of India's attitude toward a major Congress agitation in the first half of 1942, writes that, 'the government ... could call upon (from early 1942 onwards) growing numbers of British and Allied troops stationed in India.' to crush a nationalist movement. Sarkar, *Modern India*, p. 376. The Americans based in India were issued with 'very strict orders' to maintain a 'neutral attitude' towards 'all internal questions' in India soon after the outbreak of the 'Quit India' movement. Letter from G.W. Wren, GHQ to M.M Stevenson, India Office, GOBr, 17 May 1943, L/WS/1/1292, OIOC. Explaining the American stance, an official attached to their embassy in London wrote to the Secretary of State for India that, 'The sole purpose of the American Forces in India is to prosecute the war of the United Nations against the Axis powers.... American Forces in India will exercise scrupulous care to avoid the slightest participation in India's internal political problems, or appearance of so doing'. Letter from H. Freeman-Matthews, US Embassy, London to L. Amery, SSI, GOBr, 14 August 1942, ibid.

168 Secret letter from T. Rutherford, Governor, GOB to Linlithgow, Viceroy, 10 June 1943, R/3/1/23, OIOC.

169 Most secret WIS (II) 2 July 1943, L/WS/1/1433, OIOC.

170 Most secret WIS (II) 6 August 1943, L/WS/1/1433, OIOC.

Chapter Two
State Propaganda and Civilian Audiences in Eastern India 1939–45: Forms, Applications and Scope

The nature of the progress of the Second World War forced a number of changes in the administrative set-up in Eastern India. These were, in turn, reflected in the alteration of the scope and direction of the official public relations projects. This chapter attempts to describe these changes, and the challenges faced by the colonial authorities in arranging for the distribution of the various types of propaganda material amongst the civilian population in the region.

I. Wireless and Film Propaganda

Radio and film were widely considered to be important means of transmitting desired official messages by the late 1930s. However, the difficulties faced by the Government of India in arranging the deployment of these media during the Second World War underlined many of the intractable challenges the conflict posed in the sub-continent.

The production of radio propaganda for India remained centralised throughout the war.[1] Bulletins and programmes prepared at the headquarters of All-India Radio in New Delhi, in consultation with the military authorities, were transmitted to the provinces, where they were translated into the local vernaculars and broadcast. Initially, these radio stations presented 27 daily 'war news' bulletins in English, Hindustani, Punjabi, Bengali, Marathi, Tamil, Telegu and Pushto. With the progress of the war the number and the variety of wireless programmes increased.[2] All-India Radio's broadcasts were complemented by the transmission from England, over short-wave frequencies, of 'newsletters' in English, Hindustani, Bengali, Tamil and Gujarati by the British Broadcasting Corporation.[3]

But for a variety of reasons, the dissemination of wireless propaganda proved far more difficult to arrange. A salient problem was that the reach of the All-India Radio's transmissions, most of which were on medium-wave frequencies, was curbed by the technology available at the time. To the frustration of many officials based within the Government of India, the range of the medium wave transmitters remained inconsiderable throughout the war (see Table 2.1 below).[4]

According to one estimate made in 1943, the nine regional stations of All India Radio catered to 4 'circles' of 100 villages each and covered a mere 3600 villages.[5] Another assessment, a market research report compiled by A.C. Cossor Ltd., a British electronics company operating in India around the same time, concluded that at least 100 transmitting stations would be needed for the 'complete medium wave coverage' of the country.[6] The problem, however, was that the shortages of machinery in Britain and the shipping necessary to transport the infrastructure prevented an expansion of the broadcasting network in Eastern India. The plan to develop a new 100 kilowatt transmitter in 1942 was, for example, damaged by the loss of a large part of the equipment at sea and the manufacturer's inability to

Table 2.1 Range of transmissions from A.I.R. stations in India

Station	Type of Broadcast	Range
Peshawar	Medium Wave	15 miles
Lahore	Medium Wave	50 miles
Lucknow	Medium Wave	50 miles
Trichnopoly	Medium Wave	50 miles
Delhi	Medium Wave	80 miles
	Short Wave	500 miles
Madras	Medium Wave	15 miles
	Short Wave	500 miles
Calcutta	Medium Wave	20/30 miles
	Short Wave	500 miles
Bombay	Medium Wave	20/30 miles
	Short Wave	500 miles

Source: J.A Thorne, *Confidential report on the control during war of the press, broadcasting and films; and on publicity for purposes of the war*, New Delhi, 1939, p. 11, L/I/1/1136, OIOC.

provide replacements for eleven months.⁷ As a result, the only addition to broadcasting capacity that year was a small 10 kilowatt, medium wave station in Assam.⁸

The solution, namely of using short wave frequencies which had much longer ranges, was discounted after being constantly 'under review' in 1942.⁹ An official of the central government's Information and Broadcasting Department rationalised the decision thus:

> The ordinary commercial set in India takes wave-lengths from say 13 to 500 [megahertz]; but short-wave listening is not wanted, first because the short-waves owing to their tendency to 'fade', are unsuitable for 'community' listening, and secondly, because of the danger of tuning in, intentionally or by accident, to enemy transmissions....¹⁰

Significantly, a host of less obvious factors also played a role in influencing the decision not to use short-wave broadcasting in India for propaganda purposes. Crucial in this regard were the frequently vociferous debates relating to the deployment of broadcasts by British Allies in English and Indian languages. Reactions to the possibility of using American help in matters of broadcasting continued to be surprisingly hostile in a period when infrastructural constraints in the sub-continent had made the Government of India amenable to accepting Soviet assistance.¹¹ For example, the Government of India's External Affairs Department declared itself against the idea of broadcasts from the USA in 'any Indian language', and declared that:

> It is difficult to see what particular object would be served, and it would not be easy to [keep] any control over the sort of thing which was said.... There would be on the other hand some advantage in an English transmission to India, if we could get a satisfactory assurance that matters of broadcasts would be [confined] mostly to war material and American background and that British Indian politics would if treated at all, only be treated in a most dispassionate way, for example by objective and balanced review of American opinion ... on a particular matter.¹²

The matter of using American assistance was never really resolved and the US authorities were refused an independent role in wartime Indian broadcasting directed at civilian audiences. Indeed, even the very limited facilities allowed to them by the All-India Radio was begrudged in many quarters. A typical example of this was the reaction of Rushbrook Williams, the Director of the BBC's Eastern Services, to the fact that the OWI was being allowed to transmit two twenty minute shows for American troops in India, and four two hour long programmes for the 'local population', that included a fifteen minute long 'Voice of America' broadcast, 'variety' and music. Irked by the shows directed at civilians, as he felt these represented 'straight-forward American propaganda', Williams demanded a complete review of the situation.[13] A cautious enquiry made about the matter by the India Office evoked an extended, but rather caustic, memorandum from India. Frederick Puckle, the Secretary of the Information and Broadcasting Department, GOI., said that the AIR had no intention, wittingly or otherwise, of being a vehicle for 'pumping' American propaganda into India, and that 'properly used, American material, which interests Indian listeners, is of great value, both directly to the maintenance of confidence and public morale, and indirectly to producing the idea that this war is a war of the United Nations, and not a war of America or Great Britain or any other particular country.'[14]

Nevertheless, the Government of India's indulgence of wartime American broadcasting activities in the sub-continent remained quite limited. While the OWI was encouraged to operate through the AIR, American efforts to spread independent broadcasting was always frowned upon. In early 1944, Archibald Rowlands, the Advisor to the Viceroy of India on war administration, pointed out that there was a possibility of a dispute between the SEAC and the Government of India about an American request to operate five 'very short range transmitters in various parts of India ... in order to give their troops regular broadcast entertainment.'[15] Rowlands reported that the Indian government had raised objections and demanded that all broadcasting in India needed to be under the 'AIR umbrella' so that it could be supervised. Moreover, the authorities feared that granting a license to the Americans would bring on applications from the Chinese and Free French, whose desire to operate a large transmitter in Pondicherry was being resisted.[16] The issue was discussed further at a meeting held on the 21 March 1944,[17] and it was ultimately decided in August 1944 to allow the American authorities to set up six short range transmitters, intended only for catering to U.S. troop encampments in Eastern India.[18] The British authorities, nevertheless, remained very uncomfortable with the tone of American short-wave broadcasts directed at South East Asia, possibly because they could also be heard in the sub-continent.[19]

Another factor that militated against the wider distribution of both medium-wave and short-wave transmissions was that they could only cater to inhabitants of particular cities who owned or had access to wireless sets. The number of receivers owned by individuals remained low because of their cost,[20] and the high price of the licenses, which were required by law to be bought and maintained through bi-annual payments.[21] An estimate of the total number of receivers available in India in 1939 for 'private listening', calculated on the basis of the number of licenses issued, comes to 80,580, and tallies closely with a second, provided by the All India Radio, which put the figure at 79,580. It was estimated that these sets catered to 250,000 people.[22] And although a later estimate, made in May 1942, regarded the 'radio audience' in India to be between 1,000,000 and 1,200,000 people,[23] it remained obvious that the shortage of receivers, which stunted the expansion of the 'community-listening' schemes in rural areas, remained disappointing to many central publicity officials.[24]

An added problem was the complexity and the cost of the organisation required to maintain battery-powered sets in villages, most of which were unelectrified.[25] Indeed, the market research report prepared by Cossor Ltd had underlined the difficulties posed by the fact that electric supplies were installed in all towns with populations of 100,000 inhabitants or more, but not in small towns and rural areas, unless they were adjacent to a generating station.[26] This situation also played a role in arresting the expansion of the wireless 'community listening' scheme in Eastern India, and ultimately forced senior Indian administrators to inform the Ministry of Information in London that 'the village broadcasting plan' had been postponed till after the war.[27] An analysis of the justifications provided for this decision make interesting reading. The first reason given was the high cost of manufacturing 'suitable' wireless sets, which was blamed on the nature of AIR specifications. These demanded that each machine should have no 'operating adjustments' and thus be fixed at a particular frequency, that it be fitted with a 'time-switch' to turn it on and off at 'appropriate programme hours', that it have a 'self-contained power supply' able to 'operate the set for one hour without recharging', and last, but not least, 'have sufficient volume' for an audience of 200 persons.[28]

The second reason given for postponing the expansion of broadcasting in India was the 'desirability' of devoting available funds 'which [we]re by no means unlimited' to extending 'oral and visual propaganda'.[29] As a result, the use of wireless propaganda among the rural audiences of Eastern India remained limited, and was only deployed by senior district officials, who were supplied with wireless sets capable of tuning into short-wave broadcasts and asked to take these along during tours of the villages.[30] The results of the enduring shortages of wireless equipment within the provinces is well represented by a review prepared by the Government of Orissa. The document declared that:

> In the last report it was mentioned that the Publicity Department were in correspondence with the Government of India to get free of cost 350 wireless sets for being supplied [sic] to various public institutions and private persons. The majority of these sets were to be battery-worked. In consideration of the high prices of batteries and other accessories and also of the difficulty to get them and of the large amount of other incidental expenses involved in the scheme, the Provincial Government have decided upon getting only 30 such sets of which 24 have already been released by [the] Government of India and are expected to be received and distributed according to the approved list by the first week of October.[31]

The mode of distribution of a consignment of 40,976 wireless sets received from America under the 'lend-lease' agreement in April 1943 (see Table 2.2), re-emphasised the decision to target wireless propaganda at the urban and, more specifically, educated, audiences for the rest of the war. An official explained that the 'controlled distribution' of sets did not allow them to reach listeners likely to be 'most affected' by radio broadcasts, and thus 'militate[d] against [the] successful organisation of programmes in view of educational and other limitations of [the] audience'. Therefore, a decision was

Table 2.2 The distribution within India of a consignment of wireless sets sent from America in April 1943

Distributing agency	Battery powered sets	Electric powered sets
U.S. Red Cross	75	75
Provincial governments for 'controlled use'	339	58
British forces	2,198	2,600
To dealers for commercial distribution	3,983	31,618

Source: Secret telegram from the External Affairs Department, GOI to the SSI, GOBr, 27 April 1943, L/I/1/970, OIOC.

taken to rely on the commercial distribution of receivers through dealers and be 'reasonably sure ... of reaching well educated sections of the population, who do generally respond to and appreciate programmes'.[32]

Notably, although some efforts aimed at spreading rural broadcasting in India using alternative technologies were maintained, these met with little success. One plan, referring to the constraints presented by the high costs of receivers, suggested another way by which AIR could reach the 'ears of the village people': the technique of 'rediffusion', which was prevalent in Malta and 'relayed [broadcasts] by land wire to a loudspeaker set up in a prominent position in the village.'[33] And even though the proposal did not evoke much interest within the Department of Information and Broadcasting initially,[34] discussions about the uses and spread of 'Radio Relay Services' were resumed between 1945 and 1946.[35]

Yet, these debates, detailing the frustrations arising within certain quarters of the Ministry of Information and the India Office, London, and the Information and Broadcasting Department, New Delhi, from the inability to expand the scope of wireless propaganda, should not be allowed to detract us from the influences of the official attitudes existing at other levels of administration. District officers, notably, quite often regarded radio receivers to be an administrative nuisance, especially during the unsettled political and economic conditions of 1942 and 1943, and would regularly confiscate privately owned radio sets when rules about their use in public and the bans about listening in to certain channels were repeatedly flouted.[36] It becomes obvious from the secret despatches exchanged between local officials, their provincial superiors and the military authorities in Eastern India that officers based in the districts and sub-divisions preferred the 'controlled use' of radio-sets, where they could determine the programme selection and often even the audience.[37] Therefore, the most common form of wireless propaganda in the sub-divisional towns and villages of the region was through machines taken on tour or those operated with the assistance of batteries brought in by touring groups of publicity officials. In areas with a significant military presence, or of interest to the army authorities, these civilian publicity teams were accompanied by Civil Liaison Officers and a representative of the Eastern Command (and later the South East Asia Command), who were usually given the role of 'observers'.[38]

The deployment of film publicity in Eastern India provided several challenges to the authorities as well. Film propaganda, imported or internally produced, set aside for distribution amongst civilian audiences within the country remained the preserve of yet another arm of the Government of India's Information and Broadcasting Department: the Central Board of Information. In 1939, its officials arranged a number of special privileges for the import of 'suitable' propaganda films by distributors operating within India. Notable concessions were announced so as to encourage the relevant companies to order short documentary films (not more than 2,000 feet in length), dealing with any 'aspect of the war'. These were classed as 'educational films' and were thereby entitled to a full refund of customs duty. The Board's preference for 'documentary shorts' persisted throughout the war, not least because its officials felt that these contained a 'powerful incentive towards mass education and enlightenment.'[39] Other significant concessions were also provided. Distributors were, for instance, allowed to bring in a copy of a long feature film free of customs duty on top of their normal import quotas, when they imported 'in the ordinary way of business' films certified 'suitable for war purposes and propaganda'.[40]

A Film Advisory Board was set up by the Central Board of Information in June 1940. This new body, which was dissolved in January 1943, was made responsible for arranging the production of short propaganda films by the Bombay film industry, and the dubbing into Indian languages of the documentaries received from Britain and other Allied countries.[41]

The Central Board of Information also separately arranged the production of films. However, since it did not have the requisite equipment to do this in the first two years of the war, it was forced to

Table 2.3 The Government of India's total expenditure on film publicity between 1940 and 1945 (in rupees)

Financial Years	Expenditure
1940–41	124,010
1941–42	461,433
1942–43	730,180
1943–44	1,027,588
1944–45	1,974,552
1945–46	2,524,523

Source: Memorandum on Film Publicity, pp. 3–4, L/R/5/295, OIOC.

collaborate with private organisations. It reached an arrangement in July 1940 with Twentieth Century Fox Corporation (India) Ltd., which undertook to produce edited versions of British Movietone News in Indian languages after the Government of India guaranteed the corporation against losses till Rs.35,000. This scheme turned out to be a failure, since the documentaries, which dealt almost completely with European issues, failed to draw the desired audiences. It was abandoned after two years. Though the Board tried to encourage the various film-producing firms in India to undertake the production of a propaganda newsreel as a 'commercial proposition', their failure to do so was reflected in the Government of India's offer of financial support for the venture. Subsequent attempts to negotiate 'the cheapest and the best' proposition possible led, yet again, to an arrangement with the Twentieth Century Fox Corporation, which offered to produce fortnightly newsreels in English, Hindustani, Bengali, Tamil and Telegu. The first issue of the series, which was named the Indian Movietone News, appeared in September 1942 and the scheme survived the war without major modification (it was converted to a weekly newsreel and renamed the Indian News Parade a year later).[42]

From the second half of 1942, the members of the Board of Information also began to produce film propaganda in a government unit called Information Films of India. The films made here till the end of the war included 'documentary shorts' (films 1,000 feet long), as well as 'quickies' (films 250 feet long), in English, Hindustani, Bengali, Tamil and Telegu.

Moreover, the rationing of celluloid to the Indian film industry from the first quarter of 1943, by the Government of India's Industries and Civil Supplies Department, allowed the Board of Information to demand from September that year that all Indian film producers prepare 'one full-length instructional picture' for every two full-length 'entertainment films' made by their firms. The script for these films

Table 2.4 The number of copies of the Information Films of India and the Indian News Parade released every week between 1943–45

Type	English	Hindustani	Bengali	Tamil	Telegu
IFI 'shorts'	26	41	7	9	4
INP	26	43	7	9	4

Source: Memorandum on Film Publicity, pp. 11–12, L/R/5/295, OIOC.

had to be approved by the central government's Information and Broadcasting Department, which ensured that 'the necessary propaganda material' figured to a 'substantial extent'. In all, 35 films were produced by the Indian film industry under this arrangement, which was discontinued in December 1945.[43]

But, as in the case of wireless broadcasting, a number of problems needed to be tackled to ensure the smooth deployment of film publicity. Shortages of infrastructure affected both production and distribution, and although the former was relatively easy to deal with, problems persisted throughout the war.[44] And the complication of not having appropriate channels for transporting films for screening often turned out to be quite impossible to surmount. For example, the Film Advisory Board's channels and the Central Board of Information's 'gigantic' film distribution network, which supplied 1,400 cinema houses in British India, remained rather limited throughout 1939–45, as it catered primarily to the inhabitants of the major cities and the larger towns where the cinemas were largely located. Moreover, the relationship between the official film production units and the owners of the theatres showing Indian films remained uneasy throughout the war, as many establishments baulked at the prospect of screening propaganda newsreels, even though they were initially supplied free of charge by the Government.[45] The resolution of the problem was ultimately provided by the promulgation of the Defence of India Rule 44A, in May 1943. This law, which was strictly enforced, required every cinema proprietor in British India to exhibit 'at each performance after the 14th of September 1943' one or more propaganda films approved by the Central Government 'the total length of which was not less than 2000 feet'.[46] However, this policy strained the relations between cinema owners, Indian and European, and the authorities even further.[47]

The attempts to spread the scope of film publicity in rural areas threw up another set of problems and these turned out to be remarkably more difficult to address. The initial attempts to use trucks fitted with 35mm projectors were limited by the fact that these vehicles could only operate in areas accessible by road.[48] In order to deal with this situation, the Government of India sanctioned the 'Village Publicity Scheme' on an all-India scale in 1942, with the aim of distributing film propaganda in areas which did not have cinema halls and could not be reached by motorised vans. The scheme was to be based on the use of 16 mm projectors, which were portable, run by batteries, easy to operate and capable of catering to 600 people at a time.[49] The project was, nevertheless, impaired by the enduring shortage of suitable transport available to the publicity authorities; a problem that could only be marginally redressed during the wartime period. In 1939, Bengal had 6 'motor cinema vans', 8 'bullock vans' and 4 boats fitted with projector sets;[50] Bihar had six propaganda vans 'with itinerant cinemas',[51] while Assam and Orissa had no mobile film units at all.[52] By 1945, in comparison, the number of motorised vans in Bengal was increased to 10, Bihar had the services of 8, while Assam and Orissa had 6 each.[53]

There were other problems as well and even a project like the 'Village Publicity Scheme', which was deployed with the blessings of the central and provincial headquarters, suffered from shortage of requisite equipment and spare parts, especially battery packs.[54] A direct result of this situation was that, in contradiction to its professed goal, the touring 'film detachments' attached to the scheme tended to be deployed in very specific locales, namely *mofussils* and villages located near major lines of communication and major towns, so that spares and re-charged or replacement battery packs could be easily picked up. Moreover, the available detachments were regularly sent to districts that were considered strategically important, and they were used to tour villages providing labour to the defence works on the Burma front and Assam, and villages near troop concentrations. To the chagrin of some provincial officers in charge of public relations projects, local military commanders would sometimes also 'temporarily requisition' film units in order to entertain the troops under their command, thereby putting their publicity schedules out of joint. Therefore, despite its perceived uses, the available film technology during wartime and the great primacy given to military indents ensured that its reach remained much more limited than many central and provincial publicity officials would have hoped.[55]

Strikingly, this did not seem to bother the sub-divisional authorities and local boards too much. Reviews from Assam and Bihar, for instance, questioned the usefulness of highlighting the successes of Allied mobilisation, with images of bumper harvests and the supply of great quantities of grain, in regions affected by the adverse economic conditions arising from famine in Bengal. Indeed, one document pointed out that it was having the 'antipathetic effect' of abetting theories about the army being responsible for food shortages.[56] There were, of course, exceptions to this rule, but these generally tended to be officers in charge of select localities, containing the 'priority' sections of civilian population; such officials remained keen to highlight all that was being done by the wartime administration for these social groups. Notably, however, great efforts were made even in these sub-divisional towns and villages to carefully vet the audience for such film shows, with potential trouble-makers, defined generally as those not holding wartime ration cards, being denied entry.[57]

II. Print and Oral Publicity

Much of the print propaganda targeted at the civilian audiences in Eastern India was produced or arranged by agencies of the Government of India's Information and Broadcasting Department: the Public Information Bureau and, to a lesser extent, the organisation of the All-India Radio.[58] Apart from publishing pamphlets, leaflets and a fortnightly paper called *Indian Information*, the Bureau liaised with the representatives of all the major Indian newspapers in order to secure publicity for a wide range of official measures. While much of this official print publicity was prepared in the Government of India's printing presses, use was also made of the publishing facilities owned by the provincial governments and a number of private establishments.[59] The Bureau also provided, or 'suggested', pamphlets and posters for exhibitions arranged by the various departments of the central and the provincial governments, and one of its officers was permanently detailed with the Civil Defence Department, a purely wartime body created in 1941, to assist its co-ordinators in their attempts to arrange the production of 'ARP publicity'.[60] The authorities in charge of the All India Radio made the texts of their news programmes available in the form of journals, which were published in English, Urdu and Hindi.[61]

The scale of production of wartime print publicity was significantly lower in the provinces. This was caused in large measure by the restricted capacities of the provincial publicity departments. For instance, the Government of Bengal's Publicity Department had a staff of 30, who under the supervision of a Director, published the *Bengali Weekly* in Bengali and English (20,000 copies of the former and 5,000 of the latter). In addition, it concentrated on arranging for the duplication into Bengali, often with the assistance of the presses owned by the Calcutta Committee (an organisation composed of the European business interests in Bengal), of material sent by the Bureau of Public Information.[62] Bengal's Publicity Department remained moribund till it was expanded and 'livened up' in 1944 by R.G. Casey, the new Governor of the province.[63]

Table 2.5 The Government of India's expenditure (in rupees) on printing, 1939–43

Year	GOI Presses	Provincial Presses	Private Presses
1939–40	4,131,148	Figures unavailable	79,677
1940–41	5,701,039	80,989	202,164
1941–42	8,411,454	80,827	662,068
1942–43	13,871,092	1,113,390	1,818,810
1943–44	Figures unavailable	1,172,837	2,205,749

Source: Memorandum on printing, 30 August 1944, War History of the Labour Department, GOI, L/R/5/291, OIOC.

Similarly, in 1939 the Government of Bihar's Publicity Department had a staff of only 8 men who 'attempt[ed] little beyond the issue of communiqués and press notes',[64] and its weekly periodical, the *Dehat* (brought out in Urdu, Bengali, Hindi and English), was irregularly published.[65] The publicity structures in Assam, a major base for the Allied army, were even more threadbare, and, therefore, remained dependent on the 'Talking Points' provided by the Bureau of Public Information and the All-India Radio news broadcasts for information.[66] And even though the Government of Orissa's Publicity Department sponsored the creation of songs, slogans and poems, and published them in leaflet form, much of its efforts were devoted to reproducing propaganda material provided by the central government departments in Oriya.[67]

While the production of print propaganda within the provinces increased appreciably during periods of political upheaval, especially those accompanied by strikes by newspaper groups, the form and the content of such material tended to be dictated to a substantial degree by 'suggestions' made by the Government of India's Information and Broadcasting Department. For instance, Puckle, its secretary, wrote to all provincial governments after the outbreak of the 'Quit India' movement in August 1942 and suggested that 'news-sheets' of 'not more than two pages' be issued. He added that their contents:

> ... should be confined generally to news. If they are used for open propaganda, they will soon be discredited, and as matter of fact, the best propaganda is often straight news properly presented.... No attempt should be made to conceal their official origin; in fact, it might

be recognised in the title.... The news-sheet should not bear the same name as, or merge in any other way into, existing official publications, either Provincial or Central.... When a sufficient number of newspapers resume publication in any area, the official news-sheet should be discontinued, and it should be made clear from the start that this is what will happen.[68]

Reviews of the provincial publicity activities suggest that these directives were generally followed. The Government of Bihar, for example, began to bring out a short newsletter in English, titled the *Patna Daily News*, along the lines recommended by Puckle since all the English dailies in the province refused to publish the official 'press notes' on contemporary events.[69]

Arranging for the distribution of print propaganda, or the oral transmission of the messages contained in it, was far more complicated. Although district officers were asked to rely during lecture tours on pamphlets and newsletters provided by the central publicity organisations, the methodical distribution of these documents initially proved a real challenge due to the wartime transport bottlenecks.[70] Lecture tours were, of course, hardly new in the region, and J.M.G Bell's tour diary, a good example of an ICS officer's duty roster during the European chapter of the war, shows how he toured his district in Bengal disseminating 'war news' in clubs, *hats* and 'railway markets'.[71] But, the Japanese entry into the war immediately upped the scale of official tours and the effect of this was a series of temporary adaptations. In the front line province of Assam this took the form of a reliance on BBC and AIR news broadcasts, and T.T.S Hayley, the ICS officer responsible for building up the provincial propaganda organisation, mentions how he:

> ... issued to all the publicity officers what was called the 'Publicity Points Handbook'. This consisted of paragraphs, all numbered, of various publicity points arranged under headings. The handbook was loose-leaf and as new publicity points were written, they were sent out for inclusion. A Publicity Committee was formed, with the Chief Secretary as its chairman, which met every week and passed my publicity points for the handbook. It also decided what policy should be carried out for the next week and I would then inform the various publicity officers as to what sections of the publicity points duly translated from 'Basic English' into the local language should be interlarded with their news broadcasts each day. They picked up the

news from the radio. There was much more to the publicity campaign, but this was the chief feature of it.[72]

The mechanisms required to disseminate print and oral propaganda were expanded over time. 'Travelling exhibitions' were introduced, and these were arranged by the Government of India with the co-operation of the provincial publicity departments. In the industrial town of Jamshedpur, for instance, this took the form of a 'war demonstration train' which exhibited models of 'all the weapons of modern warfare'.[73] The scheme was deemed to be a success and a special 'Defence Exhibition train' was taken on a prolonged tour of Bihar in 1942. This contained models of Allied warships, tanks, aeroplanes, ammunition shells, bombs, carbines, wireless sets and telephone exchanges.[74] In Calcutta the scheme also took the form of trucks carrying the remains of two Japanese bombers and the anti-aircraft guns that had been used to shoot them down. At the head of the procession a van fitted with loudspeakers described the 'terror weapons' present in the Indian armoury and the damage these could impart to enemy planes.[75]

As a result of the expansion of the publicity networks in Eastern India, the Provincial and District War Committees were re-constituted and then asked to arrange the distribution of 'leaflets, pamphlets and other publicity materials', the broadcasting of 'war news ... through loud speakers', 'posters ... [and] war picture exhibitions', and 'study circles' in schools and colleges. A report enumerating the activities of these bodies in Orissa described how officials had employed 'songsters in the rural areas to sing songs' and distributed leaflets containing these songs 'through the watch and ward committees [and] village *chowkidars* in those villages where songsters are not available at present'. In addition, '50 war songs, 6 war *pallas* and 2 war dramas ... [printed] in the form of pamphlets' were 'supplied to the District Officers and Subdivisional Officers for distribution to *Jatra* parties, *Pallawallas* and Theatrical parties in their respective areas', and 'Liaison Assistants' were made responsible for touring the districts in search of suitable theatrical groups, who were then subsidised by the provincial government.[76] Moreover, 'magic lanterns' shown by the touring officers of the Government of Orissa's Agricultural Department in village fairs 'and other gatherings in rural areas' remained an enduring feature of the official publicity activities in the province.[77] In Bihar, similar activities were organised by the District Officers and Commissioners, who formed *Muhalla* Committees and employed 'News Wardens' for the purpose.[78] In Assam, the local bureaucrats created a 'province wide news-service' by requisitioning private cars and equipping them with loudspeaker units.[79]

However, this complex array of publicity networks did not always function as smoothly as officials hoped, with difficulties being caused by the presence of financial, manpower and supply constraints at all levels of the administration. The official history of the Bureau of Public Information mentions, for example, how the organisation increased its staff between 1939 and 1945, but not sufficiently to meet its enormous responsibilities: the number of officers went up from 7 to 57; non-gazetted staff from 59 to 286 and 'inferior staff' from 38 to 210. The review pointed out that though the Bureau's staff were given 'partial relief' after 1942, when the other branches of the Department of Information and Broadcasting were expanded and the Publicity Planning and Co-ordination Board was set up, the pressure of work placed on the Bureau continued to be significant. In 1944, for instance, the organisation was receiving 'nearly 300 services by cable, radio, airmail and seamail', which its employees had to analyse, reformulate and disperse amongst a range of distributive agencies in India: the departments of the central and provincial governments; official and 'private' publicity organisations; the press; educational institutions and libraries; chambers of commerce; technical and scientific associations; legislators; authors; paid publicists; and 'experts in various fields'.[80] Other central government departments were affected as well. The Civil Defence Department concentrated all its wartime publicity activities in the main 'urban centres' between 1942 and 1945 because it lacked the funds to create networks in the villages.[81]

Similar difficulties persisted at other levels of administration too. A report from Bengal complained, for instance, that a single propaganda van had to cover three districts in the province and that the District War Committees were allotted an annual budget of a mere hundred rupees each.[82] A civil servant who had been based in Mymensingh mentions in his memoirs how he had held 'propaganda meetings' at only the 'primary' police stations in his sub-division.[83] When the administrators in Bihar 'celebrated' the Allied Victory in North Africa in Patna and Ranchi town with 'large free feedings and distributions of clothes to the poor' and 'free cinema performances', their primary hope was that the 'good news' would seep into the villages.[84] The surrender of Italy was 'celebrated' in an identical fashion and with the same intent.[85] And the progress of the 'Grow More Food' scheme, which was inaugurated in 1942, was stunted by the shortage of personnel. In Orissa, the charge of co-ordinating the scheme throughout the province was initially given to one officer. However, his incapacity to tour the district 'effectively' forced the authorities to give the responsibility to the District Agricultural Supervisors. This, however, brought about a very slight improvement in the situation, as the districts of Cuttack, Ganjam, Sambalpur and Koraput had the services of only one supervisor each. Reviews of their activities reported that over a year they, along with the staff of the Revenue Department and officials of the National War Front, had managed only to release some 'press communiqués and useful leaflets' amongst cultivators, and to organise 17 short-lived agricultural exhibitions.[86] Similarly, the Government of Orissa's Assistant Publicity Officers (each district was assigned one officer), who were on tour 20 days a month, were able to address meetings only in 'important central places' and 'urban areas' in the localities.[87] Strikingly, even a review of the wartime role of the National War Front, a relatively well-funded body, declared that the organisation's effectiveness had been substantially impeded by the lack of the requisite manpower and machinery. While supporting a call for a 'complete re-organisation' of the body, it mentioned that to be effective the organisation would need to be provided with at least one 'properly equipped propaganda van' per district.[88]

The pressures on the civilian publicity authorities, drawn usually from the already over-worked district bureaucracy, were increased further by the military authorities' dogged insistence that the greatest emphasis be given to targeting the villages near their encampments, and the Eastern Command's demands in this regard could not be ignored since the military's priorities were given unquestioned precedence by government officials in New Delhi. Moreover, the presence of regular military intelligence reports from the units located in region, which described the 'co-operation provided' by local officials to the General Headquarters, prevented the district administrators from disregarding the army's demands and they were, therefore, usually left with very little time and few resources to visit the 'non-priority' sections of the civilian population.[89]

As a result, all attempts by the Government of India and the provincial administrations to regularise or intensify their public relations campaigns from 1942 onwards forced them to rely increasingly on the assistance of the municipal and local boards, as well as a range of non-official organisations. For example, the widespread nervousness in Calcutta resulting from the rapid Japanese successes in Burma caused publicity officials attached to the Civil Defence Department, GOI, to turn to the city municipality's *bustee* workers.[90] Similarly, the National War Front, an organisation created and run by the Government of India's Department of Information and Broadcasting primarily for the purpose of expanding official propaganda activities in the countryside,[91] remained dependent on the manpower provided by the local administrations.[92] Indeed, the Front's enduring shortage of staff ultimately forced it to concentrate on bolstering the efforts of the Provincial and District War Committees', by providing these bodies access to additional infrastructure and funding, instead of setting up parallel publicity networks in the localities.[93]

The diversity of the non-official agencies drafted in to bolster the state's public relations efforts amongst specific civilian audiences displayed the increasing complexity of the tasks being sought to be addressed, as well as the sometimes contradictory pulls of administrative necessity. Some of the agencies, like the managements of the big European establishments and the British-owned press had, of course, been old allies.[94] The Calcutta Committee, for instance, had assisted the Government of Bengal since 1940 by cultivating a number of 'small *mofussil* papers' through regular advertisements. In return the newspapers published 'editorial matter' and utilised a 'weekly survey of the war' provided from official sources.[95] In addition, the body, later renamed the Commercial Distributing Committee, also arranged for the distribution of the 'Talking Points' amongst the Managers and Head-Clerks of the *mofussil* branches of Calcutta firms, ordering them to spread the information available amongst their 'less educated customers of all classes',[96] and arranged for 'propaganda talks' in Bengali and Hindi for their workers in the factories and the bustis of Greater Calcutta.[97] Other business groups, notably organisations like the Indian Tea Association, the Indian Jute Mills Association, the Indian Mining Association and the United Planters Association, also helped distribute publicity material in the factories,[98] while a newspaper group like the *Times of India* played an active role in the creation of official propaganda material.[99]

While the escalation of the Second World War, by its spread to Asia, caused these organisations to increase the scope of their activities, the Government of India's choice of new allies often outraged the managements of the industrial concerns.[100] Conspicuous in this regard were the central government's efforts to use the assistance of the Communist Party of India and the Radical Democratic Party to popularise a 'pro-war' stance amongst the industrial workers, in the hope that this would weaken their support for the Congress organisations and thereby pacify industrial labour. However, a combination of factors, not least, the hostility of provincial officers, district administrators and the factory managers, as well as the party cadres refusal to parrot the politbureau's line, caused the scheme to be limited to very specific localities and contexts. Thus, while CPI and RDP members were often not allowed to operate within the factory limits, they were encouraged, especially during 1943, to assist central government publicity officers in working class neighbourhoods.[101] But rather than assisting the state's propaganda efforts, the activists attached to these parties tended to weaken the various official public relations schemes due to their inclination to organise agitations around local difficulties, thereby forcing the administrators to set aside sorely needed bureaucratic manpower, that could have been deployed for rural publicity projects, for the difficult task of tailing and, whenever possible, arresting them.[102]

III. Food and Medical Aid

The supply of material benefits by government, always an important means of mollifying discontent during disturbed economic times, took on an unprecedented significance during the shortages of essential goods that accompanied the war against Japan. Indeed, by mid-1942, the distribution of subsidised or free foodstuffs, domestic fuel, cloth and medicines was widely considered in official circles to be an indispensable way of maintaining morale amongst the civilian population generally, and the so-called 'priority sections' in particular.[103] But the adoption of such audience-specific distributive strategies forced the Government of India to increasingly centralise the collection and allocation of all types of essential goods. Growing numbers of officials attached to the central government's Food, Supply and War Departments were posted within, or made to tour, Eastern India with the purpose of ensuring or supervising the purchase or requisitioning of necessities, and the provinces with elected ministries saw the creation of new, autonomous bodies. In Bengal, for instance, a 'Directorate' of Civil Supplies was formed in 1942, and its head 'was given ample latitude in laying down and carrying out his own policy .... [and] the Governor made it clear that the Director's work ... not be interfered with by the [provincial] Ministers'.[104]

The centralisation of the collection and allocation of food and other necessities offered several administrative advantages in wartime. It allowed the Government of India to collaborate more effectively with General Headquarters (India), usually through its War Department, in provisioning the Allied army in Eastern India, particularly during 1942, when local food supplies and goods needed to be tapped for army needs.[105] With the expansion, and stabilisation of, the production of military supplies, the food situation eased somewhat, but items like cloth, woollens, mineral fuels, chemicals and medicines continued to be in short supply for civilians. Fuels like petroleum and coal were primarily stockpiled for military transport and industrial production, and the rapidly falling stocks of medicines, a situation exacerbated by the cutting-off of imports from outside India, were carefully managed so as to improve the health of the army detachments and military labour serving on the eastern front.[106]

Crucially, however, increased central government control over the allocation of resources also resulted in a number of administrative challenges, notably with regards to the competing demands from the different official distributive agencies. In the context of the endemic wartime shortages, these often proved almost impossible to co-ordinate or resolve. Nevertheless, a number of audiences were consistently targeted throughout 1942 and 1945, with the state's civilian employees at the different levels of administration being a major beneficiary.[107] 'Cost price grainshops', in which food grains were sold at subsidised rates, were opened, for example, for the workers of the Government of India's presses in Calcutta, Simla and Aligarh from 1942. The central government bore the resultant losses, which amounted to Rs. 340,737 by 1944.[108] Comparable schemes were initiated for the 'essential workers' of the Indian railways and a 'countrywide network' of shops was created for them, which provided the 'necessaries of life ... at concessional rates, as a form of relief in kind to counteract the high cost of living.'[109] By November 1943 there were 510 such shops (of which 127 were mobile), about 730,000 employees held ration cards, and an estimated three and a half million people were aided (among whom 963,000 *maunds* of food were sold).[110]

Similarly, reports suggested that the port authorities in Eastern India had maintained 'the steadfastness and loyalty of labour' through 'vigorous propaganda', which included the provision of housing, security of food supply at concessional rates, and dearness allowances,[111] made available with the assistance of bodies like the

War Transport Board, the Regional Transport Controllers, the Port Committees and the Priorities Committees.[112] The different ranks of provincial civil services were also targeted through special schemes. Departmental channels were used to distribute the resources, in the form of money and food, allocated by the Government of India for the local police forces in 1942 and 1943, in recognition of the 'remarkable rise' in the cost of living and the 'increased arduousness of police duties' in Eastern India.[113] From March 1943 onwards, the Governments of Bihar and Bengal also arranged to supply subsidised food to all their civil servants earning less than Rs.200 a month.[114]

Workers attached to the 'war-industries',[115] which was a wide category used to refer to both central, provincial and municipal government establishments as well as range of private business interests,[116] also benefited from the central allocation of essential goods. All these establishments, like the civil services, had been dubbed an 'essential public-service' from February 1941 onwards. This allowed the colonial authorities to 'legally' deploy coercive measures with a view to preventing 'mass migrations ... as a result of panic' from industrial areas.[117] But it soon became obvious that other strategies would be necessary to keep the expanding labour at their posts (see Table 2.6). The distribution of 'dearness' allowances and essential goods proved successful in maintaining a working labour force, even though lightning strikes could never really be completely eradicated during such disturbed economic times.[118] The widespread

Table 2.6 Average daily number of workers employed in factories (covered by the Factories Act of 1934) between 1939 and 1945

Year	British India	Bengal	Bombay
1939	1,751,137	571,539	406,040
1940	1,844,428	593,425	480,604
1941	2,156,377	648,711	611,943
1942	2,282,288	672,721	651,375
1943	2,436,312	695,043	711,525
1944	2,522,753	708,641	736,464
1945	2,642,977	744,418	735,774

Source: Tables II and III from M.N. Gupta, 'Health of the Industrial Worker', in B.L. Raina (ed), *Official History of the Indian Armed Forces in the Second World War 1939–45 (Medical Services): Preventive Medicine (Nutrition, Malaria Control and Prevention of Diseases)*, Kanpur, 1961, pp. 724–725.

belief in the efficacy of these new schemes is potently highlighted by the combined efforts of bureaucrats attached to the central services, provincial and district employees, the army authorities, the factory managers, the trade unions officials and political activists to regularise them, even though squabbles about the exact role of each group persisted right till 1945. However, the famine in Bengal, and the attendant economic problems it caused in Eastern India as a whole, forced major changes in official strategies, notably, the creation of a chain of centrally provisioned shops providing subsidised and/or free food and goods in all the major industrial centres.[119] In the United Provinces the system was operated through a 'card ration basis' for shops run jointly by the central and provincial government officials,[120] whereas the Government of Bihar was assisted by the Tata group in the distribution of daily necessities in Jamshedpur.[121]

Similar schemes were also targeted at the expanding mining and plantation industries, which were considered critical to the war effort due to the widespread loss of imports.[122] And even though the mines and plantation proved more difficult to provision, mainly due to transport problems, efforts were consistently made to keep up food and medical supplies to these establishments. In Assam, for instance, much attention was paid to the needs of those employed in the petroleum and tea industry, while official initiatives in Bihar and Bengal tended to be targeted at the coal and mica mines, as well as the tea plantations.[123] In addition, concerted official efforts were made to ensure that employers introduced special welfare provisions for their workers and complied with these. Reports from the districts of Bihar would often mention, for example, how they had regularly resorted to the Tea Districts Emigrant Labour Act (Act XXII of 1932) to force recruiting agencies attached to the various companies to offer medical attention, subsidised food and regular wages for those tea-garden labourers who had been used in military construction projects in Assam.[124] Similarly, an ordinance was promulgated by the Government of India in January 1944, which successfully allowed the authorities to intervene in the administration of the coal mines and force the constitution of a fund to provide for a variety of facilities – anti-malarial schemes, hospitals, good housing, water supplies and mobile cinema units catering to 'recreational needs' – for colliery labour in Bengal, Bihar and Assam.[125] The significance given to increased coal production, labelled an 'essential war effort' in 1943, was also underlined by the targeting of special anti-malaria operations at the coalfields, which was organised by the Government of India, with military assistance, through the Malaria Institute of India from 1944 onwards.[126]

Another group to be accorded great prominence throughout 1942 and 1945, was the unskilled labour force involved in the various military and civilian building projects carried out in Eastern India. This group was recruited from specific tribal regions of Bihar, Bengal and Orissa. In March 1942, therefore, the Government of India's Labour Department set up Provincial Labour Supply Committees in these provinces, which were made responsible for regularising employment-levels. This was achieved by the creation of district and regional committees, manned by local bureaucrats, to organise 'facilities and amenities' for labourers and their households.[127] The benefits offered took the form of free food, money (in addition to any arrears in pay on return to the village), medical attention, and free transport by train and buses (private bus operators were assigned stocks of petrol for the purpose) to 'road side places nearer their homes'.[128] In Bihar, the immediate effect of the formation of the new committees was to allow the Sub-Divisional Officers in the Santal Parganas to arrange specific projects intended to arrange food and shelter for all returning labourers at government camps,[129] and their counterparts in Ranchi to supply medicines to the hospital in Lohardaga and free food for those workers who had been taken sick while working in the eastern front or during repatriation to their villages.[130]

Such schemes, and the required scale of recruitment, were regularised and developed over the course of 1943, notably by the introduction of mobile rationing and medical units, which were financed by a combination of central and provincial funds and provisioned by the Food Department and the office Director General of the Indian Medical Services. During the period of the famine in Bengal, the Commissioner of the Chota Nagpur Division, was like his divisional counterparts in Orissa and Bengal, given access to a special fund of one hundred thousand rupees, which was intended to allow the quick provision of relief, without 'undue paperwork', in case there was a sudden emergency.[131] In addition, chains of dispensaries were created for the purpose of treating labourers working in building projects in the frontier regions of Assam and Bengal.[132]

The amount of time, effort and resources spent by the authorities on targeting the 'priority groups', necessarily meant that very little time could be spared to deal with the 'general' civilian population. Officials had been aware of this, and Theodore Gregory, the

Permanent Economic Adviser to the Government of India, for instance, had noted in January 1943 that it was going to be impossible to arrange comprehensive rationing schemes for even the entire urban population.[133] The result was a situation where general distributive schemes could never be regularised despite the persistence of continued economic difficulties, with officials only managing to attend to severe local problems, and very often this was done in a sketchy manner due to the enduring shortage of material and official manpower resources. During the 'free-trade' period between May and July 1943, for instance, when the prices of food shot up because of the forcible removal of all protectionist barriers within Eastern India by the Government of India, the main official response was to indiscriminately requisition the stocks of private entrepreneurs, often without any compensation. This, in turn, encouraged traders and suppliers to secret their stocks away, causing a further deterioration of the food supply situation.[134]

The weaknesses of official policy amongst the 'general' civilian population was even more cruelly exposed as the famine conditions progressed in Bengal. During this period, resources could only be arranged for the poor based, or arriving, in the cities and selected district towns of Eastern India, and the Final Report of the Famine Enquiry Commission pointed out that the prominence given to the needs of the industrial workers caused a delay in the initiation of rationing measures for the poorer sections of the 'non-productive' civilian population. The Government of the United Provinces arranged schemes for the poorest 60 per cent of the province's urban population;[135] the Bihar administration opened 'poor shops' where cheap food grains were sold to assist the 'poorer classes' in the district capitals,[136] and Bengal, the focus of the famine, witnessed the establishment of 'gruel kitchens' and shops selling subsidised food in Calcutta and a few district capitals.[137] Indeed, the Famine Inquiry Commission reported in 1945 that apart from Greater Calcutta, only two other towns in Bengal – Chittagong and Kurseong – had seen a 'true system of rationing'. The demands on the authorities in Eastern India had been so great during 1943–44, that it had not been possible to implement schemes of controlled distribution even in Dhaka, a town with a population of more than 200,000 inhabitants.[138] The situation was allowed to deteriorate in the rural areas to such an extent that Archibald Wavell, the Viceroy, ordered in November 1943 that the army be deployed to counter the effects of famine in the Bengal countryside.[139] The scale of the crisis in rural Bengal was considered so great that a number of Indian voluntary agencies were allowed to undertake relief measures, even though it was recognised that many of them had 'doubtful' political affiliations.[140]

In fact, the responses to, and the very enormity of the challenges faced during, the Bengal famine underlines the biases of wartime official distributive policies in Eastern India. The prospect of famine relief measures was given increasing significance in 1943 by senior policy makers within the Government of India and the GHQ (India), since they had begun to fear that the ever-increasing number of refugees migrating towards the cities of Eastern India presented potential strategic and public health risks. Relief camps in rural areas, but well-connected to the cities and ports, were touted as a good solution, not merely because they could easily be provisioned but, interestingly, also because they offered the authorities the chance to keep the scale of suffering away from the attention of 'impressionable city folk and the international and national press',[141] thereby avoiding further panic migrations and the resulting pressure on modes of transport that were militarily important.[142] Moreover, officials hoped that the camps, which tended to be located away from major military bases, would allow any outbreaks of disease to be contained locally.[143]

In fact, official fears that migrants escaping the famine conditions might spread 'disease and distress' amongst both military personnel and the 'priority' civilians, and the resultant medical policies, ultimately bared the dangers of adopting an audience-specific approach in the field of public health in Eastern India. The predominant policy ever since the outbreak of the war had been to strengthen the military medical establishment, usually at the expense of the civilian sector. This affected all branches of the Indian medicine, both public and private, especially when it became very apparent that the IMS and IMD were going to be unable to fulfil the military's requirements. The result was the recruitment of a number of 'special categories' of medical officers, which included, amongst other things, the recruitment of European doctors in India and Britain (October 1940); the transfer of assistant-surgeons in the IMD to the IMS under the emergency commissioning scheme (June 1941); the introduction of medical graduates in state-managed and company-managed railways (October 1941); the employment of specialists on special terms (January 1942); the introduction of women medical practitioners (January 1942), and the transfer of civilian anti-malaria officers to military duty (February 1942). The enduring shortages of medical personnel finally forced the authorities to draw on medical licentiates, operating amongst civilian establishments, in 1943. This forced the creation of a completely new medical service, which would allow 'inferior' medical qualifications to be accommodated within the army. This body, the Indian Army Medical Corps, pulled more practitioners out of the civilian medical services, thereby weakening it further.[144]

In the context of the Bengal famine, and the epidemics that attended it, these infrastructural trends created a situation where the civilian medical services in Eastern India proved unequal to the task of organising an appropriate reply to emergencies. This forced the various military medical corps to buttress the civilian infrastructure in various ways. At one level, the military was forced to take a direct role in medical relief, with troops and specialised medical units being given orders and resources to arrange comprehensive relief schemes.[145] At another, they assisted the civilian medical units to be provisioned and run more effectively, with quite dramatic consequences. In November 1943, the military authorities released an experienced IMS officer, so that he could take over the duties of a Director of Public Health. He was followed, in the first half of 1944, by seven other colleagues into the Bengal medical services. By 15 November 1944, this military assistance had allowed the civilian authorities to open 582 new hospitals, 195 mobile medical units and 1,352 'satellite medical centres'.[146] However, a combination of factors, especially the requirements of the Allied army based in the front, the continuing shortage of medical manpower and an easing of epidemics connected to the famine conditions in Bengal, caused the special anti-famine measures to be withdrawn by May 1944, to the great consternation of many district officials and the aid-recipients in the province.[147]

Strikingly, officials remained aware that Bengal, being the main focus of the famine conditions, was luckier than the other provinces in the region in receiving military assistance to tackle a crisis that was threatening to disrupt administrative functioning. Although districts in Assam, Bihar, Eastern United Provinces and Orissa had, of course, suffered greatly from a host of severe epidemics and the official efforts to tackle the problems in Bengal by moving food stocks from these provinces, these did not bring in any appreciable military assistance. While food distribution and public health measures in the towns and villages near military encampments or battle-fronts in Assam, Bihar, Orissa and UP were ratified by the civilian and military officials, vast swathes of rural Eastern India were denied any lasting state-sponsored distributive schemes.[148] And even though attempts were sometimes made by British and Indian officials attached to the local civilian administrations to redress some of these difficulties, by the general distribution of released food-hoards, such efforts tended to remain spasmodic on account of a variety of reasons. Prominent amongst these was the military authorities' ability to keep an eye out for such 'insubordination', the central government's continued willingness to pass punishments on the basis of the army's reports and, not least, the continuing shortages of all manner of civilian administrative staff.[149]

IV. Concluding comments

The uses and effectiveness of the official policies of propaganda in Eastern India during the Second World War have to be assessed ultimately in the light of how challenges were prioritised and sought to be tackled during the conflict. From 1942 onwards the scale of the Japanese threat and economic dislocation in Eastern India, both of which caught the colonial state totally unawares, caused a series of panicky responses, intended ultimately only to allow the smooth mobilisation of the war-effort at the expense of all other competing administrative concerns. Yet, it was soon very obvious to bureaucrats in New Delhi and the provinces, as well as the GHQ (India), that the disruption caused by these short-term policies – and the political capital being made out of their effects – would necessarily lead to a situation where major constitutional concessions, leading to the dissolution of the *Raj*, would be unavoidable.[150] Remarkably, this attitude was fostered as much by an examination of the reactions of civilian audiences 'successfully' targeted by wartime propaganda policies, as by reports about the hostility of those left outside the purview of audience-specific distributive schemes.

The propaganda efforts organised by the Government of India between 1942 and 1945 were never intended to win the unwavering support of the civilian audiences targeted. In the context of the great economic difficulties being experienced in Eastern India, the policy was always one of offering the carrot without ever removing the stick out of view. This is clearly revealed in the Government of India's relationship with the various 'priority' groups. In the case of the junior employees of the various central and provincial services, for instance, support for the war was effectively controlled by centrally-financed salary increases, subsidies or free food, and the warning that these could be withdrawn with dangerous consequences.[151]

Similarly, the unskilled labour used in military works and industrial labour was constantly told that the financial bonuses and rations that were being provided to them and their families was dependent on their completing their contractual terms.[152]

That the resultant 'loyalty' to the war-effort was going to be necessarily solicitous was obvious to many officials. While workers were generally expected to stay at their posts, their not infrequent reversion only to lightning strikes, rather then more extreme measures, in order to get particular facets of the rationing schemes rectified, underlined the fact that their quiescence was informed by a sense of self-preservation in very difficult economic times.[153] Such an understanding was also revealed in the style of functioning of the CPI activists amongst industrial workers. The organisation, which was able to take advantage of the official policy of using their help to provision the worker's *bustis*, operated through party activists drawn from the locality in question and organised around a series of local issues and problems. Thus, CPI members often tended to be involved in the apparently paradoxical roles of both strike initiator and negotiator, which, at least from the political point of view, was a successful tactic. At the same time, government officials remained constantly aware that these communist politicians would never give up an opportunity to criticise the wartime administration, and to blame the authorities for the food shortages, defective distributive schemes, and the ever-present threat of the use of military and police force.[154]

In fact, the state's complicated relationship with labour also underlined the uneasy nature of its other wartime 'alliances', particularly with the Indian industrialists. This group was never happy with the central government's policy of using communist help to reach workers, but their objections in this regard were only able to ensure official assistance to keep troublesome CPI activists off the factory floors. At another level, they were grieved by the Government of India's tendency to siphon-off their wartime profits through a variety of schemes, as well as the authorities' ability to compete with them for workers and draw them away by offering better pay and conditions. Indeed, the competition between official and industrial recruiting agents was most notable in the coal and tea industry, and whereas European business interests seemed willing to make relatively great sacrifices for the war-effort, perhaps because they stood to lose more from a Japanese take-over, Indian companies tended to baulk at any significant loss of profits.[155] Special measures, like the Excess Profits Tax and the special sub-clauses of the Defence of India

Regulations, which prevented re-investment of wartime gains in certain sectors had remained immensely unpopular.[156] Also, there were fears that the sterling balances would not be repaid in full by Britain; in a period of political renegotiation, these restrictions were adroitly denounced by Indian business groups as the stifling of 'legitimate national aspirations' of the Indian nation.[157] This disjuncture in interests was also quite clearly indicated by the reports of Indian business houses supporting a variety of anti-government agitations, not least against the scorched-earth policy, which, of course, among other things, threatened factories and stockpiles of raw materials owned by them.[158] Such opposition was, over time, increasingly tempered by a realisation that some sort of transfer of power was inevitable, became much more pronounced and complex, and businessmen were very visible in their tendency to back the various nationalist schemes of post-war development.[159]

But while the Government of India was able to pursue the seemingly paradoxical, yet effective, policy of ensuring the mobilisation of the war-effort through the deployment of a complex inter-mixture of propaganda and threats of extreme penalties amongst specific civilian audiences, its hold over rural administration was fatally weakened in a variety of ways. For instance, there seemed little doubt in a wide variety of official communications that the authorities' wartime priorities had caused great economic and social distress amongst the 'general' rural population. While the inhabitants of the bigger urban centres in Eastern India, which tended to house big military bases, were relatively well provisioned, civilians based in the smaller *mofussil* towns and 'non-strategic' villages were generally left to their own devices to fend with the vagaries of an unstable economy. And the crisis in rural Eastern India in 1943 was accentuated by the official decision to feed the region's cities and urban centres at the expense of its villages.[160] In provinces like Assam, Orissa, Bihar, and the princely states surrounding it, such policies resulted in localised famines.[161] There was also a corresponding fall in general health standards, which was underlined by the series of severe epidemics that hit the region between 1943 and 1945. One report referring to the fall in morbidity from the disease in the Raniganj area pointed out that 'available statistics of malaria morbidity have shown a steady decline in Raniganj coalfields since 1944. This reduction is more real than apparent as no such corresponding reduction is manifest in the rural areas of the neighbourhood.'[162] Notably, such views were by no means isolated.[163]

The problem, as it unfolded for the authorities, especially the local administration, arose from the fact that such official inactivity attracted a variety of tenacious critics. The middle classes, especially the poorer groups who were dependent on fixed salaries, remained active throughout the war, and often tapped into agitations being carried out by other sections of rural society, especially the poor agricultural labour.[164] However, the standard local administrative response, forced usually by the demands of local political activists or 'spokespeople', was to attempt to release hoards of food, which, in turn, strained their relationship with the richer elements of rural society, a class which had benefited from spiralling food prices and had, specially in regions like Bihar, Eastern United Provinces and Orissa, provided some of the government's staunchest allies. In this manner, official measures intended to tackle local economic problems had the effect of further isolating an already apprehensive loyalist element,[165] whose support for the war-effort had dwindled, or was at least downplayed, in the context of the heightened rural political activism aimed against the wartime administration.[166] The effectiveness of this political mobilisation in the localities was indicated by the multiplying of attacks on subordinate government servants in the sub-divisions and their allies,[167] and the difficulties experienced by officials in apprehending those involved in these attacks, not least because of the unwillingness amongst the loyalist elements of the rural populace to act as informers for fear of reprisals.[168]

Other indicators highlighted the colonial authorities' awareness of, and apprehensions about, the negative consequences of these economic, social and political trends as well. At the level of the central government these anxieties were revealed by the marked shifts in attitude towards the Indian constitutional position. Referred to in one context as the disappearance of the distinction between 'war publicity' and 'publicity for Government activities',[169] the change in position was represented by an acceptance of the inability to thwart nationalist plans to link constitutional demands with the war-issue. As a result, offers of dominion status were replaced by promises of independence after the end of the war. The Cripps mission, though a failure in the sense that it did not engender an agreement in 1942, introduced a characteristic political language which was to be reiterated for the rest of the war. According to the Government of India's Information and Broadcasting Department, this change of strategy was necessary because the 'efforts at making politically minded India war minded ha[d] failed'. Its officials, thus, 'strongly' recommended a change of policy and advised the provincial authorities to give 'political sugar coating on war quinine. Make victory certain and desirable for India's future. Draw a picture of India after victory from every angle especially that of Independent India, stressing always that freedom of India is difficult without and before victory.'[170] Consequently official propaganda in 1942 would frequently refer to the British 'willingness' to grant India 'complete freedom' after the war, and that they would allow the 'Indians themselves' to decide the form of government. The one pre-condition for the 'complete relinquishment of British responsibilities' that was to be reiterated was that the 'principal elements in India's political life' would have to agree about the form of the country's future constitution.[171]

At the level of district and sub-divisional administration, the general increase in hostility against colonial rule was acknowledged by the tendency to readapt centrally-prescribed messages. This re-telling of messages, whenever it occurred, tended to be affected by a variety of concerns, conspicuously a resolve to counter – through denials and arguments – a wide variety of 'disruptive rumours', which caused local officials to downplay, if not completely ignore, certain themes. This trend first became obvious in the localities where the scorched earth policy or the widespread requisitioning of land for military use was carried out. District and Deputy Magistrates, worried at their subordinates being upset by the fact that these scheme affected their families, kept underlining the scale of compensation that was being arranged,[172] and ignored, or downplayed, some the 'nationalist' and 'internationalist' messages that the Bureau of Public Information sought to distribute.[173] Again, in the context of the food shortages of 1943, reports suggested that local publicity officials, attached both to the provincial services and the District Local Boards, felt uncomfortable about the mass screening episodes of the Indian News Parade that combined snippets of Allied victories in South East Asia with images of the ever-improving transport and food-supply networks in India.[174] In other cases, district officers fearful of food riots within their spheres of influence, quietly put aside the lecture notes provided by the provincial headquarters and Bureau of Public Information, and desisted from making grandiose promises of providing economic relief, attempting instead to tackle the situation with the use of force against 'hoarders'.[175] Interestingly, the publicity distributed before such activities further weakened the Government of India's publicity messages. Instead of re-assuring its audience that things were being rapidly brought under control, as the central government would have preferred, local officials in the badly affected localities, who were usually not constrained by military supervision, appealed to the local landlords and merchants that they voluntarily surrender their hoards so as to 'curtail the possibility of food riots', which would be violent and cause 'the destruction of both public and private property and life'.[176]

Indeed, the problems caused by the administrative trends between 1942 and 1945 were also reflected in the roles accorded to the state policies of censorship amongst civilian audiences. These were no longer merely seen as a way of enhancing the impact of official publicity by proscribing information inimical to it, but as a means of gathering intelligence about the effectiveness of the various official public relations schemes, especially amongst the 'priority' audiences. The next chapter examines these interconnections between state propaganda and censorship in greater detail.

Notes

1 There was, of course, the additional question of arranging for 'political warfare broadcasts' to be targeted against Japanese occupied territories in Burma and South East Asia, which was given increasing attention with the improving Allied strategic position and the formulation of plans for the recapture of Burma. Indeed, an *ad hoc* committee was set up in late 1943 to discuss the issue, and this was composed of Lt Col S.R. Hunt from the GHQ, Charles Burns from the Department of Information and Broadcasting, GOI, John A. Galvin from the Far Eastern Bureau, and with Eric Robertson acting as Secretary. Its main terms of reference were to draw up a working plan for the 'preparation and presentation, as AIR services, of broadcasts directed to the countries east of India' in languages not understood in India, in Indian languages and in English, as well as to examine the question of pooling available transmitter resources. The Committee decided that in making its decisions it would be guided by the principle that the responsibility for broadcasts to South East Asia in languages not understood in India would rest with the Far Eastern Bureau, whereas all the other broadcasts would be controlled by the Government of India. See, Report of the Ad Hoc Committee on Working Arrangements for Political Warfare Broadcasts from India, 4 December 1943, L/I/1/936, OIOC. The topic of the arrangement, deployment and limitations of political warfare broadcasts against the Japanese is an important one, but it remained largely unrelated to the question of organising radio publicity for civilian audiences in Eastern India. Moreover, the subject is a vast and complex one, deserving separate attention, rather than a few paragraphs in the present analysis. Thus, the question of 'political warfare' is not studied in this monograph.

2 J.A. Thorne, *Confidential report on the control during war of the press, broadcasting and films; and on publicity for purposes of the war* [hereafter *Thorne Report*], New Delhi, 1939, pp. 11–12, L/I/1/1136, OIOC.
3 At the outset of the war the BBC concentrated on preparing radio broadcasts only in English and Hindi. Bengali programmes began to be included from November 1941. See telegram from the Information and Broadcasting Department, GOI to L. Amery, SSI, GOBr, 15 November 1941, L/I/1/942, OIOC. Between January and April 1943, 'newsletters' in Tamil and Gujrati were also incorporated in the organisation's Indian language services. See telegrams from the Information and Broadcasting Department, GOI to L. Amery, SSI, GOBr, 31 January 1943 and 30 April 1943, ibid.
4 This important facet of broadcasting in India, especially during the wartime period, has even been ignored by the best available studies of the topic. See, for instance, P.S. Gupta, *Radio and the Raj, 1921–47*, Calcutta 1995.
5 Letter from F. Puckle, Secretary, Information and Broadcasting Department, GOI to R.W. Brock, MOI, 11 February 1943, L/I/1/970, OIOC.
6 *Report on Broadcasting in India*, Research Department, A.C. Cossor Ltd., London, c.1943, L/I/1/970, OIOC.
7 Report on the development of broadcasting in India for the second half of 1942, from the Information and Broadcasting Department, GOI, to the SSI, GOBr, 26 January 1943, p. 4, L/I/1/967, OIOC. Similar problems continued over 1943, despite an improvement in the Allied strategic position. For instance, great problems were faced in setting up the AIR station in Patna (Bihar), due to shortage of steel required for constructing the transmitter tower and receiving centre buildings, as well the fact that twenty three cases of material for the transmitter were lost at sea on account of enemy action. Report on the development of broadcasting in India for the first half of 1943, from F. Puckle, Department of Information and Broadcasting, GOI, to SSI, GOBr, 27 July 1943, p. 5, L/I/1/967, OIOC. The opening of the Patna station was particularly ill-fated as seven cases of the replacement material for the transmitter was again lost at sea. Report on the development of broadcasting in India for the second half of the calendar year 1943, from G.S. Bozman, Department of Information and Broadcasting, GOI, to the SSI, 21 February 1944, p. 6, L/I/1/967, OIOC. Intimation was finally received from the Secretary of State for India's office that the required replacement material for the 5 kilowatt transmitter would only be supplied by March or April 1945. Report on the development of broadcasting in India for the first half of the calendar year 1944, from T.G.P. Spear, Department of Information and Broadcasting, GOI, to Under Secretary of State for India, GOBr, 8 August 1944, p. 5, L/I/1/967, OIOC.
8 The station was opened on 16 of July 1942, and there seemed to be much relief that this was done on schedule. Report on the development of broadcasting in India for the second half of 1942, from the Information and Broadcasting Department, GOI, to the SSI, GOBr, 26 January 1943, p. 4, L/I/1/967, OIOC.

9 Secret telegram from the Information and Broadcasting Department, GOI, to the SSI, GOBr, 5 June 1942, L/I/1/970, OIOC.
10 Letter from F. Puckle, Secretary, Information and Broadcasting Department, GOI, to R.W Brock, Ministry of Information, GOBr, 11 February 1943, L/I/1/970, OIOC.
11 A recommendation was made in May 1942 that broadcasts in Hindustani and Punjabi from Russia be used to counter the effects of transmissions from Berlin and Tokyo. The attitude of Government of India officials in this regards is truly surprising, as they remained more than willing to accept the risk of the Soviets using Indian revolutionaries in the transmission of programmes. Secret telegram from the External Affairs Ministry, GOI, to SSI, GOBr, 12 May 1942, L/I/1/969, OIOC. A formal request in this regard was made to the government of Soviet Russia on 26 June 1942. See, copy of secret telegram, sent to Foreign Office, GOBr, 7 July 1942, L/I/1/969, OIOC. Soviet assistance in the field of broadcasting was used well into the war. See, letter from A.F. Morley, India Office, GOBr, to A. R. Dew, Foreign Office, 18 February 1944, L/I/1/969, OIOC. The closing down of broadcasting stations in the Dutch East Indies, Singapore and Rangoon by March 1942 meant that Axis radio stations were 'almost completely controlling the air in the East.' It was, therefore, felt that alternate, and powerful, radio transmitters would be needed to challenge Axis claims, especially because the transmitters at Delhi and Chungking 'being low powered c[ould] only offer slight resistance'. Secret telegram from the Department of Information and Broadcasting, GOI, to SSI, GOBr, 10 March 1942, L/P&J/8/119, OIOC. The reception of broadcasts from Russia was good and they were, thus, considered useful for counter-propaganda purposes. Secret telegram from the External Affairs Ministry, GOI, to the SSI, GOBr, 12 May 1942, L/I/1/969, OIOC.
12 Secret telegram from External Affairs Department, GOI, to the SSI, 17 May 1942, L/I/1/955, OIOC.
13 Rushbrook Williams complained that 'I cannot help feeling that the use of all this American material in a space which can plainly be devoted wholly or in part to British material, is distinctly unfortunate. Plainly there is a good case for 'shows' for American troops, who cannot listen in to their own signals from the United States. But need AIR give time for 'straight American propaganda for the local population'!' [sic]. Letter from R. Williams, Director, Eastern Service, BBC, London, to the A.H. Joyce, India Office, GOBr, 5 February 1943, L/I/1/954, OIOC.
14 Memorandum by F. Puckle, 10 February 1943, L/I/1/954, OIOC. Puckle concluded by declaring that '... All India Radio, or rather the Government of India, must be accepted as the best judges of what its audience needs, and what it will listen to. In radio, more than any other form of propaganda, you can take the horse to the water, but you can't make him drink – not, at any rate, as long [as] a radio set has knobs. And remember also that the Indian audience is about 85% Indian'. Ibid., p.9.
15 Extract from confidential weekly newsletter produced by A. Rowlands, Advisor to the Viceroy of India on War Administration, c.February-March 1944, L/I/1/954, OIOC.

16 Rowlands seemed annoyed by the Government of India's delay in offering broadcasting time to the American authorities on AIR transmitters. He declared that 'I must say I think the Government of India are making very heavy weather about this: the stations would only cover a range of 50 miles and I understand the Americans already operate such stations in the U.K.' Ibid.

17 The meeting was attended by Rowlands, Air Marshal Sir P. Joubert, the Chief of Information and Civil Affairs, SEAC, G.S. Bozman of the Information and Broadcasting Department, GOI, Major General Cawthorn, DMI, GHQ (India), and a Major Jackson from the US army. Major Jackson forwarded the American request for five 50 watt stations in Agra, Delhi, Karachi, Calcutta and Assam, 'on wave lengths approved by the Chief Engineer, All India Radio, The distance covered by the transmissions would be about 15 miles.' Minutes of meeting in Rowlands' room on 21 March 1944, L/I/1/954, OIOC. An attached minute about the meeting referred to the problems created by Cawthorn's 'deep-seated suspicion of everything American.' Note by Mr. Morley, GOBr, c.March 1944, ibid.

18 Letter from S.S. Bajpai, Information and Broadcasting Department, GOI, to A.F. Morley, GOBr, 24 August 1944, L/I/1/954, OIOC.

19 A good example of British hostility towards American broadcasting activities is provided by the particularly acicular assessment of the Indonesian Section of the Pacific Bureau of the OWI, which covered 'the whole of the East Indies, both British and Dutch, the Philippines, British Malaya and whilst the Burma section is being built up, Burma itself.' See, Report by D. Bowes-Lyon, Member, Political Warfare Mission, Washington, 28 February 1943, p. 1, L/I/1/955, OIOC. Bowes Lyon was very critical of the Section Head, a Mr. Van der Bos, a Dutch national, and a British staff member called Mr. G.E.P. Collins, both of whom he called 'anti-Dutch and anti-British'. He took particular exception to the fact that the territories covered by the section were being constantly assured of their coming independence and declarations 'that their freedom will come from the United States of America and that their liberator will be President Roosevelt.' Ibid. Bowes-Lyon also directed his ire at the Director of the Pacific Bureau, Mr. Owen Lattimore, whom he considered 'to be in a curious double role, being a high official of a United States Government Agency and at the same time, political adviser to General Chiang Kai Shek.... He thus serves two masters. He is such a Sinophile that.... He is opposed to the return of Colonial Government after the war. The Indonesian Division operates therefore not only under his authority, but under his inspiration.' Ibid., pp. 1–2.

20 The high price of receivers was often blamed for the difficulties in spreading the scope of wartime broadcasting. See, for instance, departmental note, Department of Information and Broadcasting, 31 August 1944, L/I/1/939, OIOC. A receiver cost Rs. 200 upwards, and the license fee had to be paid twice a year. Although plans had been to produce cheap receivers, these did not come to fruition during the war. Indeed, as late as March 1945, a communication from the Government of Britain's Economic and Overseas Department declared that 'It had been hoped

earlier that surplus radio equipment and stores might, on the conclusion of hostilities, enable British manufacturers to fabricate for India and her Colonies the cheap set envisaged. It seems very doubtful however from discussions which have taken with the Post Office whether this hope will materialise. It is true that there will be millions of surplus valves and condensers, but these components alone do not make up the sum total of the requirements of a wireless set with a tropical finish suitable for Indian conditions. The view taken by the Engineer-in-Chief of the Post Office is that an increase in the prices of receivers suitable for community listening in India is more probable than a decrease'. Letter from J. Thomson, Economic and Overseas Department, GOBr, 2 March 1945, L/I/1/958, OIOC.

21 Between June and December 1940, the amount collected from radio license fees was Rs. 730,090; and between June and December 1941 the figure stood at 896,690. Letter from F. Puckle, Secretary, Department of Information and Broadcasting, GOI, to Under Secretary of State for India, GOBr, 20 February 1942, L/I/1/967, OIOC. These revenue receipts were more or less maintained throughout the war, with amounts ranging from Rs. 800,000 to Rs. 1,000,000 being brought in every half year. See, L/I/1/967, OIOC. Importantly, the relative stability of the monies brought in by the radio license fees is a good indicator of the fact that there were no major changes in the number of receivers in private ownership during the Second World War.

22 *Thorne Report*, pp. 12–13, L/I/1/1136, OIOC.

23 Secret telegram from External Affairs Department, GOI, to SSI, 17 May 1942, L/I/1/955, OIOC.

24 It was estimated, in February 1943, that there were about 150,000 receiving sets in the whole of British India, with a 'comparatively small' number of 'community sets in villages and in public places in towns'. Memorandum by F. Puckle, Department of Information and Broadcasting, GOI, 10 February 1943, L/I/1/954, OIOC. A year later, G.S. Bozman, then Secretary of the Department of Information and Broadcasting, complained that there were only 180,000 licensed/registered receivers in British India and a 'very limited number of listeners', especially because of an inability to reach the vast bulk of the rural population. Memorandum entitled 'Development of Broadcasting in India', by G.S. Bozman, Secretary, Department of Information and Broadcasting, GOI, c.1944, L/I/1/968, OIOC.

25 In the first few years of the war, two types of batteries were used: AMCO and EXIDE. The former was considered better as it worked a set for thirty five hours, had an average life of three and a half hours and experienced no technical problems. The EXIDE battery, in comparison, could only run a set for twenty five to thirty hours, had an average life of one and a half years and had a 'heavy sulphation' problem. A new type of battery, called the DELCO battery, was brought into use in August 1943, and was, by the end of 1944, considered to be giving very good service. Report of the Delhi Rural Broadcasting Scheme for the period between October 1941 to March 1944, attached to letter from P.N. Thapar, Joint Secretary, Department of Information and Broadcasting, GOI, to the

Under-Secretary of State for India, GOBr, 11 June 1945, p. 6, L/I/1/967, OIOC. These batteries had to be recharged in centres located in the cities and the bigger towns. While the Government of India remained responsible for batteries taken on tour by officials, the local boards were made responsible for maintaining and recharging the batteries for receivers used in community listening sets. Unfortunately, complaints about delays in recharging or replacing batteries, often caused by the wartime shortages and military demands, remained frequent. In 1944, for instance, AMCO batteries were unobtainable in the market and EXIDE batteries were very scarce, with the DAGENITE, LUCAS and DELCO varieties being the only ones available. Report on the Delhi Broadcasting Scheme for the year 1944–45, attached to a letter from M.A. Hussain, Deputy Secretary, Department of Information and Broadcasting, GOI, to the Under Secretary of State for India, GOBr, 20 June 1946, p. 4, L/I/1/967, OIOC. For a good description of the difficulties faced with the maintenance of batteries, also see *Report on Broadcasting in India*, Research Department, A.C. Cossor Limited, London, c.1943, L/I/1/970, OIOC.

26 *Report on Broadcasting in India*, Research Department, A.C. Cossor Ltd., London, c1943, L/I/1/970, OIOC.
27 Letter from F. Puckle, Secretary, Information and Broadcasting Department, GOI to R.W. Brock, MOI, 11 February 1943, L/I/1/970, OIOC.
28 *Report on Broadcasting in India*, Research Department, A.C. Cossor Limited, London, c.1943, L/I/1/970, OIOC.
29 Letter from F. Puckle, Secretary, Information and Broadcasting Department, GOI to R.W. Brock, MOI, GOBr, 11 February 1943, L/I/1/970, OIOC.
30 Intelligence report from commercial and other channels on war propaganda between April and June 1942, c.1942, L/I/1/1015, OIOC. Also see, consolidated statement of work done in the districts by the District War Committees and others during the period from June to August 1943, MSS EUR E. 360/20, Macdonald papers, OIOC.
31 Statement of the work done by the Provincial [Orissa] War Committee during the period from June to August 1943, MSS EUR E. 360/20, Macdonald papers, OIOC.
32 Secret telegram from the External Affairs Department, GOI, to L. Amery, SSI, GOBr, 27 April 1943, L/I/1/970, OIOC. There was an acute shortage of wireless sets in Great Britain between 1942 and 1945. The few available for civilian use were usually needed for consumption in Britain. India's needs in these years were met through intermittent supplies from the United States. *Report on Broadcasting in India*, Research Department, A.C Cossor Ltd., London, c.1943, L/I/1/970, OIOC. Another assessment of the supply situation declared that 'With the impending cut-back in war production in the United States it is probable that the production of wireless receivers will shortly be resumed In the United States steps are being taken to meet Empire needs including those of India by the release of sets already manufactured The quantities covered by this decision are, however, small. These American and British sets are fairly expensive. They would probably suffice to satisfy ... the large towns and the wealthier

members of the Indian community.' Letter from A.F. Morley, India Office, GOBr, to Mr. Tomkins, 5 October 1944, L/I/1/958, OIOC.
33 Departmental note, Department of Information and Broadcasting, 31 August 1944, L/I/1/939, OIOC.
34 Bozman had doubts about the practical value of the scheme in India. He explained: 'The size of the country alone, let alone climatic difficulties which affect all land lines, would make me hesitate'. Note by G.S. Bozman, Secretary, Department of Information and Broadcasting, GOI, 11 October 1944, L/I/1/939, OIOC.
35 The issue was brought into focus once again by the F.M. Chinoy & Co. Ltd., a Bombay-based concern, which indicated to the Government of India in July 1945 that it was keen to introduce 'wire broadcasting' in the cities and towns of India. See, letter from F.M. Chinoy, Director, F.M. Chinoy & Co. Ltd., to the Director General, Post and Telegraphs, India, 31 July 1945, L/I/1/939, OIOC. The Department of Information and Broadcasting's reaction to the suggestion was not negative. Bozman explained that: 'Our attitude is likely to be generally benevolent but we shall, of course, wish to keep a fair measure of control over the programmes to be relayed'. Letter from G.S. Bozman, Secretary, Department of Information and Broadcasting, GOI, to A.H. Joyce, India Office, GOBr, 3 August 1945, L/I/1/939, OIOC.
36 For instance, officials in the United Provinces confiscated 45 radio sets in 8 districts in the aftermath of the 'Quit-India' movement. Secret letter from M. Hallett, Governor, Government of United Provinces, to Linlithgow, Viceroy, 9 November 1942, R/3/1/78, OIOC. In Bihar and Assam, similar measures were taken during the extreme food shortages that accompanied the famine in Bengal, not least as the Japanese-controlled radio stations were regularly transmitting Subhas Chandra Bose's offer of rice. See, secret monthly reports prepared Provincial Press Adviser, Bihar, for the year 1943, PPAF 39/(vii)/1943, BSA. Also, while the policy of requisitioning private property for military use was generally never popular amongst civilian officials, essentially due to the hostility it evoked amongst local communities, the forcible collection of radio sets was considered an exception. A Deputy Magistrate based at Ramgarh, where Indian, American and Chinese troops were based, reported in 1943 that there was much 'official enthusiasm' for a drive to collect receivers for use by newly arrived army detachments, as the reduction of the number of privately owned radio sets would also prove 'administratively advantageous in law and order management'. Similar views were expressed by officials based in Deogarh, a major rail-head for the transport of troops eastwards. Correspondence between the district magistracy and local military commands, Bihar, United Provinces and Bengal, c.1943, WSF 65/i/43, BSA.
37 Extracts from secret reports by District Magistrates in Bihar, Eastern United Provinces and Assam, c.1943, WSF 63/iii/43, BSA.
38 Secret notes from the Deputy Magistrate of Dumka, GOB; the Deputy Commissioner of the Santhal Parganas, GOB, and the Commissioner of the Chota Nagpur Division, GOB, c.October 1943, WSF 55/2(vii)/1943, BSA.

39 Moreover, an official memorandum explained that the 'propaganda motif necessary to influence mass opinion on new and revolutionary ideas is ... the basis of the Documentary [sic] and subtle technique combined with psychological treatment give it a great advantage over other and more direct methods of propaganda. Because of this, the Documentary [sic] is ... [considered the] ideal vehicle through which propaganda about the war can be conducted on the widest possible scale.' Memorandum on Film Publicity, pp. 3–4, L/R/5/295, OIOC.

40 The concession with regards to the import of long feature films was cancelled on 1 July 1944. Ibid., pp. 2–3.

41 The Film Advisory Board, with its headquarters in Bombay and a branch in Calcutta, consisted of the representatives of both the Indian and the foreign film industries based in the country, and the importers of British and American films. These individuals were 'honorary' members and they were assisted by only one paid member of staff: a full-time secretary. The dissolution of the body in January 1943 was heralded by the GOI Information and Broadcasting Department's insistence on increased official control over all aspects of the production, and the distribution, of wartime film propaganda. Ibid., pp. 5–6.

42 It became clear in 1941 that the various foreign newsreels were unsuitable for the 'public' in India without 'some intermixture of Indian items'. An attempt was made to 'regain its ... popularity' by having Indian events filmed and incorporated occasionally among 'foreign items', but 'the percentage of the latter being still very high the circulation dropped to such a level' that the arrangement between the Board of Information and the Twentieth Century Fox corporation failed. The total expenditure for the new scheme agreed between the two was expected to be Rs.400,000, while the expected income was calculated at Rs. 250,000. The Government of India undertook to reimburse all the losses suffered by the corporation. Each documentary was about 800 feet long and its material was gleaned from a variety of sources: the 'Indian footage' was supplied by cameramen stationed in different parts of India; the 'troops footage' was arranged by the GHQ's Directorate of Public Relations, and 'foreign footage' was taken from British and Allied newsreels. Ibid., pp. 8–9.

43 The 'Instructional Film Scheme', as the arrangement was known, was discontinued with the removal of governmental control over the import and distribution of raw film. Ibid., pp. 10–11.

44 For instance, endeavours to set up a unit in August 1944 to produce cartoon propaganda films in collaboration with the Board of Information were impaired by a lack of resources and manpower. No films were produced by the body during the war and the first issue came out in May 1946. Memorandum on Film Publicity, p. 17, L/R/5/295, OIOC.

45 Memorandum on Film Publicity, pp. 2–6, L/R/5/295, OIOC.

46 The classes of 'approved films' included all issues of the Indian News Parade, the British Movietone News, British Paramount News and Universal British News. The Government of India's film unit, called Information Films of India supplied 302 films 'for the purposes of DIR 44A'. Of these 302 films, 104 were produced by the I.F.I. itself. The others

were received from other bodies: 101 from the Ministry of Information, London; 7 from 'War Department organisations'; 14 from RKO Radio Pictures, Bombay; 19 from the Soviet Film Distributors, Bombay; 4 from the Belgian Consul; 4 from the Australian Government and 39 were supplied by 'the trade'. Ibid.

47 The rentals, which began to be charged from 15 September 1943, brought in Rs 191,770 in 1943, Rs 1,185,938 in 1944 and Rs 1,853,000 in 1945. Ibid., p. 16. District Magistrates, who were in charge of ensuring the 'proper' screening of films in the towns that served as their headquarters, would often point out that local cinema proprietors were dealt with through threats of stiff prison sentences under the provisions of the Defence of India Rules. In almost all cases, this seemed to have the desired effect of stifling dissent. However, in one case, in the town of Muzaffarpur, a week's strike by the theatre operatives, who packed up and left, was tackled by the employment of military film crews till the auctioning of the premises provided a new, and more pliable, management. Extracts from secret reports by District Magistrates in Bihar, Eastern United Provinces and Assam, c.1943, WSF 63/iii/43, BSA.
48 Memorandum on Film Publicity, p. 15, L/R/5/295, OIOC.
49 The scheme was first started in Bombay which in early 1941 had purchased one hundred 16mm projectors for the purpose. After a publicity conference held in July 1941, the Information and Broadcasting Department obtained financial sanction to expand the scheme all over India. The Government of India contributed 25 per cent of the non-recurring cost and 33 and a half per cent of the recurring annual costs of the scheme, while the provincial governments paid the balance. Ibid., p. 14, L/R/5/295, OIOC.
50 *Thorne Report*, pp. 15–23, L/I/1/1136, OIOC.
51 Secret letter from T. Stewart, Governor, GOB to Linlithgow, Viceroy, 29 August 1941, R/3/1/21, OIOC.
52 *Thorne Report*, pp. 15–23, L/I/1/1136, OIOC.
53 Memorandum on Film Publicity, p. 14–15, L/R/5/295, I.O.L.
54 Ibid.
55 See, secret monthly reports prepared Provincial Press Adviser, Bihar, for the year 1943, PPAF 39/9(vii)/1943, BSA.
56 Extracts from secret reports by District Magistrates in Bihar, Eastern United Provinces and Assam, c1943, WSF 63/iii/43, BSA.
57 See, for instance, secret notes from the Commissioner of the Chota Nagpur Division, GOB, c.1943, WSF 55/2(vii)/1943, BSA.
58 *Thorne Report* , p. 5, L/I/1/1136, OIOC.
59 There were five Government [of India] presses in all: Calcutta and Simla had two each, while the fifth was in Delhi. Memorandum on printing, 30 August 1944, War History of the Labour Department, GOI, L/R/5/291, OIOC. In 1943, the pressures on the Government presses caused the South East Asia Command's new paper, the *S.E.A.C.*, to be printed in the facilities of the *Statesman* group. See secret telegram from the War Department, GOI to L. Amery, SSI, GOBr, 15 November 1943, L/I/1/1050, OIOC. Also see note on SEAC paper, 26 February 1944, ibid.

60 Initially this meant the production of propaganda contradicting claims in German radio programmes, but from 1942 it also included attempts to 'strengthen morale' by '... not merely ... educat[ing] the citizen in the technical aspect of A.R.P., but [by] inspir[ing] and retain[ing] confidence in an emergency' using all available forms of publicity. War History of the Civil Defence Department, pp. 125–133, L/R/5/286, OIOC.
61 *Thorne Report*, p. 11–12, L/I/1/1136, OIOC.
62 The Government of Bengal arranged for the weekly distribution of 2,000 copies of the 'Talking Points', a publication of the Bureau of Public Information, amongst officials based in the localities in 1940. Telegram from Home Department, GOI .to L. Amery, S.S.I., 14 February 1941, L/I/1/1017, OIOC.
63 R.G. Casey, *An Australian In India*, London, 1947, pp. 28–29.
64 *Thorne Report*, p. 9, L/I/1/1136, OIOC.
65 Recollections of S. Solomon, ICS, Bihar, pp. 83–85, MSS EUR F. 180/24, OIOC.
66 Describing the situation existing in his province, Hayley declared that 'We had no system of propaganda in Assam, and I took it upon myself to organize a province wide news service, combined with propaganda'. Recollections of T.T.S. Hayley, p. 9, MSS EUR F. 180/3, OIOC.
67 See, for instance, statement of work done by Provincial [Orissa] War Committee during the period from June to August 1943, MSS EUR E. 360/20, Macdonald papers, OIOC.
68 Confidential express letter from F. Puckle, Secretary, Department of Information and Broadcasting to the Chief Secretaries of all provincial governments, 28 August 1942, PPAF 49/42, BSA.
69 Departmental memorandum from N. Senapati, Joint Secretary, Political Department, GOB to Chief Secretary, GOB, 22 October 1942, PPAF 11/1942, BSA.
70 See, for instance, circular letter from Y.A. Godbole, Chief Secretary, Bihar to all District Officers, 1 March 1942, PPAF No. 20/1942, BSA.
71 Tour diary of J.M.G. Bell for the months June to December 1940, Bell papers, CSASA.
72 Recollections of T.T.S. Hayley, p. 11, MSS EUR F. 180/3, OIOC.
73 *Searchlight*, 25 February 1942.
74 *Searchlight*, 24 March 1942. Also see the issue of the newspaper dated 2 April 1942.
75 Report in *Amrita Bazar Patrika*, 29 December 1942.
76 Between June and August 1943, the Liaison Assistants touring the Ganjam, Puri and Cuttack districts were able to engage '7 *Jatra* parties, 2 blind singers, 1 *daskathia* boy and 1 street singer'. Statement of work done by the Provincial [Orissa] War Committee during the period from June to August 1943, Macdonald papers, MSS EUR E. 360/20, OIOC.
77 Memorandum on the war effort in Orissa, undated, Ansorge papers, CSASA.
78 Every District and Subdivisional Headquarters in Bihar had a *Muhalla* Committee, whose members assisted in the distribution of official propaganda in print or orally. Letter from N. Senapati, Provincial Press Adviser, GOB to the Secretaries of all District and Subdivisional War

Committees, 2 March 1942, PPAF No. 4/1942, BSA. Also see, departmental note, Political Department, GOB, 5 January 1942, ibid.
79 Recollections of T.T.S. Hayley, I.C.S, Assam, MSS EUR F. 180/3, pp. 9–10, OIOC.
80 Apart from publishing and releasing the Talking Points, the *Indian Information* and a variety of booklets and posters (in 1943, for example, it distributed 20 million 'photogravures'), its other duties included the preparation of the *War in Pictures* in 12 languages (which 'at one time' had a circulation of one and a half million copies each month), and releasing communiqués to the Indian and international press (compared to the quarter million words issued to the Indian press in 1939, the Bureau released 'several million' in 1944). See, secret War History of the Bureau of Public Information, 1939–45, GOI, pp. 1–7, L/R/5/295, OIOC.
81 A review of the wartime efforts declared that, 'The bulk of India's 388,000,000 people live in 700,000 villages, but it was decided to restrict propaganda to urban areas. The enemy ... was unlikely to waste bombs on remote villages scattered over a million square miles, and to equip these would have entailed enormous public expenditure'. War History of the Civil Defence Department, GOI, p. 126, L/R/5/286, OIOC.
82 Report from Bengal, 13 August 1941, L/I/1/1015, OIOC.
83 Recollections of S. Rahmatullah, ICS, pp. 20–29, MSS EUR F. 180/14a, OIOC.
84 Secret letter from T. Rutherford, Governor, GOB to Linlithgow, Viceroy, 25 May 1943, R/3/1/23, OIOC.
85 Secret letter from R.F Mudie, Governor of Bihar to Linlithgow, Viceroy, 24 September 1943, R/3/1/23, OIOC.
86 The distribution of exhibitions was as follows: 4 in Cuttack, 2 in Puri, 2 in Balasore, 4 in Sambhalpur, 2 in Ganjam and 3 in Koraput districts. *Annual Report of the Agricultural Department, Orissa for 1943–44*, Cuttack, 1947, pp. 74–75, V/24/202, OIOC.
87 Consolidated statement of work done in the districts by the District War Committees during the period from June to August 1943, MSS EUR E. 360/20, Macdonald Papers, OIOC.
88 Private and secret letter from A. Wavell, Viceroy to L. Amery, SSI, GOBr, 9 January 1945, L/I/1/842, OIOC.
89 For instance, O.M. Martin, an ICS officer who had been posted in Bengal during the war, mentions how district officials 'did a lot of propaganda throughout the villages' around strategic areas like Chittagong and Noakhali. Memoirs of O.M. Martin, ICS, p. 314, Martin papers, CSASA. Also see WIS (II), 19 June 1942, L/WS/1/1433, OIOC; Letter from J. Herbert, Governor, GOBe to Linlithgow, Viceroy, 8 May 1942, MSS EUR F. 125/42, OIOC; *Report on the Police Administration in the Province of Assam for the year 1943*, Shillong, 1943, p. 3, V/24/3259, OIOC; Note on the war in Assam, 1939–45 by H.F.G. Burbridge, IPS, undated, no pp., MSS EUR F. 161/32, OIOC, and *Review of the working of village authorities constituted under the Assam Rural Self-Government Act, 1926, for the year 1944–45*, Shillong, p. 1, V/24/373, OIOC.
90 *The Calcutta Municipal Gazette*, 17 January 1942.

91 Personal and confidential memorandum from A.H. Joyce, India Office to A. Wavell, Viceroy, 17 December 1943, L/I/1/842, OIOC.
92 Private and secret letter from A. Wavell, Viceroy to L. Amery, SSI, GOBr, 9 January 1945, L/I/1/842, OIOC.
93 See, for instance, consolidated statement of work done in the districts by the District War Committees and others during the period from June to August 1943, MSS EUR E. 360/20, Macdonald papers, OIOC. It was estimated in December 1943 that almost half of the seven and a half million rupees allocated to the Front by the Government of India had been 'absorbed' by 'grants to the provinces'. Personal and confidential memorandum from A.H. Joyce, India Office to A. Wavell, Viceroy, 17 December 1943, L/I/1/842, OIOC.
94 Associations like the Calcutta Committee, the Cawnpore Committee, the Bombay Committee and the Madras Committee, all of which were composed of the important industrialists in the respective provinces, helped spread 'official news' among their employees. See appendix B to the confidential progress report on the working of the Calcutta Committee, L/I/1/1017, OIOC.
95 Note on the Working of the Public Relations Sub-Committee, June to November 1940, by G.W. Tyson, Deputy Chairman, Calcutta Committee, c.December 1940, L/I/1/1017, OIOC.
96 Telegram from the Home Department, GOI to L. Amery, SSI, GOBr, 14 February 1941, L/I/1/1017, OIOC.
97 Note on the working of the Public Relations Sub-Committee, June to November 1940, by G.W. Tyson, Deputy Chairman, Calcutta Committee, c.December 1940, L/1017, OIOC. The Committee distributed 3,554 copies of 'Talking Points', 161 copies of 'Misleading Statements', 116 copies of 'Weekly News Reports' and 15,000 'photogravure' posters per week. Confidential report on propaganda work in India, Ceylon and Burma, May-July 1941, c.August 1941, ibid.
98 Major companies like the Burmah-Shell Oil Company, Assam Railways and Trading Company, Brooke Bond India Limited, Lipton Limited, Mackinnon and Mackenzie Company, Bird and Company, Dunlop Rubber Limited, Imperial Chemical Industries, Imperial Tobacco Company, Lever Brothers Limited, Shaw Wallace and Company, Tata Iron and Steel Company, and Andrew Yule and Company Limited Appendix B to the confidential progress report on the working of the Calcutta Committee, L/I/1/1017, OIOC.
99 The *Times of India* group worked closely with the Government of India's Home Department, and assisted in the production, and presentation of official anti-Congress propaganda. This is discussed in detail in Chapter Four of this monograph.
100 See, for instance, TDMR for 1940, 1941, 1942, 1943, 1944 and 1945, MS 86/V/8/11, DUA. Also see, private official letters from Calcutta to Thomas Duff, c.1945, MS 86/V/7/13, DUA.
101 The communists were rarely allowed to take out propaganda lorries with loudspeakers in Calcutta and Bombay. When permission was given by officials, the vehicles were confined to working class localities and, interestingly, excluded from 'middle class' areas. *People's War,* 10 January

1943. Though the Government of India had hoped to use the assistance of the CPI and the RDP to rally support for the Allied war-effort, the bureaucrats in the localities remained unenthusiastic about the scheme because the local cadres attached to the parties usually sought to 'popularise' the Second World War by involving themselves in agitations over parochial problems, most notably shortages of all varieties of essentials, unpopular wartime measures and agrarian relations. The communist cadres' attempts to organise agitations to redress local difficulties arose from their attempts to increase their support-base and the fact they often came from the local communities they were fighting on behalf of. An Intelligence Bureau report stated that it was clear that 'their [CPI's] policy includes no plan or intention of doing anything towards assisting Government in strengthening support for the war and a spirit of resistance if by their action they cannot at the same time add to the prestige and influence of the Party'. Summary of Communist Activity, IB, GOI, July 1942, HPF(I) 7/5/42, NAI. Clashes between the RDP's cadres and the district administrators remained less frequent, primarily because the party, which was established in 1940, had a thinly spread organisational network in Eastern India. For instance, its branch in Orissa, which was set up only in the second half of May 1943, represented nothing more than a 'unit' in Cuttack, the provincial capital. CSFR(1) and (2), May 1943, Orissa, HPF(I) 18/1/43, NAI. Nonetheless, reports from the localities where members of the RDP were active suggested the existence of tensions between the district officers and the party cadres. CSFR(2), June 1942, Bengal, HPF(I) 18/6/42, NAI.

102 The Government of India frequently communicated its displeasure to the provincial governments in Eastern India, between 1942 and 1944, about the local officials' tendency to arrest CPI activists, who were seen by many civil servants within central government as being a powerful weapon against the Congress. See S. Bhattacharya, 'The Colonial State and the Communist Party of India, 1942–45: A Reappraisal', *SAR*, 15, 1, 1995, pp. 48–77.

103 It needs to be pointed out here that while it was relatively easier to ensure the acceptance of food, domestic fuels and cloth amongst civilian audiences, the official efforts at targeting medical aid proved to be much more complex. Although civilians drafted into the wartime projects in Assam and Burma accepted preventive medical measures, like smallpox vaccination, quite easily, probably as these were made mandatory for their recruitment, the dissemination of 'western' medicines in other contexts often proved far more challenging. While the scope of 'western' medical science had been successfully expanded in India during the 1930s and 1940s, notably through the incorporation of locally prominent *vaids* and *hakims* into the colonial medical establishment and by the introduction of the scheme of subsidising medical practitioners in rural areas, some of its preventive practices, like vaccination and inoculation, continued to be difficult to popularise or forcibly introduce. The challenges faced in this regard are powerfully highlighted by the difficulties experienced during efforts to extend vaccination among patients in famine camps, where the primary malady

was malnourishment: the issue was finally tackled by tying up the free distribution of food and cloth with their acceptance of vaccination. However, civilian attitudes during severe epidemics could be – and often were – strikingly different: people would generally become more willing to accept preventive operations and oral prophylactics. This state of affairs was, of course, becoming increasingly apparent during the course of the twentieth century, with the demand for vaccinia vaccines and medicines like quinine going up during severe outbreaks of diseases like smallpox and malaria. It is in this particular context that the opposition to the wartime state, which began to be attacked and criticised for being unable to provide medical aid during emergencies, needs to be located. For a good study of official medical relief measures during the Bengal famine, see Chapter XVIII in B.L. Raina (ed), *Official History of the Indian Armed Forces in the Second World War 1939–45: Medical Services (Administration)*, Kanpur, 1953, pp. 405–414.

104 Memorandum submitted by S.P. Mookerjee, ex-minister, GOBe, to the Woodhead Committee, 15 August 1944, Nanavati papers, NAI. The powers given to the employees of the Government of India's Directorate of Civil Supplies in Bengal, especially the Food Grains Purchasing officers, to control the movement of rice in the region was widely criticised by many political organisations and personages during the deliberations of the Famine Enquiry Commission. See, for instance, memorandum submitted by the Bengal Provincial Hindu Mahasabha to the Woodhead Committee, c.1944, ibid.

105 The central Food Department was instrumental in arranging food supplies for the troops based in Eastern India from a variety of sources. In 1942, food tended to be purchased, or even requisitioned locally. However, by 1943 increasing efforts were made to bring in tinned and dry rations for the defence services and the labour employed in military projects. See, B.P. Srivastava, 'Nutrition', in B.L. Raina (ed), *Official History of the Indian Armed Forces in the Second World War 1939–45 (Medical Services): Preventive Medicine (Nutrition, Malaria Control and Prevention of Diseases)*, Kanpur, 1961, pp. 91–97. The provisioning schemes deployed for British Indian army detachments based in Eastern India is discussed in detail in Chapter Five of this monograph.

106 Most of the drugs and medicines sold in India before 1939 had been imported from Britain. The outbreak of the war caused these supplies to be cut off, which led in turn to severe shortages and rampant profiteering in these commodities. This forced the Government of India's Industries and Civil Supplies Department and the Health Department to play an increasingly important role in the distribution of all varieties of 'essential' drugs. Memorandum on drugs control, undated, pp. 1–3, attached to War History of the Industries and the Civil Supplies Department, GOI, L/R/5/290, OIOC. As the Medical Stores Department was till 1943 a part of the British India army, the allocation of drugs and medicines to different government organisations basically remained a military function. The situation did not really change despite the marked changes brought about, in 1943, by the division of the Medical Stores Department into two independent branches: one, under the Director

General of the Indian Medical Services was to cater to civilian needs; while the other, under the control of the Director of Medical Services, was intended to serve the requirements of the armed forces. However, the needs of the latter organisation continued to be given precedence, and the requirements of the armed forces were allowed to determine the allocation of the available drugs and chemicals till the end of the war. B.L. Raina (ed), *Official History of the Indian Armed Forces in the Second World War 1939-45, Medical Services: Medical Services and Equipment*, Kanpur, 1963, pp. 3-192.

107 Extract from the record of the proceedings of the National Defence Council, c.November 1942, HPF(I) 3/84/1942, NAI.

108 Memorandum on work arising out of work in the stationery and printing department, undated, War History of the Labour Department, L/R/5/291, OIOC.

109 Though the 'dearness allowances' sanctioned to the railway workers were steadily increased during the war, 'the danger of inflation necessitated a revision of the Government's attitude in regard to relief in cash' and forced the rapid expansion of the organisation of 'railway grainshops'. War History of Mechanical Department's (Railways) Activities, pp. 28-29, L/R/5/293, OIOC.

110 The 'relief per card holder' (measured by the difference between the railway shop price and the local *bazaar* price) ranged in the autumn of 1943 from Rs. 9/11 *annas* to Rs. 14 per month. The Railway Department also sanctioned to the temporary railway staff (whether employed on munitions or railway work) a bonus of one day's pay for each completed month of continuous employment. In the spring of 1941 the first dearness allowance was given to the workers with 'back effect from September 1940'. It was subsequently increased the 1 November 1941, on 15 of June 1942 and yet again on 1 February 1943. Note on staff matters, undated, War History of Mechanical Department's (Railways) Activities, L/R/5/293, OIOC.

111 As against 117,478 tons of imports in July 1943, Calcutta handled 254,102 tons in August 1943. *History of the War Transport Department, July 1942 to October 1945*, GOI Press, New Delhi, 1946, p. 4, L/R/5/297, OIOC. Of the six ports in India those in Chittagong, Vizagapatnam and Cochin were placed under the control of the Government of India's War Transport Department. All the other ports were controlled by individual Port Trusts. Secret War Department History: Transportation and Movements (September 1939–December 1944), 3 September 1945, p. 10, L/R/5/280, OIOC.

112 Secret War Department History: Transportation and Movements (September 1939–December 1944), 3 September 1945, p. 4, L/R/5/280, OIOC.

113 Secret War History of the Home Department, pp. 25-28, L/R/5/289, OIOC. Also see secret weekly intelligence reports from the DIG, GOA, for the weeks ending 3 June 1943 and 9 June 1943, PF 174/58/42 (C), NAI; Extract from the record of the proceedings of the National Defence Council, c.November 1942, HPF(I) 3/84/1942, N AI, and Note by D Pilditch, IB, Home Department, GOI, 10 December 1942,

PF 174/58/42 (C), NAI. As a result of the grant made by the central Home Department, the Government of Bihar announced an immediate increase in pay for its police forces. Constables were given an extra Rs. 5 a month, armed police given an increase of Rs. 3 a month and 'ordinary police' were given an additional Rs. 2 a month. The province's 57,000 chowkidars were awarded a 'war bonus' of Rs. 2 per month. Letter from T. Rutherford, Governor, GOB to Linlithgow, Viceroy, 13 February 1943, R/3/1/23, OIOC.

114 Secret letter from T. Rutherford, Governor, GOB to Linlithgow, the Viceroy, 12 July 1943, R/3/1/23, OIOC. The Government of Bengal provided its junior employees with 72,898 *maunds* of rice along with a significant quantities of 'wheat products' in 1943. Letter from T. Rutherford, Governor, GOBe, to Linlithgow, Viceroy, 2 October 1943, R/3/2/49, File No. 2, Coll. ix, OIOC. Sir Thomas Rutherford held the Governorships of two provinces in 1943: he was Governor of Bihar till 5 September 1943 and was then shifted to Bengal, to replace Sir John Herbert (who resigned due to ill health), on 6 September 1943 (he held the Bengal Governorship between 6 September 1943 and 21 January 1944). R.F. Mudie, a senior ICS officer, replaced Rutherford and acted as the Governor of Bihar between 6 September 1943 and 24 April 1944.

115 This category included clothing units, railway workshops and ordnance factories, all of which witnessed a big increase in employment figures between 1939 and 1945. For example, clothing units had 2,000 employees in 1939, a figure than swelled to 22,000 by 1945. Railway workshop workers increased from 56,000 in 1939 to 116,000 in 1945, and ordnance workers increased from 30,000 and 185,000 in the same period. See, Table II in M.N. Gupta, 'Health of the Industrial Worker', in Raina (ed), *Preventive Medicine*, p. 724.

116 This included industries like textiles; engineering; minerals and metals; food, drinks and tobacco; chemicals and dyes; paper and printing; wood, stone and glass; hides and skin, and, not least, gins and presses. Ibid.

117 See, for instance, most secret letter from the Defence Co-oridination Department, GOI to all Chief Secretaries and Chief Commissioners of provinces, 12 March 1941, HPF(I) 15/1/41, NAI. In fact, the Essential Services (Maintenance) Ordinance of 1941, which affected labour, declared that the legislation authorised an 'officer ... to prohibit any person engaged in any employment covered by the ordinance to depart, without the consent of government ... out of any such area or areas as may be specified. The ordinance makes it an offence punishable with imprisonment for a term which may extend to one year and with fine, for any person to abandon such employment or absent himself without reasonable excuse. The fact that a person apprehends that by continuing in his employment he will be exposed to increased physical danger does not constitute a reasonable excuse.' See, note on wartime legislation affecting labour, c.1941, HPF(I) 318/42, NAI.

118 Despite the passing of specific Defence of India Rules banning industrial action, short strikes remained quite common between 1942 and 1945. See, the Chief Secretaries' Fortnightly Reports from Assam, Bengal, Bihar and United Provinces for the years 1942 to 1945, NAI. This, of course,

highlighted the great difference between passing wartime legislation and having the ability or the will to implement it. In case of the industrial workers, the authorities remained unwilling to arrest them for disobeying the provisions of the DIR as they did not want to disrupt wartime production in any way, and, moreover, after August 1942, the rather restricted jail space was quickly filled by the mass arrest of Congress activists.

119 In January 1943, Theodore Gregory, the Permanent Economic Adviser to the Government of India, had noted that the rationing of the urban population was a 'formidable undertaking', and the administrative problems of such a course were too great. He advocated instead, cheap grain shops for supply to certain sections of the population. Gregory Collection, MSS EUR.D.1163/6, OIOC. Although Gregory did not identify the target population, files detailing the distribution of food aid during these disastrous months clearly indicate the industrial labour employed by the 'war-industries', apart from the state's 'subordinate services', as being the principal civilian recipients of such assistance. See, for instance, letter from T. Rutherford, GOBe, to Linlithgow, Viceroy, India, 2 October 1943, R/3/2/49, File No. 2, Coll. ix, OIOC.

120 *The Famine Enquiry Commission, Final Report*, Madras, 1945, p. 37, V/26/830/11, OIOC.

121 Secret letters from T. Rutherford, Governor, GOB to Linlithgow, Viceroy, 5 March 1943; 25 May 1943 and 12 July 1943, R/3/1/23, OIOC.

122 The increase of employment levels in different sectors, between 1939 and 1945, was as follows: cotton mills registered an increase of 34.6 per cent; the jute mills witnessed an increase of 4.3 per cent; the woollens' industry saw an increase of 114 per cent; the engineering industry grew by 26.9 per cent, and the minerals and metals industry grew by a massive 127.5 per cent. M.N. Gupta, 'Health of the Industrial Worker', pp. 724–725.

123 Secret letters from T. Rutherford, Governor, GOB to Linlithgow, Viceroy, 5 March 1943; 25 May 1943 and 12 July 1943, R/3/1/23, OIOC.

124 Letter from Rai Bahadur B.N. Singh, Deputy Commissioner, Santhal Parganas, GOB to the Commissioner, Bhagalpur Division, GOB, 5 June 1942, WSF 29(45)/1942, BSA.

125 Note on coal mines' welfare, undated, War History of the Labour Department, L/R/5/291, OIOC. For descriptions of the success of the Government of India and the provincial administrations Eastern India in forcing coal mine owners to offer special wartime bonuses, financial and material, see extracts of the correspondence between the Eastern Command and the civilian authorities, Bihar, c.1944, WSF 48/4(ii)/44, BSA.

126 The great sense of official urgency about expanding coal production caused the Government of India to bring in the military to buttress the anti-malarial operations, especially as it expected the setting up of appropriate civilian organisations to take unreasonable amounts of time. Thus, army anti-malaria units were used to start work in the larger coal fields in 1944. Interestingly, the continuing shortages of coal in the

immediate post-war period, which began to impact negatively on industrial production and civilian life, caused officially-sponsored antimalarial organisations to be detailed to Jharia, Raniganj, Pench Valley and Margherita from 1 December 1945. Note entitled 'Anti-Malaria Operations in Delhi, Jamnagar and Coalfields', Appendix X in Raina (ed), *Preventive Medicine*, pp. 374–375.

127 Brief outline of the position regarding supply of unskilled labour, undated, War History of the Labour Department, L/R/5/291, OIOC. There was a broad agreement within the different levels of the administration about the usefulness of tapping these areas for wartime workers. Apart from sharing a rather flawed belief that these sections of the population would be more attuned to working in the climatic conditions of the Assam frontier, officials located in the central government, the provincial headquarters and the districts also felt that they had few connections with organised Congress politics and that they would be able to work closely if necessary with the *santhali* population settled in Assam. See, Departmental Memoranda, c.1942, 49/(12)/1942, BSA. This view was probably connected to the great encouragement given by the authorities to tribal leaders like Jaipal Singh, whose party was backed by the Government against pro-Congress candidates in local elections.

128 Report by S.M. Naqvi, Deputy Magistrate, Dumka, GOB, 26 May 1942, attached to confidential letter from Rai Bahadur B.N. Singh, Deputy Commissioner, Santal Parganas, GOB to B.K. Gokhale, Commissioner, Bhagalpur Division, GOB, 28 May 1942, WSF 29(45)/1942, BSA.

129 Letter from Rai Bahadur B.N Singh, Deputy Commissioner, Santhal Parganas, GOB to B.K Gokhale, Commissioner, Bhagalpur Division, GOB, 5 June 1942, W.S.F 29(45)/1942, BSA.

130 Letter from J.W Houlton, Secretary, Civil Defence Department, GOI to E.C. Lee, Commissioner, Chota Nagpur Division, GOB, 8 June 1942, WSF 29 (45)/1942, BSA.

131 Secret notes from the Commissioner of the Chota Nagpur Division, GOB, c.1943, WSF 55/2(vii)/1943, BSA.

132 For instance, the decision to convert the bridle path from Palel to Tamu into a major road allowing motor transport caused the Government of India to give the Inspector General of Civil Hospitals, GOA, Rs. 45,000 for the purpose of establishing a chain of along the road, which were subsidised by further central government grants. Dispensaries were set up in Nichguard, Piphima, Zubza, Jotsoma, Kezoma, Maram, Karong, Kangpokpi, Kanglatongbi and Ghaspanti, which were provisioned by a central medical store depot based in Kohima, put under the charge of the Civil Surgeon of the Naga Hills. These establishments continued till end-March 1943, when the building activities were diverted to the Assam Trunk Road and the subsidiary roads attached it, as well as a series of aerodrome projects. The result was a new chain of dispensaries at Nowgong, Silghat, Bongaigon, Bokakhat, Numaligarh, Kumargaon, Goalpara, Neti, Digaru, Boko, Sonapur, Dabaho, Amguri, Kahara, Puranigudam (B.G.G. Road) and Bagribari (Access Road). Raina (ed), *Preventive Medicine*, pp. 788–789.

133 Gregory represented those who believed that the wartime administration could only cater to the needs of a few select groups. Gregory Collection, MSS.EUR.D.1163/6, OIOC.
134 Extracts from secret reports by District Magistrates in Bihar, Eastern United Provinces and Assam, c.1943, WSF 63/iii/43, BSA.
135 *The Famine Enquiry Commission Final Report*, Madras, 1945, p. 37, V/26/830/11, OIOC.
136 *Ibid.*, p. 4. In certain urban areas of Bihar 'really poor' people were given 2 seers of rice or wheat and a seer of pulses or maize for one rupee, 'with a strict limit as to the amount each individual can acquire'. Secret letter from T. Rutherford, Governor, GOB to Linlithgow, Viceroy, 12 July 1943, R/3/1/23, OIOC. In Bengal, the comparative comfort in the cities led to the influx of 'old men, women, deserted wives and widows with children and also out of work agricultural labourers' into urban areas in general, and Calcutta in particular. In October 1943, the number of people receiving relief was 1,18,000 in Calcutta and 8,40,000 in the *mofussils*. Letter from T. Rutherford, Governor, GOBe, to Linlithgow, Viceroy, 2 October 1943, R/3/2/49, File No. 2, Coll. ix, OIOC.
137 See memoranda submitted by the Bengal Provincial Hindu Mahasabha, c.1944, and by S.P. Mookerjea, ex-minister, GOBe, 15 August 1944, to the Woodhead Committee, Nanavati papers, NAI. 631,702 *maunds* of rice, 89,766 *maunds* of paddy and 390,300 *maunds* of wheat products were sent to the districts between 1 March and 31 August 1943 for relief measures and 'subsidised sales through controlled shops'. See table attached to letter from T. Rutherford, Governor, GOBe, to Linlithgow, Viceroy, 2 October 1943, R/3/2/49, File No. 2, Coll. IX, OIOC. Also see, confidential letter from E. Wood, Department of Food, Government of India to J.R. Blair, Chief Secretary, Government of Bengal, 15 April 1943, WSF 50(IV)/1942, BSA.
138 *Famine Inquiry Commission, Report on Bengal*, Madras, p. 149, V/26/830/10, OIOC. Between 1 March and 31 August 1943, the worst months of scarcity, 1,110,827 *maunds* of rice, 48,070 *maunds* of wheat and 941,002 *maunds* of 'wheat products' were distributed Table attached to letter from T. Rutherford, Governor, GOBe, to Linlithgow, Viceroy, 2 October 1943, R/3/2/49, File No. 2, Coll. ix, OIOC.
139 In October 1943, the official agencies were providing 'relief' to almost a million destitutes in Calcutta and the *mofussils*. However, a vast majority of the aid recipients were based in the city: 840,000 were based in Calcutta, while only 118,000 were located in the *mofussils*. Letter from T. Rutherford, GOBe, to Linlithgow, Viceroy, 2 October 1943, R/3/2/49, File No. 2, Coll. IX, OIOC. Also see, most secret WIS (II) 31 December 1943, L/WS/1/1433, OIOC. Also see, memoirs of O.M. Martin, ICS, Bengal, p. 262, Martin papers, CSASA. During the famine military and civil reports from Eastern India constantly identified the 'small village cultivator', the 'village labourer' and the 'labouring classes in towns' as being the worst hit by the crisis. See, for example, most secret WIS(II) 27 August 1943, L/WS/1/1433, OIOC. A report from the Government of Bengal highlighted the misfortunes of the 'landless labourer' in the province and '... the wreckage of the population that subsists on

charity'. Telegram from T. Rutherford, GOBe, to Linlithgow, Viceroy, 19 September 1943, R/3/2/49, File No. 2, Coll. ix, OIOC. These groups were also identified by the Woodhead Committee as the sections of the civilian population to be most badly affected by the famine of 1943–44. *Famine Inquiry Commission, Report on Bengal*, Madras, p. 2, V/26/830/10, OIOC.

140 Apart from the Indian Red Cross Society and the Friends Ambulance Unit, which worked in close collaboration with the civil medical establishment throughout the war, a number of private organisations became very active during the famine period. These included the Bengal Relief Committee, the Marwari Relief Association, the Hindu Mahasabha, the Bengal Civil Protection Committee, the Bengal Muslim League Relief Committee and the Ramakrishna Mission. See, Chapter XVIII in Raina (ed), *Medical Services (Administration)*, p. 411.

141 Correspondence between the district magistracy and local military commands, Bihar, United Provinces and Bengal, c.1943, WSF 65/1(i)/43, BSA.

142 Ibid. The attempt to prevent the clogging of rail services and road communications in Eastern India was, of course, considered a very important administrative objective since 1942. Indeed, the decision to avoid a comprehensive 'scorched earth' policy in the region was informed by an unwillingness to create a situation where people would be forced to migrate to other districts or provinces. Secret telegram from the Defence Department, GOI to L. Amery, SSI, GOBr, 31 March 1942, L/WS/1/1242, OIOC. Also see, most secret summary of case for the decision of HE, the VEC, c.April 1942, HPF(I) 230/42, NAI. Notably, even the most eulogistic descriptions of the medical relief provided by the military during the famine have not been able to ignore the strategic compulsions of the policy. One description of these activities informs us how: 'At first, some were inclined to regard the employment of troops for civil relief work as a serious interruption of their training for war. They, however, soon realised that the restoration of normal conditions in Bengal was an important military task as Bengal formed the military base and main line of communication [sic].' Raina (ed), *Medical Services (Administration)*, p. 413.

143 Correspondence between the district magistracy and local military commands, Bihar, United Provinces and Bengal, c.1943, WSF 65/1(i)/43, BSA. The movement of refugees had, of course, been considered a major strategic problem since 1942 due to its capability to spread epidemic disease. Officials were especially worried about the spread of cholera, plague and smallpox. See, note from the office of the Public Health Commissioner, GOI, to the Department of Education, Health and Lands, GOI, 25 April 1942, EHLDF 44–10/42-H, NAI. A new instrument, titled the 'weekly epidemiological telegrams', was introduced in April 1942 to keep an eye on the progress of these diseases in Eastern India. See, note from the office of the Public Health Commissioner, GOI, 9 June 1942, ibid. The telegram, dated 24 April 1942, declared that 'The Directors of Public Health send, in their weekly telegrams, only the total figures for their respective provinces for each of the diseases cholera, smallpox and

plague; but, in view of the continuous flow of evacuees from Burma, the Directors of Public Health in Bengal and Assam are supplying, at our request, figures for districts in order to enable us to keep a watch on the progress of the epidemics.' EHLDF 44–10/42-H, NAI.

144 See, Raina (ed), *Medical Services (Administration)*, pp. 13–30. The negative effects of the removal of doctors from the civilian sector to military services is indicated by a variety of sources, not least the correspondence available from the districts. For instance, see extracts from secret reports by District Magistrates in Bihar, Eastern United Provinces and Assam, c.1943, WSF 63/iii/43, BSA. The medical situation in rural Eastern India was, by all accounts, particularly strained. See, for example, précis of opinions received from certain members of the committee on the post-war plans of the Medical and Public Health Departments, c.1944, in MDF 479/44, UPSA. The wartime expansion of the military medical services in Eastern India is studied in detail in Chapter Five of this monograph.

145 Raina (ed), *Medical Services (Administration)*, pp. 405–407.

146 There were basically three types of hospitals set up: those with 100 beds, those with 50 beds and those with 20 beds. The first two categories of hospitals could be expanded in multiples of 100 and 50 respectively, and were put under the control of the district civil surgeon. The twenty-bed units, in comparison, were attached to district outdoor dispensaries, while the 'satellite centres' were outdoor clinics situated within five miles of the local dispensary, and housed in verandas, rooms lent by owners of houses or under trees in the dry season. They, like the mobile units, were placed under the control of the local civil surgeon, whose work was supervised by military officials. Three hundred and fifty six civilian doctors were involved in this exercise (this number excluded the Burma Medical Officers and two temporary assistant-surgeons brought in from the Central Provinces), and they were supported by 2,852 nursing staff in treating 229,253 hospital patients (24,551 of these were treated in Calcutta, while 203,702 given attention in the mofussil towns) till 15 November 1944. Raina (ed), *Medical Services (Administration)*, pp. 407–411.

147 References to the demonstrations against the withdrawals of these special measures in Bengal are provided in, for instance, the correspondence between the district magistracy and local military commands, Bihar, United Provinces and Bengal, c.1943, WSF 65/1(i)/43, BSA.

148 A good example of this is provided by the distribution of anti-malarial measures, especially the latest technologies and techniques, amongst civilians. The spraying of DDT, widely considered at the time to be a miracle chemical against malarial vectors, tended to be organised in centres in and near troops encampments, while the older technique of using pyrethrum, which was less effective in the short-run, was continued elsewhere. Similarly, mepacrine, the new synthetic drug being promoted at the time as an effective suppressant of the malarial parasite, was almost completely monopolised for military use, and only shared with very specific civilian groups like the labour employed in strategic projects and mines. Similar priorities also determined the wartime distribution of

quinine. See, Raina (ed), *Medical Stores and Equipment*, pp. 116–146. Also see, Raina (ed), *Preventive Medicine*, pp. 374–375.

149 The military authorities managed to keep an eye on the attitudes of civilian administrators through a variety of means. One was the military's tendency to dominate the censorship apparatus, through which it was able to monitor a great deal of the official telegraphic and postal material. Another effective way of keeping an eye on civilian activity was accorded by the fact that most official forays intended to uncover hoards of food and other essential goods after October 1942 tended to be given a military escort, often at the request of the district administrators themselves. This allowed military officers to keep an eye, and report, on the mode of allocation of released hoards. Adverse 'performance reports' could cause transfer requests, usually to the provincial capital, to be turned down, and for more junior officials, could cause a freeze – or even a cut – in wartime benefits. Indeed, appeals against such punishments often referred to the constraints placed on officials by a lack of manpower resources and local hostility. Extracts from secret reports by District Magistrates in Bihar, Eastern United Provinces and Assam, c.1943, WSF 63/iii/43, BSA.

150 The short-term nature of wartime propaganda policy is revealed, among other things, by the way the issue of post-war reconstruction was debated, publicised and then laid to rest. By 1942, it had become obvious to most officials that it would be impossible to implement the development schemes that were being advertised Thus, despite the presence of good intentions among various officials within the colonial administration, the overall picture that emerges is that the dominant concern among the colonial administration between 1942 and 1947 was to ensure that economic and political benefits continued to accrue to Britain, notwithstanding the difficulties of the Indian situation at the time. Even making allowances for over-optimism and self-delusion, rather than cynical attempts at self-serving manipulation, the balancing of Indian and British interests, was by the end of the war widely accepted to be unrealistic. Indeed, as Britain's initial economic calculations for the post-war period were rapidly upset, her wartime plans for Indian development, announced with so much fanfare, were quietly allowed to rest in their filing cabinets, while new schemes designed to allow Britain favourable access to an independent Indian economy were lobbied. For a detailed description of this topic, see, S. Bhattacharya and B. Zachariah, 'A Great Destiny': The British Colonial State and the advertisement of post-war reconstruction in India, 1942–45', *SAR*, 19, 1, 1999.

151 See, for instance, secret War History of the Home Department, GOI, pp. 25–28, L/R/5/289, OIOC. For a description of these strategies in the localities of Eastern India, see, extracts from secret reports by District Magistrates in Bihar, Eastern United Provinces and Assam, c.1943, WSF 63/iii/43, BSA.

152 Discussions about the 'effectiveness' of this strategy would frequently crop up in the discussion between the civilian and military authorities. See, for example, correspondence between the district magistracy and

local military commands, Bihar, United Provinces and Bengal, c.1943, WSF 65/1(i)/43, BSA.
153 Ibid.
154 This is discussed in detail in Bhattacharya, 'The Colonial State and the Communist Party of India', pp. 48–77.
155 The military contractors' ability to draw away colliery labour with promises of higher pay led ultimately to a crisis in coal production. See, for instance, WIS(II), 24 December 1943, L/WS/1/1433, OIOC. Initially the Government of India sought to counter the labour problem by reversing an earlier decision about not letting women work in the mines. This, however, proved insufficient to tackle the coal production crisis, the reversal of which was declared to be a 'war priority' by the end of 1943 as the shortages had begun to affect industrial output in other strategic industries like the cotton and jute mills. Yet, this did not signal an improvement in relations between the industrialists and the authorities, as the other official tactics to make workers more 'productive' and 'stable', that is the initiation of welfare and health schemes, were made the responsibility of the industrialists. The Government of India's role was limited essentially to supervising the implementation of these special projects, and in the context of a difficult strategic situation, central government officials proved extremely eager taskmasters. Indeed, the coal mine owners were also forced to contribute towards the cost of running special anti-malarial units operating in the mines. They expressed much unhappiness at this 'arm-twisting'. See, for example, extracts from secret reports by District Magistrates in Bihar, Eastern United Provinces and Assam, c.1943, WSF 63/iii/43, BSA. Also see, note on coal mines' welfare, undated, War History of the Labour Department, L/R/5/291, OIOC.
156 One of the indicators of the growing tensions between the Government of India and the industrialists on this account is revealed in the complaint that industries with 'Congress leanings' preferred to pay out 'excessive bonuses' and dearness allowances to staff rather than pay money to the authorities in the form of Excess Profits Tax. See, Appendix A in most secret WIS(II), 23 July 1943, OIOC.
157 See, File 235 in P. Thakurdas Papers, NMML. Of course, the fears about the sterling balances were by no means misplaced: the British government's doubts regarding its ability to pay back the sterling balances were deliberately sought to be hidden from the Indian public, as it was considered extremely dangerous for confidence in Britain's financial stability, in terms of its effects on educated and business opinion in India, and consequently on the Indian participation in the War Effort. See L/F/7/2861, OIOC.
158 Strictly secret report entitled 'Congress and 'Big Business'', 28 February 1944, L/P&J/8/618a, OIOC.
159 Bhattacharya and Zachariah, 'A Great Destiny'.
160 The tendency of officials to sacrifice the needs of the rural areas at expense of urban needs, with the acquiescence, if not active collaboration, of non-official Indians, is clearly revealed in the various depositions submitted to the Woodhead Committee, which are luckily

preserved in the papers of Sir Manilal B. Nanavati. See, Nanavati papers, NAI.
161 The only exceptions in the Orissa region seem to be a few tribal pockets that provided unskilled labour for military works. Orissa province and the princely state of Travancore, in Southern India, were affected by famine conditions, which were accompanied by severe epidemics of malaria, cholera and smallpox. See, for instance, Raina (ed), *Preventive Medicine*, p. 775. The creation of rather serious famine conditions in Bihar was regularly noted in military intelligence. One report mentioned, for example, that the inhabitants of some villages in Bihar had not tasted rice for months, and that this had caused them to revert to eating edible bulbs and pulses ordinarily used to feed cattle. See, most secret WIS (II), 18 June 1943, L/WS/1/1433, OIOC. Military intelligence would regularly point out that both East Bengal and Assam were seriously affected by famine conditions. Indeed, the levels of starvation in these regions was high enough to encourage suicides, prostitution and child selling. The army complained that 'hundreds of deaths' in villages surrounding military camps was making Indian soldiers apprehensive about the effects of shortages upon their families. Most secret WIS(II), 20 August 1943, L/WS/1/1433, OIOC. Vinita Damodaran is one of the few to point out that the famine conditions in Bengal were replicated in parts of Bihar. See, V. Damodaran, 'Azad Dastas and Dacoit Gangs: The Congress and Underground Activity in Bihar, 1942–44', *MAS*, 26, 3, 1992. However, more detailed work needs to be carried out about the development, the social costs and the political effects of the extension of famine conditions in the provinces of Assam, Bihar, Orissa, Madras, Bombay, and Central Provinces and Berar. Notably, it is often forgotten that parts of Bombay, CP and Berar and Hyderabad state suffered from very serious food shortages as well. In Bombay, for instance, a state of scarcity was declared in all the villages of Athani and Parasgad Talukas, in Belgaum District, in early 1943 (the declaration was cancelled on 1 October 1943). Scarcity was also declared in Karmala, Madha, Pandharpur, Sangola and Malsiras Talukas of the Sholapur district from 9 February 1942, and was extended to Sholapur taluka from 18 January 1943 (the declarations were only withdrawn in January 1944). Famine was also declared in Bijapur district, where famine was declared in 1942, which caused a large migration from the area, calculated at one eighth of the district population. Scarcity relief works – in the form of stone quarries, metal breaking units, tank and road building schemes – were started to tackle the situation and by the end of July 1943, it was reported that more than 90,000 labourers were involved. Moreover, 23 kitchens were opened to feed about 18,000 destitutes. See, *Annual Report of the Director of Public Health for the Government of Bombay, 1943*, Bombay, 1945, p. 41, PHDF 23–10/1945 – P.H., NAI.
162 This was the opinion of the Chief Sanitary Officer, Raniganj Mines Board of Health, quoted in *ibid.*, p. 375. The general rise in mortality from disease – especially malaria – has been described by Arup Maharatna. See, A. Maharatna, 'Malaria ecology, relief provision and regional variation in mortality during the Bengal famine of 1943–44, *SAR*, 13, 1,

1993. The disastrous effects of delayed relief provision have also been noted by scholars like Amartya Sen and Paul Greenough. See, A.K. Sen, *Poverty and Famines: An essay on Entitlement and Deprivation*, Oxford, 1981, and P.R. Greenough, *Prosperity and Misery in Modern Bengal: The Famine of 1943–44*, New York, 1982.

163 References to the scale of epidemics in the localities of Eastern India are provided in extracts from secret reports by District Magistrates in Bihar, Eastern United Provinces and Assam, c.1943, WSF 63/iii/43, BSA. Also see, correspondence between the district magistracy and local military commands, Bihar, United Provinces and Bengal, c.1943, WSF 65/1(i)/43, BSA.

164 Wartime reports – from civilian and military sources – would frequently highlight the fact that the scarcities, and the high prices, of food and other 'essentials' had affected all these classes adversely. See, for instance, letter from T. Rutherford, Governor, GOB to Linlithgow, Viceroy, 2 October 1943, R/3/2/49, File No. 2, Coll. ix, OIOC. Also see most secret WIS(II) 19 February 1943, most secret WIS(II) 27 August 1943, most secret WIS(II) 22 October 1943, secret WIS(II) 12 January 1945 and secret WIS(II) 22 June 1945, L/WS/1/1506, OIOC.

165 I.H. Macdonald, an ICS officer posted in Orissa, mentions in his memoirs how civil servants responsible for requisitioning grain were always accompanied by bodyguards since their duties were unpopular, especially because they were done with 'a certain element' of coercion. Memoirs of I.H. Macdonald, p. 41, Macdonald papers, OIOC.

166 Most secret WIS(II) 17 December 1943, L/WS/1/1433, OIOC. Also see secret history of the Congress party, September 1939–May 1945, no pp., Appendix B to secret WIS (II) 1 June 1945, ibid.

167 Ibid. Also see CSFRs from Assam, Bengal, Bihar and Orissa for 1942, 1943 and 1944, for regular references to attacks on the members of the subordinate civil services.

168 H.E. Bruce, the DIG of the Eastern Range mentions, for instance, how '... terrorists made it impossible to find witnesses brave enough to give evidence in court. The bandit leaders did more maimings than murders – and the prevalence of noseless villagers was remarkable.' See remarks made by H.E. Bruce about statement made by R.D.K. Ninnis, IPS, in appendix B of his memoirs. MSS EUR C. 282, OIOC.

169 Secret War History of the Bureau of Public Information, GOI, 1939–45, p. 14, L/R/5/295, OIOC.

170 Secret telegram from the Department of Information and Broadcasting, GOI, to L. Amery, SSI, GOBr, 23 December 1942, L/I/1/942, OIOC.

171 For an early example of such publicity material see, note titled 'Teh [sic] Indian Constitutional Issue'. Appendix B to most secret WIS (II), 15 December 1942, L/WS/1/1433, OIOC.

172 See, for instance, letter from R.P.N. Sahi, Deputy Commissioner, Chota Nagpur Division, GOB to E.O. Lee, Commissioner, Chota Nagpur Division, GOB, 15 May 1942, WSF 17 (xix)/1942, BSA.

173 For an example of centrally-prescribed Governments Press communiqué regarding the 'scorched-earth' policy and the requisitioning schemes, see draft press communiqué, 21 March 1942, WSF 198/1942, BSA. The

communiqué was released to the press without modification. See, *Searchlight*, 15 April 1943. The Government of India also thought it useful to refer to the Russian and Chinese experiences of the 'scorched earth' policy in order to explain its relevance in India. See, Secret War History of the Bureau of Public Information, GOI, 1939–45, p. 9–14, L/R/5/295, OIOC.

174 Letter from the President, Bihar Branch of the National War Front, to the Provincial Press Adviser, GOB, 16 July 1943, in PPAF 32/1943, BSA.

175 These attitudes are revealed in the local officials' responses to a letter from E. Wood, the Additional Secretary to the Food Department, GOI, where provincial and district officers in Bengal and Bihar were encouraged, amongst other things, to 'emphasise and re-emphasise that the Government of India ha[d] set up the Food Deptt. [sic] whose job [wa]s to see that no one starves ... and that if food [wa]s found to be short in any place, the Food Department w[ould] produce the goods'. Confidential letter from E. Wood to Chief Secretaries of Bengal and Bihar, c.September 1943, WSF 50(iv)/1942, BSA. Responses from the district headquarters and sub-divisional capitals of both provinces attests to widespread cynicism towards Wood's suggestions. Even officials based in the tribal belts, which had been the focus of official food-relief and health operations (due to the fact that these areas were important recruiting grounds for the 'labour battalions' involved in the construction of strategic projects), doubted the advisability of promising 'too much' in the likely case the administration could 'not deliver'. Indeed, it was widely feared that an incapacity to fulfil official promises of food aid would stoke 'popular anger' and possibly 'cause the explosion of riots'. See secret notes from the Deputy Magistrate of Dumka, GOB; the Deputy Commissioner of the Santhal Parganas, GOB, and the Commissioner of the Chota Nagpur Division, GOB, c. October 1943, WSF 55/2(vii)/1943, BSA.

176 However, such appeals seemed largely ineffective, causing the use of official force to extract the surplus food. See extracts from secret reports by District Magistrates in Bihar, Eastern United Provinces and Assam, c.1943, WSF 63/iii/43, BSA.

Chapter Three

An Ancillary to Propaganda: State Censorship and the Civilian Population in Eastern India 1939–45

Studies dealing with wartime censorship in India have generally stressed its proscriptive aspects and emphasised cases where nationalist, usually pro-Congress, tracts were banned. They have, as a result, tended to ignore the official disagreements about the deployment of censorship measures between 1939 and 1945, as well as the other administrative uses accorded to such policies. This chapter highlights the significance given to collecting information, not least about the working of various official propaganda policies, through wartime censorship schemes located at the different levels of administration.[1]

I. The Structures of Official Wartime Censorship in Eastern India

Military interests played a dominant role throughout the Second World War in developing, or directing the establishment of, the censorship structures utilised by civilian administration in Eastern India. For instance, the management of postal and telegraphic censorship remained a military preserve throughout 1939 and 1945. An army official, the Director of Military Operations and Intelligence, guided policy in this regard and his influence was accentuated within the central government by the deputation of two army officials as the Chief Telegraph Censor and Chief Postal Censor respectively.[2] They arranged for the establishment of postal and telegraphic censorship in the provincial capitals and the seaports of Eastern India,[3] and the officials appointed by them were made responsible for screening national and international mail (letters and telegraphic messages) and for reporting any weaknesses discovered in the system.[4]

The military authorities remained equally predominant in directing the nature of postal and telegraphic censorship in the localities, despite the comprehensive powers given to the local officials in this regard through Section 25 of the Emergency Powers Ordinance of 1940.[5] Though the Postal Department officials, District Magistrates and Sub-Divisional Officers were empowered, under Section 5 of the Government of India's Telegraph Act, to prohibit the transmission of 'sensational telegrams',[6] the imposition of comprehensive schemes facilitating the screening of internal mail remained a military prerogative throughout the war. As a consequence, the relevant infrastructure was established only in localities considered by the army to be of strategic worth, particularly in situations where specific political or economic crises were deemed to be capable of threatening the Allied war-effort. For instance, the outbreak of the disturbances in August 1942 caused the local military authorities to initiate the censorship of internal mail in the troubled localities in Eastern India.[7]

Comparable measures were introduced in the region during the first quarter of 1943, when the region was faced with a severe food shortage. Arrangements were made in March 1943 to permit the examination of postal communications in the 'areas to the south (and the east) of the Brahmaputra river and the east of the Ganges river'.[8] However, these schemes remained ephemeral and were discontinued as soon as threats from particular crises were considered to have receded. A permanent, but 'limited scheme', of internal censorship was maintained only in particular areas of Eastern India between 1943 and 1945: the localities with significant troop concentrations and the major industrial centres.[9] No attempt was made during this period to establish structures facilitating the 'continuous' screening of postal communications throughout the region, as it was decided that the necessary censorship measures would be shuffled between localities from 'time to time' without warning.[10] Internal postal and telegraphic censorship was finally discontinued on 30 September 1945, though the examination of international mail arriving from, and being directed to, a few selected countries was maintained till the end of the year.[11]

The civilian officials in charge of the censorship of wireless broadcasting, films and the Indian press also remained answerable to the military representatives posted at the Home Departments of the central and provincial governments and at the District Headquarters. The central government had retained wide powers over wireless broadcasting within the sub-continent under the Government of India Act of 1935, which meant that the provincial Governors General could prevent the transmission of programmes considered to be a 'grave menace to the peace and tranquillity of India'.[12] While this proviso ensured the maintenance of the ascendancy of the government's views during the dissemination of wireless propaganda, official control over all facets of broadcasting policy was ensured by the fact that all the transmitting stations in India were controlled by the All-India Radio, which was an arm of the Government of India's Information and Broadcasting Department. Furthermore, the official censorship duties with regard to domestic broadcasting were simplified by the paucity of wireless transmitters available in the sub-continent, all of which were located in a few big cities. With the outbreak of the war, the Controller of Broadcasting in India became the Chief Broadcasting Censor and he was assisted by the Directors of the AIR stations in the provinces, who were made responsible for local censorship. These officials were instructed to work in close association with the Provincial Press Advisers and the relevant military authorities, and were made responsible for examining, and modifying, the scripts of the speeches made by local 'dignitaries'.[13]

The challenge over the air-waves came from a completely different source: the various Axis radio stations in Germany (Berlin), Italy (Rome) and Japan (Tokyo), as well as the 'enemy-controlled broadcasts' from Bangkok, Vichy France, Saigon, Holland and Luxembourg.[14] Although problems were also initially experienced with Allied broadcasts from Britain and China (Chungking), which were found to be repeating Axis claims while denying them, these were rectified by the Government of India's liaison officers connected to the Government of Britain's Ministry of Information, the British Broadcasting Corporation and the Chinese government.[15] While many of the broadcasts from hostile nations were 'jammed' by powerful transmitters located in the Allies' colonial possessions in South East Asia in the first two years of the war, the Japanese conquest of these regions in 1942 forced a suspension of these efforts, principally because the transmitting stations in India did not possess the appropriate technology.[16]

The Government of India attempted to redress this shortcoming by arranging for some of AIR's short-wave transmissions to clash with the Axis broadcasts.[17] But the bulk of the responsibility for ensuring that people did not tune into enemy radio programmes fell upon the officials in the provinces. Ironically, their task was simplified by the very infrastructural constraints which had stunted the wartime development of the radio as a medium of official propaganda: the shortage of wireless receivers, the high cost of wireless licences, the lack of electricity in the vast majority of villages in Eastern India and the high cost of maintaining battery-powered sets. Legal provisions to prevent the dissemination of enemy broadcasts 'at full blast' by the licensed owners of wireless receivers were made available by the Government of India to officials at all levels of the administration from 1940 onwards.[18]

Unlike the task of screening radio broadcasts transmitted from within India, the examination of the contents of commercially-produced films, books and newspapers was complicated by the fact that they were produced and distributed primarily by a variety of private commercial establishments. In all these cases the Government of India sought to deal with the complexity of the task by delegating the responsibilities to the local administrations. Film censorship, for instance, remained a provincial function throughout 1939–45. Boards of Censors in Bombay, Calcutta, Madras and Lahore provided licences to films, without which they could not be exhibited at any theatre in India. In addition, District Magistrates were given special powers by the provincial governments to suspend the certificate of any film they considered to be unsuitable for local reasons.[19]

However, the greatest amount of attention was paid by the authorities to regulating the print media. Most of the 'All-India' papers, as the major papers published in English and the vernaculars from the provinces were known, were controlled by European firms and considered to be loyal to the British war-effort. But the majority of the Indian owned papers were regarded with suspicion by the colonial administrators.[20] The censorship of Indian-owned papers was made the responsibility of the Chief Press Censor and the Press Adviser to the Government of India, who were assisted by the Provincial Press Adviser (usually an Indian Civil Service officer based in the provincial capital) and District Press Advisers (usually the District Magistrate or the Deputy Magistrate). Among other laws, the Press and Registration of Books Act of 1867 attempted to regulate printing presses, newspapers and books published in India. Its third and fourth rules declared that all publications in India needed to have 'printed legibly' the name of its printer, publisher and the place of printing. The legislation also decreed that it was necessary for all owners of publishing facilities to acquire licenses for the premises.[21]

The existing press laws were strengthened further by the Defence of India Rules, which were brought into force immediately after the outbreak of the Second World War, and provided the colonial officials with comprehensive powers to proscribe all potentially threatening

Table 3.1 A comparison of the circulation figures of the British and the Indian owned newspapers published in English in 1939

Type of newspaper	British owned	Approximate circulation	Indian owned	Approximate circulation
Dailies	6	154,782	25	266,400
Weeklies	3	71, 750	32	187,400
Total	9	226,532	57	453,800

Source: J.A Thorne, *Confidential report on the control during war of the press, broadcasting and films; and on publicity for purposes of the war*, New Delhi, 1939, p. 19, L/I/1/1136, OIOC.

printed material.[22] The sub-rules of this legislation, when used in combination with pre-existing ordinances, made a comprehensive corpus of powers available.[23] In addition, Section 13 of the Emergency Powers Ordinance of 1940 offered quite arbitrary powers to the authorities.[24] The Defence of India Rules were similarly combined with pre-existing ordinances, principally the Criminal Law Amendment Act and the Indian Penal Code, to present the colonial administration with comprehensive powers for the arrest of political activists, the prohibition of meetings and processions, and the banning of political parties. The Emergency Powers Ordinance of 1940, aimed at facilitating the suppression of any local or national 'revolutionary movement', vested further powers with the provincial authorities.[25]

II. The Working of the Structures of Official Wartime Censorship in New Delhi and the Provincial Capitals

Even though the bureaucrats attached to the Government of India, the provincial headquarters and the district administrations collaborated in creating structures of censorship, proscribing the discussion of certain topics and impeding the information released by specific political parties, they debated the validity of particular measures and often implemented them according to their own administrative requirements. The officials located at various levels of the state agreed, for instance, on the importance of collecting intelligence through the examination of postal communications. This consensus was in large measure a result of the incapacity on the part of government's publicity agencies operating in Eastern India to create any comprehensive and lasting channels of information about the reactions of the civilian populace to all forms of official propaganda,[26] which had forced the authorities to rely on a range of informal, and often inconstant, sources of feedback. For example, reports regarding the adequacy of the BBC's Indian language services were obtained by the Government of India's Information and Broadcasting Department and Home Department through the City Magistrates, Directors of the All India Radio Stations and a selected number of senior Indian government servants, all of whom would garner such information from their social peers.[27] Use was also made of 'commercial and other channels', whose members would be encouraged to send regular reports to the relevant departments. However, a perusal of these reviews, which were all sent by 'observers whose business br[ought] them into constant contact with ... middle-class trading classes', reveals that the information contained in them dealt almost entirely with the attitudes of the dwellers of the principal urban centres, especially its well-to-do inhabitants.[28]

By contrast, the intelligence gained through the examination of postal communications and the press in Eastern India was important for what it revealed of the attitudes of the 'masses'.[29] Such official efforts became more significant between 1942 and 1945, when the region became an actual base of operations. It was hoped that the information would, among other things, increase the effectiveness of official propaganda by providing feedback on the adequacy of the publicity material distributed amongst different civilian audiences, and on the rumours that needed to be countered. The information thus collected was considered so valuable that the activity was kept secret and letters were very rarely confiscated, unless they contained details of military installations, troop movements, panic resulting from bombing raids, outbreaks of extreme violence in the localities, 'underground' literature, or, between 1942 and 1945, coins.[30] According to G.R. Savage, a Central Intelligence Department officer, postal censorship was seldom publicised since it allowed the collection of 'a great deal of intelligence of value'.[31] The practice of juggling schemes of comprehensive postal censorship between districts, and establishing the necessary structures without prior warning had a similar logic: the design was to prevent the affected civilians from being discouraged from transmitting their views about wartime conditions in their correspondence.[32] The collection of information in this manner was institutionalised between 1942 and 1945. During these years, censors based in the localities of Eastern India sent 'weekly censorship reports' regularly to the Government of India's

Chief Censor, as well as to the Magistrates' offices and military commanders, who would in turn forward them to their superiors in New Delhi. The analyses would be used by the district authorities to pinpoint potentially hostile political activity, investigate the hoarding of food by merchants, gauge the morale of the subordinate services and develop schemes to counter prevalent rumours.[33]

While there was widespread agreement within the bureaucracy about using postal communications as a source of intelligence, the official dealings with the press varied considerably. Civil servants attached to the central government and the provincial headquarters generally remained unwilling to use the Defence of India Regulations to gag the press, and preferred less blatant methods of control. They felt that banning the hostile elements of the 'All-India' press or censoring them 'heavily' would only create 'sullen-ness' and cause the press not to publish 'what the government wanted published'. The outcome would be 'less news and less comment' creating a 'vacuum ... to be filled ... by rumour and the enemy radio': 'the house swept and garnished' would be 'invaded by devils far worse than those ... expelled.'[34]

The most notable of the indirect attempts to direct the tone of the press was the establishment of the 'advisory system', whose functioning was primarily 'based on the voluntary and loyal co-operation of the Press',[35] and aimed to encourage the 'internal regulation' of the Indian-owned newspapers. The Government of India's Chief Press Censor initiated negotiations for the organisation of the system with the All India Newspaper Editors' Conference in 1940 on the basis that the government would be 'prepared to modify or withdraw prohibitory orders in return for satisfactory responses from the Press as a whole that they would refrain from anti-war propaganda.' The resultant 'gentleman's agreement' was seen as a 'great tactical gain' within the central government,[36] since it was felt that the Press Advisory Committees would act as a buffer between it and the newspapers. Linlithgow declared that the system had begun 'a recognition of the very sound principle that Editors, in the interests of the Press as a whole, should do their own censoring and exercise some control over their more extreme brethren.'[37]

The enthusiasm of the officials posted in New Delhi and the provincial capitals of Eastern India for the agreement was reflected in their unwillingness to ban the publication of newspapers, their continuing efforts to encourage editors to hand in articles for examination, and the irregularity with which they used the Defence of India Rules to punish errant publishers. Representative of this attitude were the so-called *National Herald* cases of 1942. A description of a meeting of the Provincial Press Advisory Committee held in February 1942 to consider the paper's criticism of the administration went thus:

> Majority of the Committee held that the total effect of the articles, etc. was to impede the war-effort, but in view of the assurance of the editor of the paper that he would see to it in future that articles likely, in his judgement, to have the effect of impeding the war efforts were not inserted in the *National Herald*, the Committee did not take any action itself against the paper nor recommended any course of action to Government.[38]

Commonly, in place of general bans on papers, the officials in Delhi and the provincial capitals sought to outlaw particular topics, as revealed in an examination of the themes censored between September 1939 and July 1942. A letter described how it had 'been made clear to Editors [at the Conference] in Delhi that Government are unalterably determined not to tolerate propaganda designed to prejudice recruitment, discourage subscriptions to Defence Loans or otherwise impede the prosecution of the war.'[39] Significantly, the Allied military reverses in the Far East caused the advisers to dictate, rather than prohibit, news about the strategic situation. For instance, the Government of Bengal's Press Adviser tried to discourage newspapers from 'emphasising enemy successes', and while he decided that he 'could not ask the editors to abandon all banner headlines, editors were asked 'to exercise a very careful discretion about headlines and not to give any spectacular publicity to enemy successes: a decisive enemy gain could be displayed simply in the main headlines without any unnecessary flourish.'[40]

The officials based in the central and provincial headquarters remained similarly selective in proscribing resolutions released by the Indian National Congress. Interestingly, only two of the resolutions passed by the committee on 28 April 1942 were banned, although prompt action was taken against newspapers that ignored the banning orders.[41] One of these resolutions dealt with the fall of Burma, describing how all the 'high officials' had evacuated Rangoon leaving the Indian population stranded, and warning that the 'same type of official wield[ed] authority' in India. The other dealt with the molestation of women by troops in railway compartments and the shooting of people who resisted these crimes. By contrast, a resolution dealing with the evacuation of areas for military purposes in Eastern India was not banned, even though it was extremely critical of the colonial authorities for not providing transport facilities and adequate compensation to affected civilians, and claimed, among other things, that the government measures had forced 'families ... to walk out, camp under trees, become destitute and starve.'[42]

Apart from the press advisory system, the other indirect method deployed to control the tone of the 'All-India' press was the selective grant of newsprint, which was in short supply between 1942 and 1945. The Paper Control Orders of 1942 allowed the government to ration the commodity and direct it towards the 'friendlier' sections of the press.[43] Additional Paper Control Orders were issued in 1944 to control the distribution of paper 'other than newsprint', which was being increasingly used by many newspaper establishments in 1943–45.[44] A similar approach was followed with regards to the vetting of the content of films from mid-1942. The rationing of celluloid by the Government of India's Industries and Civil Supplies Department allowed the authorities not only to restrict film to the more 'dependable' firms, but also to dictate the content of some of the films being made within the country.[45]

Great attention was paid also to controlling the various 'sources' of press information. According to F. Puckle, the Secretary to the Government of India's Information and Broadcasting Department, the news imbibed by the Indian press during the war originated from three 'legitimate' sources: the 'external news agencies' (the Reuters group or 'special correspondents' posted outside India), 'internal news agencies' (the Associated Press of India and the United Press of India monopolised the distribution of news within the sub-continent) and the 'special correspondents' based in various parts of India. Though the control of the news agencies was a policy continued from the inter-war years, its scope was widened between 1939 and 1945 through the introduction of new wartime legislation. The news bulletins telegraphed by correspondents based abroad were examined by censors based 'at the points of arrival in India';[46] and the various news agencies operating in the sub-continent, who catered primarily to the 'All-India' papers, agreed to hand in the bulletins and articles sent by their reporters to the central and provincial press advisory committees for examination. Correspondents were also registered with the relevant District Magistrates.[47]

Continuous efforts were also made to prevent foreign broadcasts from being repeated in the press.[48] The issue was resolved by initiating special provisions from 1942 which made it legally necessary for the Reuters group, as well as the other news agencies, to submit all 'unconfirmed news reports' derived from the various Allied wireless broadcasts to the press advisory committees for 'advice' before distribution among newspapers in India.[49] A military telegram explained that the 'full censorship of Reuters's service [in] Bombay' was 'instituted with [the] willing co-operation [of] Reuters's local representative'.[50] The publication of news derived from Axis radio broadcasts was treated as a felony. Laws were also passed so as to make it obligatory for newspapers to reveal their sources of information.[51]

Attempts to control the activities of the press were maintained throughout the conflict, but the Government of India's 'gentleman's agreement' with the AINEC came under severe strain in mid-1942.[52] The correspondence between the Viceroy and the Secretary of State for India at the time, hinted at the possibility that an increased reliance might be placed on the preventive aspects of censorship. One telegram declared that:

> It occurs to me that developments of the War near India and consequent internal trouble ... may compel you before long to impose a stricter control of internal ... press messages and comment than is at present exercised. ... You might perhaps feel some reluctance in superseding the present 'gentleman's agreement' with the Press, which so far as I know has worked fairly well, but the conditions of an emergency would amply justify more vigorous measures.[53]

Significantly, the comprehensive powers of censorship available to the authorities were utilised by officials in New Delhi and provincial headquarters during the 'Quit India' movement of August-September 1942, but – it seems – only because they had failed in their attempts to coax the press to desist from discussing particular aspects of the crisis and to rely on 'dependable' sources of news.[54] The 'Guidance Notes for officers appointed to scrutinise news relating to the Congress movement and disorders' made it clear that four topics should be omitted from all reports handed in for advice: anything that would be likely to 'incite the public to subversive activity or sabotage' and 'arouse apprehensions among the public or Government servants'; reports about jail conditions which attempted to 'glorify prisoners and represent them as martyrs'; the 'programmes and plans' of 'unlawful bodies'; and allegations of 'undue severity' in suppressing the disorders.[55]

The policy of promptly banning errant newspapers and publishing establishments was relaxed only after the Government of India considered the 'Quit India' movement to have abated. It held a series of meetings with the AINEC between September and October 1942 to reiterate its commitment to the press advisory system. The result was another agreement, whereby the central and the provincial governments undertook to allow 'greater flexibility' to the press while the newspaper editors agreed to work in 'close association' with the official censors. The scheme also allowed for all material dealing with the strategic situation to be sent to the local military censors prior to publication. This understanding allowed Linlithgow, the Viceroy, to claim, not without reason, in December 1942 that 'the press throughout India is now working under restrictions voluntarily imposed and is at least as 'free' as the press in any country at war.'[56]

Indeed, the censors based in New Delhi and the provincial capitals, who remained very sensitive to accusations of being high-handed, remained unwilling to make protracted use of the harsher aspects of preventive censorship. Instead of shutting down presses or publishing houses completely, emphasis was placed on fining them or banning the sale of particular editions of their publications. In fact, the discontinuation of publication during a difficult strategic situation was considered best avoided as it was felt that it 'would cause grave public uneasiness ... and would be most undesirable from [a] political standpoint.' Interestingly, efforts were made in December 1942 to procure shipments of newsprint from North America so that nationalist papers like the *Amrita Bazar Patrika* and the *Hindu* did not stop publication.[57]

The agreement reached in October 1942 with the AINEC provided the officials based at the central and provincial headquarters with the basis for their dealings with the press till the end of the war, as an examination of the cases of censorship proves. Great care was taken to prevent the publication of information of strategic importance, and such topics included rumours about enemy aircraft flying over Eastern India, strikes in industrial areas, acts of sabotage against railways and telegraph lines, the forcible clearing of paddy fields by the authorities to facilitate troop movements, and the 'outrages' committed by troops against the local populace.[58] In fact, the Defence of India Rules were amended so as to allow the prohibition of reports dealing with 'incidents in which troops were involved'.[59] While no efforts were made to deny, or ban the reporting of, Japanese air raids in the eastern provinces, the publication of references to official incompetence and panic among the civilians after such attacks was not tolerated.[60] In December 1942 a new section, regarding 'Air Raid Reports', was added to the Press Restrictions for War, which advised the Provincial Press Advisers that they 'should tone down or draw a veil over ... statements' such as:

> (1) 'Crowds of refugees' trekking out at night. (2) 'Whole streets' or 'vast areas' or 'thousands of homes' in ruins. (3) 'All available transport' being used to take refugees out. (4) 'The municipality or other local administration being overwhelmed' with problems. (5) 'Thousands' of people being homeless. (6) That the air raid damage is 'worse than in ...' or 'the worst since the war began'. (7) That looting or other disorders have broken out on a large scale. It follows that no reference to the following can be permitted:
> (a) Any reference to the breakdown of morale or evacuation of officials.
> (b) Any reference to the evacuation of any special class of labour, such as dockers, factory workers, etc.
> (c) The closing of food shops.[61]

Care was also taken to clamp down on the discussion of other topics. References to the 'brutality' or the 'incompetence' of the administration during specific crises were consistently sought to be proscribed,[62] and efforts were made to restrain the press from accusing the bureaucracy and the military authorities of having created the famine of 1943 through the forcible requisitioning of food. An issue of *Forum*, a weekly magazine published from Calcutta, was proscribed for publishing an article titled '1944 Horror List', which parodied the annual honour's list thus:

> ... Major Leopold Amery [had been] promoted to be lie-asion officer on behalf of His Majesty's Government in the BBC and the Indian 'AIR' force [and that the] Late Sir John Herbert, formerly Governor of Bengal, [had been] posthumously made [the] Baron of Kalighat for helping Bengal to get rid of a lot of excess population to permanently solve Bengal's food difficulties and losing his life in the endeavour.[63]

In contrast to the sensitivity displayed by the censors regarding such wartime events, a great deal of latitude was allowed with regard to discussion of the colonial constitutional and wartime policy. A report from Bengal, which is quite representative of the official reviews being sent in from the other eastern provinces, mentioned how:

The White Paper on India and Mr. Amery's speech in the House of Commons were bitterly criticised. 'Mr. Amery's pronounced predilection for Fascist methods' was underlined.... 'The perpetuation of British vested interests' was declared to be a fundamental policy of the British Government.... The speech of the Earl of Munster had a similar reception. One paper described it as 'maiden but not maidenly'; and another described the Under-Secretary as 'toeing the line of his Chief, Mr. Amery and his Grand-Chief, Mr. Churchill'. The speech of Lord Samuel which was published *in extenso*, was strongly criticised: 'The accusation that the Congress has turned totalitarian comes with ill-grace from those, Lord Samuel included, who are declaring India to be unfit for a democratic form of Government' was a typical comment.[64]

A striking manifestation of the central and provincial governments' willingness to accept not insignificant levels of nationalist criticism was the decision to allow special quotas of newsprint to be set aside for moderate pro-Congress papers, such as the *Sansar*, a Hindi daily started in September 1942 and published from Benares (United Provinces). An official communication mentioned that the paper's initial request for a quota of newsprint had been refused since it was a new newspaper, but:

> The case of the newspaper was referred to the Principal Information Officer in order to find out whether the newspaper served any special purpose or was of interest from any special point of view which would justify the grant of a newsprint permit. The Principal Officer stated that although it was a pro-Congress newspaper, it had always co-operated with the Bureau [of Public Information] and had given sufficient publicity to the war and departmental material supplied to it. He added that it was one of the few Congress papers which had not allowed their political ideology to confuse the Indian issue with the war in general. In view of the remarks of the Principal Information Officer and pressing demands from ... Mr. Sri Prakash, M.L.A., it has recently been decided after consultation with ... the Newsprint Advisory Committee to allot a monthly ration of 1 ton of newsprint to the *Sansar*.[65]

III. The Working of the Structures of Official Wartime Censorship in the District and Sub-Divisional Capitals

Unlike the press advisers based in New Delhi and the provincial capitals, who would repeatedly warn a paper before finally proscribing one or more of its issues, the district officials tended to take immediate action against errant printers or publishers. Whilst the press advisory committees in the district capitals, which were established in the last quarter of 1940, remained theoretically under the direction of the Government of India's Chief Press Officer, their day to day working devolved to local bureaucracies, who tended to adapt centrally prescribed censorship policies according to their own needs.[66] Although the local officials were able to monitor the activities of the bigger newspapers published in the district capitals, and indeed utilise them to gauge the 'popular mood' – because their editors remained willing to co-operate with the local Press Advisory Committees and register their correspondents with the Magistrate's office – the control of the vast number of 'less reputable' vernacular papers published in the *mofussils* was rendered difficult due to the shortage of personnel. What made matters worse for the local administrators was the smaller newspapers' tendency to 'pirate' material, often out of context, from the 'All-India' press,[67] to publish local rumours and claims made in Axis news broadcasts,[68] and to refuse to hand in material for examination.[69] A typical official complaint went thus:

> Certain of the Indian language papers indulged in giving an undesirable twist to news, so as to show that the Allies were on the run in Burma and things were going very badly for them; but the better type of newspapers refrained from this and published news in a straightforward manner.[70]

The difficulties faced in policing a plethora of small vernacular papers in a period of severe economic and political stress, and the fear that the views espoused in them might stoke disturbances, caused the local administrators to adopt an uncompromising stance. Officials would often go beyond the 'limits' agreed upon in New Delhi between the Government of India and the AINEC while dealing with these establishments,[71] and the action taken against them would take various forms: the imposition of forcible pre-censorship; the temporary or permanent banning of publications, and the prosecution or imprisonment of their correspondents, editors and proprietors.[72]

The frequent necessity for these measures was recognised by the officials in New Delhi, and thus overlooked by them. A review prepared by the Secretary to the Government of India's Information and Broadcasting Department declared, for example, that:

Table 3.2 Circulation figures of vernacular newspapers (entirely owned by Indian firms) in 1939

Type of newspaper	Newspapers published in a single Indian language	Approximate circulation	Newspapers published in two or three Indian languages	Approximate circulation
Dailies	87	543,600	14	54,100
Weeklies	116	597,850	11	47,700
Total	203	1,141,450	25	101,800

Source: J.A Thorne, *Confidential report on the control during war of the press, broadcasting and films; and on publicity for purposes of the war*, New Delhi, 1939, p. 19, L/I/1/1136, OIOC.

Speaking broadly, the policy of the Government of India has been to encourage the Press to govern itself, and Provincial Governments, sometimes with reluctance, have followed this example. It must be remembered that the control of the Provincial Press is primarily a Provincial responsibility and that local conditions do not always make it easy for a Provincial Government to take the same view of the needs of a case as the Government of India.[73]

The attitude of the local officials towards the dissemination of other forms of hostile information remained equally firm. While they made minimal use of the legal provisions provided by the Government of India to prevent the dissemination of enemy radio broadcasts in public in the first two years of the war, since it was feared that this might drive the activity 'underground', the situation changed dramatically after the Japanese entry into the conflict in December 1941. Action now began to be regularly taken against 'people ... [who] when tuning in to Axis broadcasts turn[ed] their receiving sets at full blast, so that the bulletins c[ould] be heard at a considerable distance'.[74] Those considered to be guilty of intentionally disseminating 'matter derived from enemy sources' in this manner were prosecuted by the application of the Defence of India Rule 38A.[75] In the localities of Bihar, as in the other eastern provinces, official press notes were released warning owners of radio sets that it was an offence to 'disseminate enemy broadcasts either orally or by permitting visitors to hear them or to tune in at full blast so as to let passerby [sic] hear'.[76] In times of extreme political or economic strain, the district authorities would also often resort to the confiscation of radio receivers,[77] or mete out severe punishments to individuals found guilty of 'merely listening' to Axis broadcasts. According to K.K. Banerjee, a sessions judge posted at Muzzafarpur (Bihar) in 1942, people would often be arrested and given long stints in prison for tuning into enemy radio stations.[78]

The district administrations also regularly banned meetings and processions organised by Congress members. Individuals considered to be 'emissaries from Mr. Gandhi' would often be arrested or prohibited from entering particular districts.[79] The widespread nervousness amongst the district officials in the provinces of Eastern India between 1942 and 1945 also caused them to impede, if not ban, events organised by 'agitators' with no ostensible political links, and activists attached to other political parties, most notably the Communist Party of India, the Radical Democratic Party of India and the Hindu Mahasabha. Reports from Assam mentioned, for instance, how a 'number of ex-agitators from the Oil-fields [sic] were externed from the upper districts of the Assam Valley lest their conduct should be prejudicial',[80] and that action was being taken against 'rumour-mongers' in Lakhimpur district (some of whom were ultimately thrown out of the locality).[81] Comparable measures were resorted to in Bihar, where 'unruly agitators were excluded' from all important industrial areas by the implementation of Section 144 of the Criminal Procedure Code.[82] This legislation was also regularly used to prohibit meetings and processions arranged by the local branches of the Hindu Mahasabha, since these events were considered capable of fomenting communal violence.[83]

Though the Government of India had hoped to use the assistance of the CPI and the RDP to rally support for the Allied war-effort, the bureaucrats in the localities remained unenthusiastic about the scheme because the local cadres attached to the parties usually sought to 'popularise' the Second World War by involving themselves in agitations over parochial problems, most notably shortages of all varieties of essentials, unpopular wartime measures and agrarian relations.[84] District officials in Assam,[85] Bengal,[86] Orissa[87] and the United Provinces,[88] refused to accept such activism, which was seen as being capable of encouraging outbreaks of violence against the loyalist sections of the rural elite, whose assistance was considered indispensable by the local administrations.[89] Therefore, it was still common to find the gagging of the local communist press, the arrest of party cadres, and the denial of licences for processions and public meetings arranged by the CPI's members.[90] Moreover, on the rare occasions when permission for meetings was given, the organisers were asked to give written undertakings that they would not discuss specific issues.[91]

Clashes between the RDP's cadres and the district administrators remained less frequent, primarily because the party, which was established in 1940, had a relatively thinly spread organisational network in Eastern India. For instance, its branch in Orissa, which was set up only in the second half of May 1943, represented nothing more than a 'unit' in Cuttack, the provincial capital.[92] Similarly, a report sent from Bihar as late as March 1943 mentioned how the Indian Federation of Labour, the RDP's labour front, was 'endeavouring to bolster up their claims to represent industrial labour through affiliation of existing unions. A number of sugar mill unions are being registered. Efforts to form teachers' unions are not meeting with much success.'[93] Nonetheless, reports from the localities where members of the RDP were active suggested the existence of tensions between the district officers and the party cadres. A report from Bengal complained, for example, that the enthusiasm of RDP activists:

> ... who [we]re prepared to conduct anti-Fascist or anti-Japanese propaganda, [wa]s ... principally directed to the party programme to which such propaganda forms in effect only an adjunct. What may be described as helpful continues to be accompanied by very much more which is unhelpful or almost prejudicial.... Many officials, in fact, continue to look with considerable disquietude upon the activities of persons professing to be 'anti-Fascist' and are convinced that their willingness to support efforts to rally public opinion against the Japanese is little more than a cloak for the establishment of their own influence....[94]

Contemporary government files reveal that district officials remained unimpressed by such activities, and that they ordered the arrest of party activists considered to be inordinately keen to utilise agitations organised around local issues.

IV. Concluding comments

The effectiveness of censorship measures targeted at civilian audiences was, like the propaganda schemes deployed at the time, encumbered by the acute shortage of manpower resources during the war. As a result, the mechanisms developed to deal with the press, the news-agencies and the publishing houses remained dependant on their willingness to hand in material for examination to the Central, the Provincial or the District Press Advisory Committees. The system was also based on their acceptance of official suggestions about what not to print. Unfortunately for the colonial authorities such co-operation was rarely forthcoming. As a consequence, any disciplinary action that was taken was targeted against the errant establishments after the objectionable material had appeared in print. This legal loophole was used regularly by the Indian-owned sections of the newspaper industry to report topical issues, the mention of which transgressed the wartime press instructions. A good example of this was the authorities' experience in 1942 with Shyama Prasad Mookerjee's extremely critical letter of resignation from the Bengal Ministry headed by Fazlul Huq. The seventeen page letter, addressed to the Governor of Bengal and the Viceroy, censured the country's 'alien rulers' for creating a political stalemate and thereby forcing the Congress to launch an agitation, for suppressing this 'political movement' with unnecessary 'brutality'; the 'illegality' of the 'collective fines' imposed in areas affected by the 'Quit India' movement; the inadequacies of the official relief measures after the cyclone in Midnapur, and the forcible requisitioning of domestic cattle from the stricken area for feeding the army.[95] Not unnaturally, the authorities in Delhi and the provinces of Eastern India did not want the letter to be publicised.[96] But the newspapers gave the document great prominence,[97] even as the Government of Bengal prepared to warn the press that 'they would publish it at their own risk'.[98] Significantly, the only official response was to release a second warning that the document not be given further publicity.[99]

Mookerjee's letter of resignation also provides us with a good example of another ploy often used by the proprietors of Indian newspapers from 1942 onwards to avoid official retribution for publishing articles which contravened the wartime press instructions. This involved combining criticism of the administration with denouncements of Japanese expansionism in Asia, which caused the Press Advisers, especially those attached to the central and provincial headquarters, to debate the propriety of the articles with other officials and sometimes ignore their publication. A discussion of the tone of Mookerjee's letter declared, for instance, that:

Reading the letter as a whole however, there is little ... to which serious objection can be taken, or which offends against the ordinary expression of political views and suggestions for the improvement of a situation which, in any view, cannot be regarded as satisfactory. It can moreover be argued that the purpose underlying the letter is to secure wholehearted co-operation in resistance to a common enemy and whether the means whereby this should be attained are regarded as reasonable and proper.[100]

The debates within official circles between November and December 1942 about the danger posed by the letter allowed the press enough time to publicise the document and the issues it dealt with, even though a decision was ultimately taken to prohibit further discussion of it.[101]

Contemporary reviews of the working of the press between 1942 and 1945 reveal that the censors based in the central and provincial headquarters were put in a similar quandary by the nationalist press, notably the papers overtly allied to the Congress and the Communist Party of India.[102] A report from Bihar pointed out, for example, how:

The 'Rashtravani' ... has written a rather objectionable editorial criticising Mr. Churchill's speech, but it is so cleverly done that action is rather difficult.... The gist of the article is that if Mr. Churchill thinks that he will be excused for using gas on German factories, because he has given a warning to Hitler, he is mistaken. If Mr. Churchill is as strong as he claims to be, why does he not hasten the defeat of the Axis powers?[103]

In a great number of these cases the editors of the relevant papers got away with mere warnings about the possibility of bans in the future.[104] The *People's War*, the CPI mouthpiece in English, was accorded greater freedom than other papers by the Government of India, which sought to encourage the communist politbureau to criticise the national leadership of the Congress, although reports underlined the unhappiness caused within government circles by the tone of the paper.[105] The official incapacity to proscribe the criticism levelled against the Raj was also caused by the shortage of government personnel in the localities.[106] Although the local bureaucrats tried to redress the situation by directing the available supplies of newsprint amongst selected establishments, their efforts failed due to the press's capacity to overcome the resultant shortfall through purchases of good quality paper from the black market.[107]

However, the failures of official wartime censorship needs to be examined in another context: the capacity to collect political information. While analyses of the press provided significant bulk to the reports prepared by officials based in the provincial and district headquarters, the ineffective policing of newspapers in the localities had the effect of impeding attempts to gather intelligence from the smaller, especially vernacular, publications. This administrative shortcoming was powerfully illustrated by the civil servants' tendency to base reports on analyses of the 'All India' press and the major, primarily English, newspapers published in the district headquarters.[108] Similarly, attempts by the overstretched local bureaucracies to gather information from the examination of postal communications remained spasmodic,[109] a situation exacerbated by the central War Department's decision to shuffle the additional wartime structures of censorship amongst selected – usually only strategically important – district and sub-divisional capitals.[110]

This, of course, meant that information could, and was, collected about the attitudes of specific 'priority' groups towards the local political and social situation, official propaganda schemes and their expectations from the authorities, which proved useful in certain administrative contexts.[111] For example, information gleaned from all manner of postal communications, including the notes attached to money orders sent by workers to villages, often enabled local officials to effectively identify troublesome trade union activists operating in the war industries; detect and counter damaging 'rumours', locate epidemic outbreaks of contagious disease, and spot serious snags in the networks set up to distribute food and medical aid, thereby allowing them save scarce time and resources. But, these activities also permitted the authorities to be aware of the fact that the strategy of mobilising 'war-workers' and members of the subordinate services through material benefits, along with the threat that these would be reduced or removed altogether if required, was yielding a 'dubious loyalty'. The tone of the correspondence being sifted seemed to assure the censors, and the military and civil officials assessing their reports in the provincial headquarters and New Delhi, that the removal of the wartime distributive schemes, along with the shedding of wartime labour and bureaucracy, was going to cause widespread civil unrest. Such reports, which underlined the falling official morale due to the increasing attacks on officials attached to the subordinate services and an inability to arrest the assailants due to an inability to find witnesses, also nurtured fears about the growing influence of the

Congress and its 'communistic' allies.[112] This, in turn, affected both the impetus and tone of the official publicity onslaught against the party between 1942 and 1944, which is examined in the following chapter.

Notes

1 A good example of the approach this study is seeking to avoid is provided by Aurobindo Mazumdar, who declares that 'With the imposition of [the] Defence Ordinance the constitutional machinery set up in 1937 as well as the normal operation of the laws were suspended. The Ordinance was of such a sweeping character that it was extremely difficult for any newspaper to discharge its functions normally.... The newspapers had to undergo a series of restrictions imposed at different levels – central, provincial and local.' See, A. Mazumdar, *Indian Press and Freedom Struggle, 1937–42*, Calcutta, 1993. Apart from treating wartime censorship as a purely restrictive policy, Mazumdar's work, like most other studies in the field, tends to ignore its operation in the locality, concentrating selectively, instead, on the attitudes within the central and provincial headquarters. However, it is important to point out here that one exception to the general rule is provided by Barrier's classic work, which has pointed out that centrally-prescribed censorship policies tended to be adapted locally, but unfortunately avoided researching this assertion in any detail. See, N.G. Barrier, *Banned: Controversial Literature and Political Control in British India 1907–1947*, Columbia, 1974.
2 J.A. Thorne, *Confidential report on the control during war of the press, broadcasting and films; and on publicity for purposes of the war*[hereafter *Thorne Report*], New Delhi, 1939, p. 16, L/I/1/1136, OIOC.
3 Most secret letter from War Department, GOI to Home Department, GOI, 10 February 1944, HPF(I) 20/1/44, NAI.
4 In July 1940 the Government of India discovered that wartime postal and telegraphic censorship was being evaded by persons smuggling correspondence into Goa, from where messages were being transmitted to Europe via South Africa. This weakness was rectified with the assistance of the South African government, which initiated effective censorship structures to examine, and subsequently prohibit the transmission, of all suspect correspondence from Goa. Moreover, summaries of the censored messages were sent to the Chief Censor's office in India. Secret letter from Chief Censor, GOI, to Chief Censor, Government of South Africa, 29 July 1940, HPF(I) 88/1/41, NAI.
5 For a detailed description of the powers endowed by Section 25 of the Emergency Powers Ordinance of 1940 see secret letter from R. Tottenham, Additional Secretary, Home Department, GOI, to the Chief Secretaries of all provincial governments, 2 August 1940, PDGF 69/12, BSA.
6 Departmental note from N. Senapati, Provincial Press Adviser, GOB, to the Chief Secretary, GOB, 26 March 1942, PPAF 4/1942, BSA.
7 Departmental note, Home Department, GOI, c.August 1942, HPF(I) 20/18/45, NAI.

8 The structures of censorship consisted of 'static censor stations' at all the major river crossings and these were supplemented by 'mobile censor units' based at these stations. Most secret WIS(II), 9 April 1943, L/WS/1/1433, OIOC.
9 Departmental note, Home Department, GOI, c.1943, HPF(I) 20/18/45, NAI.
10 Departmental note by R. Tottenham, Additional Secretary, Home Department, GOI, c.March 1944, HPF(I) 20/1/44, NAI. This plan was supported by the Government of India's War Department. See departmental note by W.A. Wright, Secretary, War Department, GOI, 1 March 1944, HPF(I) 20/1/44, NAI.
11 Censorship of 'civil first class terminal mails' and telegrams exchanged between India and Hong Kong, Macao, Burma and Malaya was maintained throughout 1945, primarily due to the insistence of the SEAC leadership. Confidential letter from War Department, GOI, to the SSI, GOBr, 1 October 1945, HPF(I) 20/18/45, NAI.
12 Regulations for the control of broadcasting in war, General Staff Branch, [December] 1938, L/MIL/17/5/4257, OIOC.
13 *Thorne Report*, p. 18, L/I/1/1136, OIOC.
14 Secret letter from F. Puckle, Secretary, Information and Broadcasting Department, GOI to the Chief Secretary, GOB, 7 January 1942, PPAF 4/1942, BSA. Broadcasts were also targeted at India from Singapore and Rangoon from May 1942. See list of broadcasts from Axis controlled radio stations attached to express letter from F. Puckle, Secretary, Information and Broadcasting Department, GOI to the Chief Secretary, GOB, 10 July 1942, WSF 142/1942, BSA.
15 Secret letter from P.N. Thapar, Deputy Secretary, Information and Broadcasting Department, GOI to the Chief Secretaries of all provincial governments, 24 December 1941, PPAF 4/1942, BSA.
16 Secret telegram from F. Puckle, Secretary, Information and Broadcasting Department, GOI to L. Amery, SSI, GOBr, 10 March 1942, L/PJ/8/119, OIOC.
17 Express letter from F. Puckle, Secretary, Information and Broadcasting Department, GOI to the Chief Secretary, GOB, 10 July 1942, WSF 142/1942, BSA.
18 Confidential letter from R. Tottenham, Additional Secretary, Home Department, GOI to all provincial governments and Chief Commissioners, 7 March 1942, WSF 43/42, BSA.
19 *Thorne Report*, pp. 16–18, L/I/1/1136, OIOC.
20 The three newspapers considered to be most trustworthy by the Government of India were the *Times of India* published from Bombay, the *Mail* published from Madras and the *Civil and Military Gazette* in Lahore. Circular letter from Linlithgow, the Viceroy to the Governors of all the provinces, 30 November 1940, L/PJ/8/791, OIOC.
21 Appendix 1 in M. Gopal, *Freedom Movement and the Press: The Role of Hindi Newspapers*, New Delhi, 1980.
22 See appendix to express letter from R. Tottenham, Home Department, GOI to all provincial governments, 20 November 1940, L/PJ/8/791, NAI.

23 Strictly secret circular from R. Tottenham, Additional Secretary, Home Department, GOI to all provincial governments, 16 May 1942, L/PJ/8/791, OIOC.
24 Secret Memorandum on Press Control, GOI, c.August 1940, attached to secret letter from Y.A. Godbole, Chief Secretary, GOB to all District Officers; all Divisional Commissioners; all Superintendents and Additional Superintendents of Police; the Inspector-General of Police and all Deputy Inspectors-General of Police, 9 December 1940, PDGF 69/12, BSA.
25 Secret letter from R. Tottenham, Additional Secretary, Home Department, GOI to the Chief Secretaries of all provincial governments, 2 August 1940, PDGF 69/12, BSA.
26 See, for instance, secret minutes of the Central Intelligence Department conference held in Delhi between 9 and 11 March 1942 to consider improvements in [the] Security Intelligence organisation, c.March, HPF(I) 21/7/42, NAI.
27 See note by H.J. Evans, Deputy Commissioner of Delhi, 22 May 1940; Note by R. Ahmed, Director, AIR, Lahore, to A.S. Bokhari, Controller of Broadcasting, AIR, 20 May 1940; weekly report from Director, AIR Lucknow, 18 May 1940; Secret telegram from Home Department, GOI to L. Amery, SSI, GOBr, 16 September 1941; Secret telegram from the Information and Broadcasting Department, GOI to L. Amery, Secretary of SSI, GOBr, 15 January 1942; Telegram from Information and Broadcasting Department, GOI to L. Amery, SSI, GOBr, 31 January 1943, L/I/1/942, OIOC.
28 See, for instance, extracts of letters received by the Director-General of Information, GOI, c.1941, L/I/1/1015, OIOC.
29 Secret Censorship Regulations, India, Defence Department, GOI, 1939, L/MIL/17/5/4258, OIOC.
30 A problem which plagued the colonial administrators throughout 1942–44 was an acute shortage of coins, specially those of smaller denominations. Officials in Eastern India would regularly attempt to seek and prosecute hoarders of coins, the paucity of which was considered to be having an adverse effect on civilian morale. Postal censorship in Assam would regularly reveal attempts by *Marwari* merchants and shop-keepers to smuggle coinage out of the province. One particularly striking case was an attempt by an agent of the Assam Oil Company to post 960 one *anna* pieces to Jaipur State. The packet was intercepted by the censors. CSFR(1), May 1943, Assam, HPF(I) 18/5/43, NAI.
31 Note by G.R. Savage, CID, MSS EUR F. 161/210, OIOC. Also see note by E.J. Beveridge, Assistant Director, IB, GOI, 21 December 1943, HPF(I) 3/47/43, NAI.
32 Departmental note by R. Tottenham, Additional Secretary, Home Department, GOI, c.March 1944, HPF(I) 20/1/44, NAI.
33 See, for instance, HPF(I) 20/26/42, NAI. and HPF(I) 20/21/45, NAI.
34 Secret departmental note by F. Puckle, Secretary, Information and Broadcasting Department, GOI, 27 March 1942, L/PJ/8/791, OIOC.
35 *Thorne Report*, pp. 15–17, L/I/1/1136, OIOC.
36 Secret telegram from the Home Department, GOI to L. Amery, SSI, GOBr, 11 November 1940, L/PJ/8/791, OIOC.

37 Circular letter from Linlithgow, Viceroy to the Governors of all provinces, 30 November 1940, L/PJ/8/791, OIOC.
38 Appendix 1 to CSFR(2), February 1942, United Provinces, HPF(I) 18/2/42, NAI.
39 Express letter from R. Tottenham, Additional Secretary, Home Department, GOI to all provincial governments, 20 November 1940, L/PJ/8/791, OIOC.
40 Appendix 1 to CSFR(1) January 1942, Bengal, HPF(I) 18/1/42, NAI.
41 The Government of United Provinces 'prohibited the weekly edition and publication, sale or distribution of the paper the *Sainik*, Agra, under clause (d) of sub-rule (1) of rule 40 of the Defence of India Rules, for publishing prejudicial reports.... The paper in its issue, dated May 1, 1942, published a part of the resolution adopted at Allahabad on April 28, 1942, by the Working Committee of the All-India Congress, printing and publication of which was prohibited by the Central and the Provincial Governments...'. CSFR(1) May 1942, United Provinces, HPF(I) 18/5/42, NAI.
42 Summary of resolutions adopted by the Congress Working Committee on 28 April 1942 attached to secret telegram from the Home Department, GOI to L. Amery, SSI, GOBr, 1 May 1942, L/PJ/8/791, OIOC.
43 Note by V. Sahay, Additional Secretary, Information and Broadcasting Department, GOI, 12 May 1944, HPF(I) 3/7/43, NAI. The paper shortage became so acute in 1942 that a Paper Control Order was passed that year. Another Paper Control Order was passed in 1943 and this legislation prohibited the 'extravagant use' of paper by making it a punishable offence. For instance, posters and calendars could not exceed certain dimensions and the printing of advertising circulars and directories were prohibited by law. Memorandum on provisioning of paper, c.1944, War History of the Labour Department, GOI, L/R/5/291, OIOC.
44 Note by V. Sahay, Additional Secretary, Information and Broadcasting Department, GOI, 12 May 1944, HPF(I) 3/7/43, NAI.
45 The Government of India informed all indigenous film producers in 1943 that they would be required to produce one 'instructional film' about the war for every two full-length 'entertainment films' released by them in order to ensure supplies of celluloid to their firms. The producers were also asked to forward the scripts of these 'instructional films' to the central government's Information and Broadcasting Department for approval. Memorandum on Film Publicity, pp. 10–11, L/R/5/295, OIOC.
46 Secret departmental note by F. Puckle, Secretary, Information and Broadcasting Department, GOI, 27 March 1942, L/PJ/8/791, OIOC.
47 Telegram from F. Puckle, Secretary, Information and Broadcasting Department, GOI to L. Amery, SSI, GOBr, 3 September 1942, L/I/1/732, OIOC.
48 Secret letter from P.N. Thapar, Deputy Secretary, Information and Broadcasting Department, GOI to the Chief Secretaries of all provincial governments, 24 December 1941, PPAF 4/1942, BSA.
49 Ibid.
50 Secret cipher telegram from the Commander-in-Chief, India to the Commander-in-Chief, Ceylon, 19 March 1942, L/I/1/732, OIOC.

51 Secret departmental note by F. Puckle, Secretary, Information and Broadcasting Department, GOI, 27 March 1942, L/PJ/8/791, OIOC. Also see, confidential letter from R. Tottenham, Additional Secretary, Home Department, GOI to all provincial governments and Chief Commissioners, 7 March 1942, WSF 43/42, BSA.
52 Survey of the Press Advisory System, c1941, HPF(I) 3/27/1941, NAI.
53 Secret telegram from L. Amery, SSI, GOBr to Linlithgow, Viceroy, 31 January 1942, L/PJ/8/791, OIOC.
54 Order signed by R. Tottenham, Additional Secretary, Home Department, GOI, 8 August 1942, HPF(I) 8/6/1942, NAI.
55 Confidential express letter from Home Department, GOI to all provincial governments, 10 September 1942, HPF(I) 8/6/1942, NAI.
56 Secret telegram from Linlithgow, Viceroy to L. Amery, SSI, GOBr, 15 December 1942, HPF(I) 3/13/1942, Part II, NAI.
57 Secret telegram from the Commerce Department, GOI to L. Amery, SSI, GOBr, 4 December 1942, L/I/1/339, OIOC.
58 See fortnightly reports on the press in the CSFRs from Assam, Bengal, Bihar, Orissa and the United Provinces for 1942, 1943 and 1944, NAI. Also see Appendix 1 to CSFR(1) October 1942, Bengal, HPF(I) 18/10/42, NAI.
59 Appendix 1 to CSFR(2) June 1942, Bengal, HPF(I) 18/6/42, NAI.
60 Note from B.J. Kirchner, Chief Press Censor, GOI to R. Tottenham, Additional Secretary, Home Department, GOI, 28 December 1942, HPF(I) 33/47/42, OIOC.
61 Attached to confidential departmental memorandum, Information and Broadcasting Department, GOI, 31 December 1942, HPF(I) 33/47/42, NAI.
62 A pamphlet written by S.P. Mookerjee in 1943 titled *A Phase of the Indian Struggle*, which repeated the allegations made by him against the colonial administration in his letter of resignation of November 1942, was 'forfeited and further publication prohibited' under the Defence of India Rules. Appendix 1 to CSFR(2), January 1942, Bengal, HPF(I) 18/1/43, NAI.
63 *Forum*, 9 January 1944. By 1945, however, the constraints regarding the discussion of the 'man-made famine' were slackened in New Delhi and provincial capitals. A good example was a book written by Ela Sen called *Darkening Days*, which referred to the ineffectiveness of official measures in 1943 and that the calamity could have been reverted under a 'national government'. The book was released by the censors for publication on 19 February 1945. See HPF(I) 20/12/45, NAI.
64 Appendix 1 to CSFR(1) April 1943, Bengal, HPF(I) 18/4/43, NAI. Amery's speech in the House of Commons came in for 'considerable criticism' in Orissa too. Appendix to CSFR(1) April 1943, Orissa, ibid. The Government of India was frequently blamed for the constitutional deadlock by the press in the other provinces as well. See, for instance, appendix 1 to CSFR(2) May 1943, United Provinces, HPF(I) 18/5/43, NAI. The press also adopted a critical tone towards the 'food-supply situation and the constitutional impasse'. See, for instance, appendix 1 to CSFR(2) January 1943, Assam, HPF(I) 18/1/43, NAI.
65 Departmental note by M. Nasrullah, Assistant Secretary, Industries and Civil Supplies Department, GOI, c.1944, HPF(I) 3/47/43, NAI.

66 Descriptions of the working the Press Advisory System within the provinces and their localities are available in HPF(I) 18/14/41, HPF(I) 14/20/41 and HPF(I) 3/27/41, NAI. Also see, Barrier, *Banned*, p. 144.
67 Confidential letter from R. Tottenham, Additional Secretary, Home Department, GOI to all provincial governments, 7 March 1942, WSF 43/42, BSA.
68 Appendix 1 to CSFR(1) June 1942, United Provinces, HPF(I) 18/6/42, NAI.
69 The Provincial Press Advisers' reports would often refer to the difficulties in getting the smaller papers in the districts and sub-divisions to hand in articles for 'guidance'. See, for instance, CSFR(2) February 1942, United Provinces, HPF(I) 18/2/1942, NAI.
70 Appendix 1 to CSFR(1) May 1942, United Provinces, HPF(I) 18/5/42, NAI.
71 Descriptions of .the working the Press Advisory System within the provinces and their localities are available in HPF(I) 18/14/41, HPF(I) 14/20/41 and HPF(I) 3/27/41, NAI.
72 See, for instance, secret letter from P.N. Thapar, Deputy Secretary, Information and Broadcasting Department, GOI to the Chief Secretaries of all provincial governments, 24 December 1941, PPAF 4/1942, BSA, confidential letter from Y.A. Godbole, Chief Secretary, GOB to R. Tottenham, Additional Secretary, Home Department, GOI 20 March 1942, WSF 43/42, BSA, and CSFR(2) December 1942, Assam, HPF(I) 18/12/42, NAI.
73 Secret departmental note by F. Puckle, Secretary, Information and Broadcasting Department, GOI, 27 March 1942, L/PJ/8/791, OIOC.
74 Confidential letter from R. Tottenham, Additional Secretary, Home Department, GOI to all provincial governments, 7 March 1942, WSF 43/42, BSA.
75 Express letter from F. Puckle, Secretary, Information and Broadcasting Department, GOI to the Chief Secretary, GOB, 10 July 1942, WSF 142/1942, BSA.
76 Departmental note by G. Murray, Political Department, GOB, 19 July 1942, WSF 142/1942, BSA.
77 For instance, officials in the United Provinces confiscated 45 radio sets in 8 districts in the aftermath of the 'Quit-India' movement. Secret letter from M. Hallett, Governor, Government of United Provinces, to Linlithgow, Viceroy, 9 November 1942, R/3/1/78, OIOC.
78 Recollections of Justice K.K. Banerjee, MSS EUR T. 79/2, OIOC.
79 See, for example, CSFR(1) February 1942, Orissa, HPF(I) 18/2/42, NAI.; CSFR(2), June 1942, Bengal, HPF(I) 18/6/42, NAI.; CSFR(1) May 1942, United Provinces, HPF(I) 18/5/42, NAI., and CSFR(2), January 1943, Orissa, HPF(I) 18/1/43, NAI.
80 CSFR(2) January 1942, Assam, HPF(I) 18/1/42, NAI. A regular check was maintained in the Digboi oil fields on 'persons resident without authority'. CSFR(1) February 1942, Assam, HPF(I) 18/2/42, NAI.
81 CSFR(1), February 1942, Assam, HPF(I) 18/2/42, NAI.
82 CSFR(2), December 1941, Bihar, HPF(I) 18/12/41, NAI.
83 See, for instance, CSFR(1), May 1942, Bihar, HPF(I) 18/5/42, NAI, and CSFR(1) October 1942, Bihar HPF(I) 18/10/42, NAI.

84 The communist cadres' attempts to organise agitations to redress local difficulties arose from their attempts to increase their support-base and the fact they often came from the local community. An Intelligence Bureau report stated that it was clear that 'their [CPI.s] policy includes no plan or intention of doing anything towards assisting Government in strengthening support for the war and a spirit of resistance if by their action they cannot at the same time add to the prestige and influence of the Party'. Summary of Communist Activity, IB, GOI, July 1942, HPF(I) 7/5/42, NAI.
85 See, for instance, CSFR(1) and CSFR(2) January 1943, Assam, HPF(I) 18/1/43, NAI.
86 See, for instance, CSFR(1) and (2), February 1943, Bengal, HPF(I) 18/2/43, NAI.
87 See, for instance, CSFR(1), January 1942, Orissa, HPF(I) 18/1/42, NAI; CSFR(1) and CSFR(2) January. 1943, Orissa, HPF(I) 18/1/43, NAI, and CSFR(1) and CSFR(2) February 1943, Orissa, HPF(I) 18/2/43, NAI.
88 See, for instance, CSFR(1) and CSFR(2) May 1943, United Provinces, HPF(I) 18/5/43, NAI.
89 Note by S.J.L. Olver, IB, GOI, 27 October 1943, HPF(I) 7/23/43, NAI. Also see note by R. Maxwell, Home Member, VEC, 31 October 1943, HPF(I) 7/23/43, NAI.
90 The Government of India frequently communicated its displeasure between 1942–44 to the provincial governments in Eastern India about the local officials' tendency to arrest CPI activists, who were seen by many civil servants in the centre as being a useful weapon against Congress influence. See S. Bhattacharya, 'The Colonial State and the Communist Party of India, 1942–45: A Reappraisal', *SAR*, 15, 1, 1995, pp. 48–77.
91 CSFR(1) and (2), January 1943, Bihar, HPF(I) 18/1/43, NAI.
92 CSFR(1) and (2), May 1943, Orissa, HPF(I) 18/1/43, NAI.
93 CSFR(2), March 1943, Bihar, HPF(I) 18/3/43, NAI.
94 CSFR(2), June 1942, Bengal, HPF(I) 18/6/42, NAI.
95 Enclosure to letter from S.P. Mookerjee, Minister of Finance, G.O.Be, to A.K. Fazlul Huq, Chief Minister, G.O.Be, 16 November 1942, R/3/2/41, File 31, Collection II, OIOC.
96 Departmental memorandum, Home Department, GOI, 5 December 1942, R/3/2/41, File 31, Collection II, OIOC. Also see, secret letter from M. Hallett, Governor, GOUP to J. Herbert, Governor, G.O.Be, 28 November 1942, R/3/2/41, File 31, Collection II, OIOC.
97 See, for instance, *Amrita Bazar Patrika*, 24 November 1942.
98 Extract from proceedings of a meeting of the Council of Ministers held at Government House, Calcutta, 23 November 1942, R/3/2/41, File 31, Collection II, OIOC.
99 Transcript of phone message from J. Kirchner, Chief Press Adviser, GOI to Assistant Secretary, GOBe, 1 December 1942, R/3/2/41, File 31, Collection II, OIOC.
100 Departmental memorandum, Home Department, GOI, 5 December 1942, R/3/2/41, File 31, Collection II, OIOC.
101 Transcript of phone message from J. Kirchner, Chief Press Adviser, GOI to Assistant Secretary, GOBe, 1 December 1942, R/3/2/41, File 31, Collection II, OIOC.

102 Though the 'Hindu Press' was largely seen as being 'pro-Congress', the *Hindustan Times*, the *Hindu*, the *Free Press of India*, the *Amrita Bazar Patrika*, the *National Call* and the Searchlight were seen as 'leading disseminator[s] ... of Congress news and views'. Secret appreciation of the 'Congress Propaganda Machinery', Home Department, GOI, 2 June 1943, HPF(I) 3/47/43, NAI. For extracts of newspapers continuing covert 'anti-war propaganda', see HPF(I) 189/42, NAI.
103 Appendix to CSFR(1) May 1942, Bihar, HPF(I) 18/5/42, NAI.
104 Examples of instances of newspapers being 'warned' for transgressing official instructions in the Chief Secretaries' fortnightly reports to the Government of India. However, the unwillingness of the Provincial Press Advisers' to ban publications is strikingly represented by the attitude of the censors attached to the Government of Bihar in the month of June 1942, which was recognised as being a period of extreme strategic difficulty throughout Eastern India. Papers like the *Rashtravani* and the *Searchlight*, which were recognised as being hostile to British rule, were let off with a mere warning even after they published articles contravening the officially prescribed press instructions. See appendix to CSFR(1) June 1942, Bihar, 18/6/42, NAI.
105 See, for instance, note from B.J. Kirchner, Chief Press Adviser, GOI to R. Tottenham, Additional Secretary, Home Department, GOI, 6 February 1943, HPF(I) 7/15/42, NAI.
106 Provincial representatives attending a conference were unanimous in their recognition of the shortcomings of the 'security intelligence organisation' and their agreement that the local branches of the CID be strengthened during discussions of the importance of a 'stricter control' of the vernacular press in the localities. Secret minutes of CID conference held in Delhi between 9–11 March 1942, c.1942, HPF(I) 21/7/42, NAI.
107 Note from Commerce Department, GOI, 7 August 1943, HPF(I) 3/47/43, NAI.
108 See, for instance, reports sent to the Government of Bihar's Chief Secretary and the Provincial Press Adviser by district officials in the province in PPAF 4/1942, BSA; PPAF 11/1942, BSA; PPAF 20/1942, BSA, and PPAF 49/42, BSA.
109 Secret minutes of CID conference held in Delhi between 9–11 March 1942, c.1942, HPF(I) 21/7/42, NAI.
110 Departmental note by R. Tottenham, Additional Secretary, Home Department, GOI, c.March 1944, HPF(I) 20/1/44, NAI.
111 For instance, it was clearly stated that the special provisions of inland censorship imposed from 1 September 1943 to the south and east of the Brahmaputra river, as well as the east of the Ganges river, at the request of the Government of Bengal and Eastern Army HQ, was intended mainly to hinder information on troop movements and alarmist rumours, and 'ascertain the general feeling and morale of civilians in the operational area'. See, most secret WIS(II), 16 April 1943, L/WS/1/1433, OIOC.
112 See, for instance, correspondence between the district magistracy and local military commands, Bihar, United Provinces and Bengal, c.1943, WSF 65/1(i)/43, BSA.

Chapter Four
The Colonial State, 'Neutrals' and the Propaganda Campaign against the Indian National Congress 1939–1944

A great volume of the print and oral propaganda deployed by the British colonial state during the Second World War was intended to challenge the Indian National Congress, with the campaign being sought to be buttressed by the involvement of a range of 'neutral' organisations at different points of the conflict. This chapter examines the development of the official anti-Congress onslaught and the changes in this strategy upto 1944.

I. The nature of the official anti-Congress propaganda campaign

The Government of India's Home Department planned the official propaganda campaign against the Congress throughout 1942–44, whereas the central Information and Broadcasting Department, the publicity bodies attached to it and the provincial authorities were given a distributory role. This meant that their involvement remained limited to advising their own subordinates about the shifts in the course of the programme.

But, the 'negative propaganda' deployed against the Indian National Congress appeared to be at times inseparable from what was considered in government circles to be 'positive propaganda': the efforts to develop a specifically wartime nationalism through a discussion of the 'moral aspects' of the conflict, the industrial benefits gained by the 'nation' as a result of the war, and the inevitability of independence 'soon after' the victory was achieved. Even senior civil servants would, therefore, sometimes complain that it was difficult to separate 'the positive and the negative sides of ... [anti-Congress] propaganda', and a report prepared in 1943 wondered whether 'any attempt at positive political propaganda must inevitably be to a considerable extent preoccupied with attacking and endeavouring to undermine the Congress position'. The response of Richard Tottenham, the Additional Secretary to the Government of India's Home Department, to this query, in the form of a jotting along the margin of the document that contained it, was that while 'positive propaganda' might have the 'effect' of damaging the Congress stand 'it would not need to be openly & explicitly so'.[1]

The official propaganda blitz directed against the Congress thus had two distinct facets to begin with: one was an overt and undisguised attack against the party; whereas the other endeavoured to question its articulation of Indian nationalism during the Second World War while ostensibly debating 'general' issues. From the latter half of 1943, the efforts to counter the criticisms of this policy by a melange of indigenous political opinion became an integral part of the campaign itself.

The germs of this official campaign were visible as early as 1940–41, when the failure of the negotiations between the party's Working Committee and the Government of India resulted in Gandhi's decision to launch a civil disobedience movement. As the agitation did not take serious proportions, Frederick Puckle, the Secretary to the Government of India's Department of Information and Broadcasting, circulated a statement to the provincial publicity authorities in February 1941 detailing the 'particulars of the instances of violence ... [that] ha[d] occurred during the course of the Congress Satyagraha movement' with the advice that:

> You will notice that there are only 15 of them [instances of violence] and that by no means all are serious: Mr. Gandhi might indeed argue that to find only 15 instances in an agitation which has been going on for four months or so and has involved about 4,000 arrests, shows the strength of the control he exercises over it. It is therefore not suggested that you take any special steps to secure publicity for this list, but, if there should unfortunately be any fresh instance of violence in your Province, the list might afford to a friendly paper a convenient peg on which to hang a lecture of the dangers of 'Non-Violent' Civil Disobedience.[2]

The official attitude towards the Congress began stiffening after the Japanese entry into the war in December 1941, and culminated in the police raid on the Congress headquarters at Allahabad, UP, in May 1942. The minutes of the meetings held by the party's national executive regarding the strategic situation in the country were confiscated, and plans began to be drawn up about how best to deploy them in official publicity. The Home Department explained in June 1942 that:

> ... we must have our plans ready and one matter that we consider of prime importance is that public opinion in England and even more in America should be prepared well in advance for any strong action we may eventually decide to take [against the Congress]. We suggest that [the] Press in England and important American correspondents should be taken into confidence with [the] object of exposing Gandhi and [the] Congress.[3]

Consequently, official propaganda began to highlight the suggestion that the 'long-term object' of the Congress leadership, despite 'opportunist changes' to meet particular situations, was to establish a permanent 'Congress-Hindu-bourgeois domination' supported by the British army or a Congress-controlled Indian army. The Cripps mission's refusal to hand over control of the defence portfolio to the party, since the Government could not allow itself to be 'led' into allowing this, was described as the reason for the 'Congress hostility to [the] British connection'.[4]

In addition, the party's opposition to the war began to be characterised as a means adopted by its leaders to obtain a 'bargain by pressure' from the British government during a period of extreme crisis, which it was claimed, was further evidence of their willingness to 'make independent terms with Japan'. Three sets of 'proof' were constantly stressed. The first was the Congress's undisguised opposition to the 'scorched-earth policy'. This was publicised as being a senseless obstruction of defence preparations and attributed to the influence of big business upon Congress; business being reluctant to forego profits from war industries and keen to do 'business after Japanese occupation'. A second 'proof' was the frequent suggestion by 'elements' within the party that Japan and India had no mutual quarrels. The third was Gandhi's emphasis on non-violence, which was represented as a belief in 'no resistance at all'.[5]

As the Government of India had secretly drawn up plans to arrest the Congress leadership by the latter half of June 1942, primacy was now given to preparing 'public opinion' for such 'strong action'. This caused a significant shift in policy, and it was now considered beneficial to underline the sway that the party's leaders, especially Gandhi, held over the other members of the Provincial Congress Committee's and the cadres. The aim was to point out how far-reaching and dangerous a Congress-sponsored civil disobedience movement could be. Not surprisingly, official propaganda now concentrated on pointing out that Gandhi was at 'the centre of the political stage and ha[d] great political influence', adding that he was going to start a 'mass movement based on the exploitation of anti-British sentiment' whose purpose would be 'to embarrass in every possible way the war effort and the defence of India'. The Government's stance was publicised as a policy of 'wait and see', with the possibility of 'action' against the Congress as a part of the Allied strategy for the defence of India, which in turn was depicted as being an integral part of their strategy in the Far-East 'as a whole' and thus a 'vital factor' in the overthrow of Japan. In addition, the Congress's incapacity to speak for India 'as a whole' was also consistently emphasised, as was the forecast that if the British left there would be a civil war which would be the 'greatest single step that could be taken to menace the victory of the United Nations'.[6]

The debates within the Government of India, and especially the Home Department, about the appropriateness of the issues highlighted in communiqués and the timing of their release, began to intensify in the following weeks. Maxwell, the Home Member in the Viceroy's Executive Council, argued that a 'public pronouncement' should be made that if the Congress 'misbehaved' it would be the 'end of them as a political party' as far as the Government was concerned. The Viceroy questioned the validity of such a policy arguing that it was politically impractical. He declared that 'there was too much of the ostrich about that line',[7] and re-iterated in subsequent correspondence that even if 'measures' were taken against the Congress during the war:

> We cannot for ever ostracise a great political party which, misguided and malevolent as it may be, still has a first-class electoral machine and commands the votes (however obtained) of an immense preponderance of [the] Hindu population of this country....[8]

However, the Congress Working Committee's pronouncements at Wardha on 10 July 1942 caused the War Cabinet to endorse the Home Member's argument that it was necessary to follow a more aggressive line towards the party. The final resolution passed by it was considered to be:

> ... too serious to ignore. The Congress Working Committee, claiming the position of an authority parallel to that of the Government, deliberately instructed people to resist the Government's action in regard to measures such as the removal of boats or vehicles. This was an

intolerable challenge, and was made worse when read together with paragraph 4 of the Resolution which said that 'All restrictions on organisation[s] for self-protection should be disregarded.'[9]

As a result a directive to the provinces explained that:

> During this time [the three weeks before the Congress meeting on 7 August 1942] the matter is mainly a problem of propaganda to mobilise opinion against the concrete proposals contained in the Congress Resolution and Gandhi as 'open rebellion'. We have to (1) Encourage those on whose support we can depend (2) Win over waverers, and (3) Avoid stiffening the determination of Congressmen; with the object either of putting pressure on the Congress to withdraw from its position, or, if action has to be taken against Congress, to secure that such action has the support of the public opinion inside and outside India.[10]

It also advised that declarations be made that 'the people of India' could choose their form of government after the cessation of hostilities and that the proposed Congress campaign could only cause 'administrative anarchy', which would be a 'direct invitation' for Japan to invade the sub-continent. The Wardha resolutions were to be criticised as an 'impractical party manifesto', to which other parties did not subscribe and which had been based on a misrepresentation of the Cripps proposals. In addition, the 'communal tangle' and the Congress's unwillingness to address it, were to be emphasised by pointing out that Rajagopalachari had been forced to resign from the party for daring to suggest that an understanding with the Muslim League was achievable. Puckle, however, counselled caution in developing these themes and stated that:

> It would be advisable at the present stage to abstain from attacking the Congress too directly, e.g by calling it a Fifth Column, etc., and certainly to abstain from attacks on individuals.... For the moment the object is to mobilise public opinion against the Congress policy as detrimental to the successful conduct of the war. Loyalists and waverers may be assured that [the] Government has the means to deal suitably with trouble and intends to use them.[11]

As the relations between the two protagonists worsened further, the Government of India decided to release two sets of proceedings of a meeting of the Congress Working Committee confiscated from the Congress' Allahabad offices in May 1942. One was the original typescript of Gandhi's draft resolution, while the other consisted of the resolutions ultimately passed on behalf of the party and included the amendments proposed by Nehru. Officials in charge of publicity were advised to accord greater emphasis to the former document, since it contained the 'outstanding sentence' which declared that 'if India were freed her first step would probably be to negotiate with Japan'. They were warned however that the documents would be a:

> ... severe shock to Indian self-respect, particularly to a great number of educated Indians who though not 100% Congressmen, admired Gandhi as [a] great and saintly Indian and respect Congress as [a] great National Institution [sic]. Avoid therefore any attacks on the honour of Indians generally [and] sympathise with Indians as honourable people who had been deceived and badly let down by a small caucus of men who have either surrendered their judgement and honour blindly into Gandhi's hands or else have placed the achievements of narrow party ends before the true welfare of the country. Blame is on this small caucus only....[12]

Official publicity thus began to brand the majority of the Congress Working Committee as 'appeasers', while the rest (Nehru included) were presented as being 'only anxious that [the Congress] resolution should be so phrased that Congress position before world opinion would not be compromised'.[13] On 4 August 1942, a day before the release of the papers, a widely-advertised communiqué described among other things the various 'problems arising out of war conditions' and pointed out that:

> ... certain hardships must, in these circumstances, fall upon the civil population is, unfortunately, inevitable; nor is this a position that is confined to India. It is also probably true that instances have occurred in which some avoidable hardship has been caused. It has always been the policy of the Government of India, however, to reduce inconvenience to the public to the minimum. Nevertheless, advantage has been taken of the position to exploit for political purposes the inevitable hardships arising from the necessary preparation of defence against aggression and to incite people to defy the orders of the Government, a course which, if persisted in, must inevitably bring the authors into conflict with the law....[14]

The Congress leadership was arrested on 8 August 1942 and the action was publicised as being a 'preventive' one, brought about by the presence of 'ample evidence' that the party had meant mischief;

the evidence took the form of 'full instructions' for the organisation of 'violent activities' circulated by the Provincial Congress Committees.[15] Additionally, the 'uselessness' of setting up a 'national government' at the time was underlined by pointing out that though the Viceroy's Executive Council was not representative in the 'ordinary sense', it was however a Government of 'representative men ... who between them' could speak:

> ... for almost every element and every activity in the life of the country. They are as good nationalists as anyone, in that their aim is full freedom for India under a constitution devised by Indians; they are democratic, in that they believe in representative institutions and the liberty of the individual. A 'National Government', in the sense of a Government representative of political parties is not possible until at least some of the major political parties find a common basis on which they can come together to form a Government. The Viceroy's Council has such a common basis, the determination to fight this war to a victorious end....[16]

The disturbances that followed the arrests gave a new impetus to the campaign against the Congress. There was now a widespread agreement within the Home Department that the party must be 'indicted' by underlining its responsibility for all the major instances of violence. As the rather serious civil disorders continued into the second half of August, the party was attacked 'by exploiting the tragic fate of policemen and other Government servants who had been brutally done to death for no fault of their own except discharging their duty'.[17] Explaining the necessity for this policy, Puckle explained that:

> When order is restored, and the country returns to normal, one of the first things which we may expect is a press campaign against the excessive use of force in dealing with the disturbances. I consider this to be inevitable. On this ground alone, there would be considerable advantage in making known what barbarities have been committed by the rioters, and also how senseless and harmful to the community in general has been much of the destruction which they have wrought. An instance which I have in mind is the destruction of the Tuberculosis Clinic in Delhi, where the poor receive treatment and advice free.[18]

Tottenham's reaction to Puckle's suggestion was to complain about the limitations imposed by the necessity for secrecy in a difficult strategic situation on the efforts to expose the Congress' misdemeanours. In a departmental note he expostulated that:

We are placed between the Scylla of not publishing news that might be of value to the enemy and the Charybdis of hiding the seriousness of the situation and thus giving the impression both in India and abroad that the measures taken [against the Congress] have been unduly severe.... We obviously must settle policy in this matter. My opinion is that once the main communications have been reasonably restored and there is thus no danger of giving the Japanese the impression that the Eastern Provinces are cut off from reinforcements, we should lift the veil and allow a good deal more to be published of what has happened in Bihar....[19]

J. Natrajan, a senior civil servant attached to the Home Department, agreed with Tottenham and advised caution while criticising the Congress, lest some of the information released be useful to the Japanese. He 'strongly urge[d] postponement of this idea of lifting this veil until we are definitely out of the wood' and declared that it was 'important that neither the extent of the damage caused nor the punitive measures taken by [the] government should be widely publicised either in this country or abroad.' Nonetheless, anticipating criticism about the severity of the government's action, he advised that it be constantly publicised that the enemy was 'at the door', and that if the disturbances were allowed to spread they would have affected the war-effort. He added that for 'purposes of broadcasting general terms like 'severe penalties' or 'deterrent punishment' should be used. We should endeavour as far as possible to show that even under great provocation British methods are not as ruthless as Nazi methods'.[20]

Puckle supported Natrajan's arguments, even though they contradicted his earlier suggestion that the available 'proof' regarding the Congress' betrayal of the Allied war-aims be released immediately. He clarified that his earlier stance had been based on:

(a) the desirability of forestalling accusations of unnecessary severity in India,
(b) the desirability of dispelling the idea, which may be prevalent in England and America, that disturbances did not amount to much,
(c) the desirability again mainly for England but also for India and U.S.A. of clearing ourselves of the charge that behind a veil of secrecy, we were out-Hunning the Huns.

He further added that:

Perhaps we should do better to go slowly in lifting the veil and rather make revelations only when they are demanded of us, leaving the full story to be told when we are safely through our troubles. That need not prevent our collecting at once all the material that we can get and examining it to see whether it should be used and if so how best....[21]

The Government of India, as a result, concentrated on disseminating propaganda contradicting the more damaging allegations against the administration, while gradually increasing the output of information about the role of Congress members in the 'Quit India' upsurge that rocked parts of the country in the last quarter of 1942. A letter sent to the provinces explained that:

> It is generally known that [the] Government have taken and used most drastic powers, but the manifestations of violence against which these powers have had to be exercised have been largely concealed, with the result that the public both in India and abroad are in danger of forming an entirely wrong impression both of the situation itself and of the measures taken to restore order.... Further there is the fact that the forthcoming meeting of the Central Legislature will afford an opportunity for much criticism and 'atrocity-mongering' under the 'privilege' of the House, and even though steps can be and will be taken to prevent its repetition in the Press, an impression may well be caused which the Government spokesmen may find it difficult to dispel within the time at their disposal unless a fuller picture of events has previously found its way into the Press.

Thus:

> ... some change is necessary in the direction of gradually giving greater publicity to what has occurred. The necessity for suppressing news that would be of value or comfort of the enemy remains; even if the 'imitation' danger has receded, there is still danger of provoking competition with what has occurred elsewhere. This risk must be accepted; but both it and the military danger can be minimised, while securing the main object of 'lifting the veil' to a certain extent....[22]

This meant, in practice, that all references to the damage suffered by military installations and 'important factories' involved in war production were avoided. Moreover, announcements that communications had been disrupted by Congress-led mobs were mentioned only after the damage had been repaired. Similarly, the threat posed by the movement to 'public utility' concerns and the difficulties caused in transporting essential commodities were referred to in 'general terms', and only after the situation had been brought under control, and all 'occurrences' were described without giving place names. Great effort was also spent in propagating articles and 'stories' about the murders of Government officials, the 'wanton destruction of valuable and useful property' and the cases where the 'public' co-operated in quelling disorders.[23]

By February 1943 the Government of India's Home Department considered the strategic situation to have improved sufficiently enough to release its 'case' against the Congress. In the form of a pamphlet titled *Congress Responsibility for the Disturbances, 1942–43*, it declared that:

> In response to demands which have reached Government from several sources, Government have now prepared a review which brings together a number of facts, whether derived from official documents or otherwise, bearing on the responsibility of Mr. Gandhi and the Congress High Command for the disturbances which followed the sanctioning of a mass movement by the AICC on August 8th, 1942. Almost all the facts presented in this review are, or should be, already within the knowledge of the public. The review does not purport to disclose all the information in the possession of the Government. In addition to the facts here stated, there is a large volume of evidence which it is undesirable to publish at present.

The document had six chapters which dealt with the background of the Quit-India movement, the motives of the Congress's Wardha and the Bombay resolutions, the 'contemplated character' of the movement, the nature of the disturbances and the part played by known Congressmen. Not unexpectedly, the draft resolutions by Gandhi were given the greatest prominence amongst all the documents confiscated in Allahabad the previous year, and were described as 'important evidence as to the working of his mind, and the reactions of the members of the Working Committee'.[24] It was also pointed out that the 'composite picture of the projected movement, as it emerged from Gandhi's writings or statements ... and from the speeches of Congress leaders' was that violence was planned and this would include:

> ... all possible forms of mass demonstration and was to be marked by a defiance of Government authority; individual items were to include interference with communications including the stopping and sabotaging of railways, interference with troop movements, the cutting of telegraph and telephone wires, incitement to strikes and the fomentation

of no-tax and no-rent campaigns, and efforts to suborn the police, the military, and Government servants as a whole from their allegiance.[25]

The pamphlet concluded that:

> In the face of all this evidence ... the evidence of the atmosphere produced by Mr. Gandhi's writings in the 'Harijan', the evidence of the speeches of the members of the Working Committee before and at Bombay, the evidence of the programmes involving violent action, the evidence of the pamphlets broadcast in the name of the Congress – only one answer can be given to the question as to who must bear the responsibility for the mass uprisings and individual crimes which have disgraced and are still disgracing the fair name of India.... [T]he Indian National Congress, under the leadership of Mr. Gandhi.[26]

Since the document was made available to the public during Gandhi's fast to protest at his arrest, some officials doubted the appropriateness of the timing of its release. One bureaucrat complained that:

> The whole theme [of the pamphlet] is directed primarily against Mr. Gandhi himself, and he is attacked in strong terms ... [T]he reactions to publishing the booklet at the present moment are to be considered. It will certainly rouse indignation among nearly all sections of the Indian public, and nobody will read it with a sufficiently cool head to take in its arguments. Government will be charged with 'hitting a man when he is down'.[27]

Other senior officials disagreed with this view, and one's rejoinder was that, 'The object of the document is to inform the public not only in India but also abroad and I do not see how the revelation of necessary facts can be made dependent on Mr Gandhi's life or death.'[28] Tottenham's support for the release of the pamphlet was reflected in his advice to maintain the collection of 'public evidence' for inclusion in a future issue of the document.[29] The first edition was 'widely' distributed: 66 copies were sent to 'accredited press correspondents'; 220 to the 'principal newspapers in all languages'; 158 to the members of the central legislature; 45 to the members of the National Defence Council; 265 to the officials of the National War Front; 96 to the various branches of All India Radio; 35 to various libraries throughout the country, and 253 to persons overseas.[30] In addition, 200 were sold through the Government of India Book Depot in Calcutta, while its branches in Assam, Bihar, United Provinces and Orissa sold 50 copies each. Subsequently, a further 4,300 were sold by the Central Bureau of Public Information and its agents.[31] The provincial publicity authorities were also given copies,[32] with the instructions that they translate and publish the pamphlet in 'local vernaculars'.[33] The Government of Orissa, for instance, printed and distributed 1,000 copies in Oriya.[34]

The Government of India released another publication in 1943, which also purported to prove the Congress's guilt. Titled *Some Facts About The Disturbances, 1942–43*, it described the attacks on railway lines, government servants, 'bomb outrages', 'senseless destruction' of property and other 'atrocities', and contained photographs of the damage wrought by the agitators. One paragraph went thus:

> From economic boycott to cold blooded murder, Government servants were called upon to suffer every torture that mobs could devise, and for no better reason than that they ... were true to their salt.... All kinds of weapons were used – stones and bottles, daggers, spears, arrows and guns and even kerosene for burning Government servants alive.[35]

In addition, official propaganda began to highlight some 'new points' in 1943. 'Important Congressmen' who were in hiding were linked to the disturbances by pointing out that they had not condemned the disorder, and it was underlined that the 'important members' of the Congress Socialist Party and the Forward Bloc who had taken part in the unrest were also members of the All India Congress Committee. It was hoped that this would serve the 'dual purpose' of 'exploding' the theory that 'orthodox Congress leaders' were not responsible for the outrages committed in 1942 and assist in 'developing the point made by the CPI that these two [the CSP and the Forward Bloc] are the real 'Fifth Columnists' and thus, incidentally, forcing the CPI itself into open opposition to at least the Congress Left-Wing'.[36]

The other new constituents of the official propaganda campaign were underlined in a set of 'guidance notes' sent by the central Home Department to the provinces in April 1943. The information contained in the document was in large measure a riposte to the criticisms that had surfaced about the pamphlets released earlier in the year, and advertised the 'countrywide demand' for the publications and the accuracy of the sources on which they were based.[37] The Governments of Bengal, United Provinces, Assam, Orissa and Bihar distributed these notes among their government servants, the provincial Public Relations Committees and publicity departments and officials of the National War Front, to serve as a basis for oral propaganda.[38] Considered a great success, a second set was brought out in October 1943 and contained, once again, information regarded as useful for countering the attacks being directed against the Government for its policy towards the Congress. For instance, there was now a common accusation that the Congress's responsibility for the events of 1942 had not been proved before an impartial judicial tribunal; in reply it was pointed out that the 'tribunal of world opinion' had passed its verdict. The decision not to release Gandhi and the Working Committee was justified by mentioning that they had not withdrawn the threat of rebellion, and that:

> It is easy [for the Congress] to come out of jail and make speeches criticising 'authoritarian government' making capital out of the food situation and deploring the absence of a 'national Government'; but what is one to think when the slightest attempt to sink differences for a common purpose, even in a single Province, is immediately condemned as 'likely to destroy the tradition of democratic rule'?[39]

By the end of 1943 some officials in the Home Department began to encourage an intensification of the campaign against the party. S.J.L. Olver, the Under Secretary, proposed that a 'separate Home Department organisation' be established to co-ordinate a 'direct attack on the Congress'. He supported Maxwell's argument that 'the most important' propaganda aim was to discredit Gandhi and the rest of the Congress Working Committee, with a view to encouraging a revolt against their leadership.[40] Tottenham advised caution, and explained that 'the general object is to develop the *positive* side [of propaganda] in the hope that this may gradually reduce the necessity of pursuing the *negative* (a directly anti-Congress) side. We are still left with the question of what *negative* anti-Congress propaganda we can and should continue with our existing resources.'[41] Tottenham supported the Chief Press Adviser's suggestions that they concentrate on 'certain essentials' rather than 'making purely debating points here and there over a wide field'. His recommendation was to give primacy to 'particular features' of Congress publicity and counter them 'in season and out of season'. He advised they should highlight the importance of the Cripps' offer and the Congress's role in turning it down, and at every opportunity debunk the declarations that the party's August Resolutions were intended to help the war-effort and the view that the Government was responsible for the political deadlock. Significantly, Tottenham asked the government publicists constantly to re-iterate that 'the majority' of the All India Congress

Committee were now free and could 'act' on behalf of the party.[42] Kirchner, the Chief Press Adviser, backed these views and proposed that only the Congress leaders (not the party itself) be discredited by continuously advertising the papers seized in Allahabad in 1942 as well as the 'Published statements during the period 1937–1939 showing the totalitarian outlook of the Congress high-command when Congress ministries were in power. The cases of Dr Khare and Mr Nariman can be cited to show what happened to Congress leaders who dared to take their own line and that the ministries were merely puppet ministries.'[43]

Describing the propaganda policy for 1944 to the Information and Broadcasting Department, Tottenham explained that:

> ... the main object of our political propaganda should be to develop some positive or constructive line (the first attempt in that direction is the stimulation of controversy about the form of India's future constitution) and thus gruadulally [sic] reduce the necessity for destructive or purely anti-Congress propaganda. At the same time anti-Congress propaganda, for which the Home Department must continue to be responsible, cannot be entirely neglected....[44]

In June 1944 the Home Department sanctioned the release of the full text of the correspondence between Gandhi and Linlithgow to counter doubts that certain facts had not been disclosed by the Government of India.[45] From this point onwards the propaganda aiming to 'prove' the Congress's responsibility for the disturbances of 1942, and the consequent dislocation of the war-effort, began to be gradually toned down. Archibald Wavell's administration veered round to the view, in the second half of 1944, that it would be impossible to ignore the Congress leadership in the inevitable negotiations after the war. Tottenham remarked, in a reference to this, that:

> ... the decision on the Wickenden Report [the report prepared in the aftermath of the 'Quit India' movement of August 1942] not to take any definite steps to bring home to the Congress leaders their responsibility for the August rebellion also implies the eventual return to legitimacy of the Indian National Congress itself and the abandonment of any idea of attempting to destroy it as a political organisation....

He added that official propaganda about the Congress would now have to address:

... the further consideration, which ... ha[d] never been made sufficiently clear to the public in India ... that Government are not opposed to any political organisation, including Congress, or to the national aspirations which inspires it, provided that it acts in a constitutional manner. All that we are opposed to and that we shall continue to resist and repress with all our power is [sic] the illegal methods which Congress, under Gandhi's leadership, ha[d] chosen to employ for the attainment of their objects and which ha[d] invariably led to violence and suffering and ha[d] retarded rather than promoted the cause of Indian freedom.[46]

The propaganda campaign against the Congress was thus abandoned in early 1945, and official publicity relating to the Congress and its attitude towards the war would now comprise of denials, and sometimes justifications for, the state's repressive policies between 1942 and 1944.

II. A Successful Public Relations Campaign?

The aims of the official propaganda campaign against the Indian National Congress between 1942 and 1944 – which essentially amounted to destroying the 'political legitimacy' of the party in the eyes of 'national and international opinion' – remained largely unfulfilled. Although the scheme was considered to be a success till August 1942, because it had encouraged some 'public men' and 'non-Congress organisations' to criticise the Congress Working Committee's 'Quit-India' resolutions at Bombay,[47] its ultimate value remained distinctly suspect. Despite the best efforts of the Government of India, the credibility of the Congress amongst its traditional constituencies remained unimpaired, no national or provincial faction within the party dared to revolt against the imprisoned Working Committee. In addition, the Central Working Committees of the other primary political parties, despite often being at odds with Congress policy, refused to endorse the government's attack against the organisation. Instead, it can be very credibly argued that the state's propaganda onslaught against the Congress had quite the opposite effect. At one level it encouraged a broad spectrum of opinion, including in many cases those opposed to the Congress standpoint, to criticise the Government of India. The discontinuation of the official attack against the Congress was to a great extent a result of this phenomenon, as the authorities discovered to their dismay that none of the established political organisations found it desirable to offer the scheme unabashed support.

Particularly revealing in this regard are the reactions of the Muslim League, the Hindu Mahasabha and the Communist Party of India to the Government of India's Home Department's pamphlet, *Congress Responsibility for the Disturbances, 1942–43*. The League labelled it as 'at best the prosecution's case containing a jumble of quotations that c[ould] be verified only by hearing the defence which [wa]s beyond the ... policy of the Government of India', while the *Vishwa Bandhu*, a pro-Mahasabha paper, declared that all its quotations from the *Harijan* had 'been torn out of context and used arbitrarily'.[48] The *People's War*, the CPI's English mouthpiece, was by far the most critical in this regard and called the publication a 'miserable stunt', adding that:

> Finding that international opinion is quickly rallying for the release of Mahatma Gandhi to save him from the jaws of death, the Government of India have come out with their charge-sheet against the Indian National Congress .... [in which] the Government relies on quoting Gandhiji out of context and seeks to make out a case through sheer suppression of the real meaning....[49]

Another article in the paper insisted that the pamphlet was:

> a piece ... full of misrepresentations and misleading statements.... Full of contradictory statements, assertions without facts and allegations without evidence, it fails to establish any charge against the Congress except the one of being a patriotic organisation and demanding a National Government to defend a country. Not only does it fail as a justification of Government policy towards the Mahatma and the Congress, but the appendix reproducing Congress resolutions of May, July and August constitute the biggest indictment of government's policy and show that the Government in attacking the Congress attacked the major anti-Axis force in the country.[50]

The Communist leadership's refusal to criticise the Congress Working Committee and accuse it of impeding the war remained particularly galling to the authorities. This caused the central Intelligence Bureau to complain, for instance, that the CPI had remained loyal to the 'pro-war' policy 'in their own peculiar fashion' after the outbreak of the 'Quit India' movement of August 1942.[51] Contrary to official hopes, Communist criticism of the government in this regard continued unmitigated. A report prepared by the military authorities in 1943 regarding the activities of the party since the lifting of the ban stated that its members were primarily concerned with 'appeasing' the Congress and that their promises of support to the administration had 'proved illusory'. The review also declared that the *People's War* 'has not hesitated to impute to Government motives of so scandalous a nature as to be more suggestive of Axis propaganda than political cooperation.'[52] On one hand this caused officials based in the localities to impede Communist activism whenever possible. On the other hand, it forced the Government of India to review its policy of attempting to deploy the CPI against the Congress, and finally to suspend these efforts in 1944.[53]

In addition, the nationalist diatribe against the colonial authorities was kept up by the sections of the 'All-India' press allied, or sympathetic, to the Congress, who took advantage of the Government of India's unwillingness to deploy comprehensive bans against them to consistently contradict the official criticisms of the party's stance and maintain a potent publicity onslaught against an 'alien' Raj. Official reports pointed out, for instance, how articles in the *Hindustan Times* had been repeatedly accusing the official publicity organisations of using 'considerable funds' to maintain an illegal vendetta against the Congress.[54] An editorial in the paper, which was representative of the tone of its disapprobation of the authorities, declared that:

> ... we are firmly convinced that whatever justification there may have been for the many-sided activities of the Information (Propaganda) Department, it now become a white elephant, and that its present activity can only corrupt the channels of thought and opinion in an attempt to perpetuate the present irresponsible and unnatural regime. When India attains her freedom the first task of the National Government will be to undo the mischief wrought so cunningly and for so long.[55]

The gradual release of the imprisoned Congress Committee members from the second half of 1944 caused increasing attention to be given to the 're-organisation' of the party machinery,[56] which in turn increased the criticism targeted against the authorities.[57]

The isolation of the colonial authorities, ranged against a variety of nationalist opposition, was powerfully illustrated by the Congress's and Muslim League's united demand in March 1945 that the National War Front, a body sponsored by the Government of India, be abolished. The issue was raised in the Legislative Assembly and Abdul Qaiyum (Congress) declared that the Front needed to be disbanded as it was utilised primarily against the 'popular political parties' rather than the Axis powers. The League's representatives agreed with this view and one, Yamin Khan, moved a resolution demanding the 'liquidation' of the official publicity organisation. This was successfully carried by 55 votes to 43. Explaining the Muslim League's stance in this regard, Liaquat Ali Khan, the Deputy Leader of the party, declared that though their intention was not to impede the war-effort, they objected to the 'prostitution of the National War Front by interested people'.[58] Significantly, a review of the working of the Front, which complained that it had failed to 'capture [the] public imagination and support', blamed its sorry state on the 'complete indifference' of the Indian political parties towards it.[59]

The wartime propaganda campaign against the Congress also underlined the widening of the existing cracks, as well as the creation of new ones, within the edifice of the colonial administration and its network of indigenous allies. Significantly, the Government of India's Home Department, which pushed for the deployment of the scheme, was forced to take responsibility for the running of the scheme throughout 1942–44, because the Information and Broadcasting Department, which was dominated by Indian civil servants, was reported to be uncomfortable with it.[60] Moreover, a senior Indian civil servant like Vishnu Sahay was excluded from the teams within the central Home Department teams that were made responsible for preparing this propaganda.[61] The difficulties experienced in maintaining the attack against the Congress were, however, particularly marked at the various levels of the provincial administration, not least because of the local civil servants' dependence on assistance from a variety of powerful rural notables, who expected the party to play a prominent role after the war.[62] For instance, reports about the nature of official vernacular publicity material produced within the provinces would routinely complain how a range of honorifics were used while referring to the members of the Congress Working Committee, especially Gandhi, in material intended to attack them.[63] Similarly, reports would mention how local papers allied to, or even sponsored by, the authorities would often refuse to follow the central Home Department's guidelines about how to depict the party's role. A notable instance of this was the *Indian Nation* in Bihar, whose tendency to publish sympathetic reports on the 'Quit India' movement forced the authorities to ultimately ban its publication.[64] References to the increased erosion of indigenous support in the province also frequently cropped up during the debates about the efficacy of attempting to utilise Communist assistance during a difficult strategic situation.[65]

All these trends also had the effect of straining the relationship between the British and Indian elements of the colonial administration: a survey of the correspondence sent by British civilian and military officials posted in the localities reveals that Indian attitudes towards the Congress made them very uneasy about the fluidity of the political situation. Indeed, military intelligence had begun to sporadically refer to the increased prevalence of collusion between junior Indian district officials – especially policemen – and local Congress activists from 1942 onwards.[66] Reports of such developments preyed on the minds of a succession of senior government officials in New Delhi; Wavell's fears about the rapid erosion of British power in the sub-continent were regularly echoed by Mountbatten's reports to London. There can be little doubt that the failed attempt at isolating the Congress leadership, and the insights this policy provided to the Government of India about the wartime weakening of its administrative edifice, often through the medium of special censorship networks, contributed to the British willingness to start negotiations for the transfer of power in India. Interestingly, the effects of these developments, especially that of the government's back-tracking with regards to the policy against the Congress, on the indigenous elements of the British Indian army contributed further to official discomfiture about the political situation. This aspect is examined in the next chapter.

Notes

1 Departmental note by S.J.L. Olver, Under Secretary, Home Department, GOI, 21 December 1943, HPF(I) KW to 43/4/44, NAI.
2 Confidential letter from F. Puckle, Secretary, Information of Broadcasting Department, GOI to all provincial publicity authorities, 28 February 1941, HPF(I) 3/10/40, NAI.
3 Telegram from the Home Department, GOI to L. Amery, SSI, GOBr, 7 June 1942, L/PJ/8/596, OIOC.
4 Ibid.
5 Ibid.
6 Secret telegram from L. Amery, SSI, GOBr, to the GOI, 18 June 1942, L/PJ/8/596, OIOC.
7 Extract from private letter from Linlithgow, Viceroy to L. Amery, SSI, GOBr, 15 June 1942, L/PJ/8/596, OIOC.
8 Secret telegram from Linlithgow, the Viceroy to L. Amery, SSI, GOBr, 26 June 1942, L/PJ/8/596, OIOC.

9 Extract from War Cabinet Conclusions 91(42), 13 July 1942, L/PJ/8/596, OIOC.
10 Confidential letter from F. Puckle, Secretary, Information and Broadcasting Department, GOI to the Chief Secretaries of all provincial governments, 17 July 1942, HPF(I) 33/53/42, NAI.
11 Ibid.
12 Secret telegram from the Information and Broadcasting Department, GOI to L. Amery, SSI, GOBr, 3 August 1942, L/I/1/756, OIOC.
13 Ibid.
14 Press communiqué released by the Government of India, 4 August 1942, L/I/1/756, OIOC.
15 Note by R. Tottenham, Additional Secretary, Home Department, GOI, 10 August 1942, HPF(I) 3/29/42, NAI.
16 Confidential letter from E. Conran-Smith, Secretary, GOI to all provincial governments and administrations, 11 August 1942, HPF(I) 3/29/42, NAI.
17 Letter from R. Tottenham, Additional Secretary, GOI to F. Puckle, Secretary, Information and Broadcasting Department, GOI, 24 August 1942, KW to HPF(I) 3/107/42, NAI.
18 Letter from F. Puckle, Secretary, Information and Broadcasting Department, GOI to R. Tottenham, Additional Secretary, Home Department, GOI, 26 August 1942, KW to HPF(I) 3/107/42, NAI.
19 Note by R. Tottenham, Additional Secretary, Home Department, GOI, 27 August 1942, HPF(I) 3/29/42, NAI.
20 Note by J. Natrajan, Home Department, GOI, 31 August 1942, HPF(I) 3/29/42, NAI.
21 F. Puckle's comments on J. Natrajan's note, 31 August 1942, HPF(I) 3/29/42, NAI [emphasis original].
22 Confidential letter from the Home Department, GOI to all provincial governments, 6 September 1942, HPF(I) 3/107/42 & KW, NAI.
23 Ibid.
24 *Congress Responsibility For The Disturbances 1942–43*, Delhi, 1943, pp. 1–3.
25 *Ibid*, p. 21.
26 *Ibid*, p. 41.
27 Note by W.H. Suamarez Smith, GOI, 18 February 1943, HPF(I) 3/79/42, Part II, NAI.
28 Note by R.M. Maxwell, Home Member, V.E.C., GOI, 18 February 1943, HPF(I) 3/79/42, Part II, NAI.
29 Note by R. Tottenham, Additional Secretary, Home Department, GOI, 24 February 1943, HPF(I) 33/15/43, NAI.
30 Statement on the distribution of the pamphlet [*Congress Responsibility For The Disturbances, 1942–43*], c.1943, KW IX to HPF(I) 3/79/42, NAI.
31 Statement showing the receipt and sale of the pamphlet [*Congress Responsibility For The Disturbances, 1942–43*], c.1943, KW IX to HPF(I) 3/79/42, NAI. The central Home Department arranged for the pamphlet to be translated into Hindi and Urdu, and offered them for sale at the price of 2 *annas* each. Express and confidential letter from R. Tottenham, Additional Secretary, Home Department, GOI to all provincial governments, 16 March 1943, ibid.

32 By February 1943, 2,950 copies of the pamphlet were prepared by the Home Department. Of these, Bengal was sent 51 copies, Bihar was provided with 26, while Assam and Orissa were sent 16 each. KW IX to HPF(I) 3/79/42, NAI.
33 Express and confidential letter from R. Tottenham, Additional Secretary, Home Department, GOI to all provincial governments, 16 March 1943, KW IX to HPF(I) 3/79/42, NAI.
34 Statement of work done by Provincial [Orissa] War Committee during the period from June to August 1943, MSS EUR E. 360/20, I.H. Macdonald papers, OIOC.
35 *Some Facts About The Disturbances, 1942–43*, New Delhi, c.1943, p. 1.
36 Note by R. Tottenham, Additional Secretary, Home Department, GOI, 25 March 1943, HPF(I) 33/15/43, NAI.
37 Appendix to letter from R. Tottenham, Additional Secretary, Home Department, GOI to all Chief Secretaries and Chief Commissioners, 30 April 1943, HPF(I) 33/15/43, NAI.
38 Letter from Bengal Secretariat, GOBe, to Home Department, GOI, 10 May 1943, HPF(I) 33/15/43, NAI. Also see letter from Civil Secretariat, GOUP. to the Home Department, GOI, 15 May 1943; letter from GOA to the Home Department, GOI, 22 May 1943; letter from the GOO to the Home Department, GOI, 24 May 1943, and letter from GOB to Home Department, GOI, 26 May 1942, ibid.
39 Appendix to confidential express letter from R. Tottenham, Additional Secretary, Home Department, GOI to all provincial governments and Chief Commissioners, 11 October 1943, HPF(I) 33/15/43, NAI.
40 Departmental note by S.J.L. Olver, Under Secretary, Home Department, GOI, 21 December 1943, HPF(I) KW to 48/4/44, NAI.
41 Departmental note by R. Tottenham, Additional Secretary, Home Department, GOI, 30 December 1943, HPF(I) KW to 48/4/44, NAI. [emphases in quotation original].
42 Ibid.
43 Note by B.J. Kirchner, Chief Press Adviser, GOI, 4 January 1944, KW to 48/4/44, NAI.
44 Secret departmental note from R. Tottenham, Additional Secretary, Home Department, GOI to P.N. Thapar, Information and Broadcasting Department, GOI, 7 January 1944, HPF(I) 112/43, NAI.
45 Letter from P.N. Thapar, Information and Broadcasting Department, GOI to J. Hennessy, Information Officer with Agent General for India in the USA, L/I/1/1133, OIOC.
46 Departmental note by R. Tottenham, Additional Secretary, GOI, 4 December 1944, HPF(I) 4/7/44, NAI.
47 Confidential letter from Home Department, GOI to all provincial governments and administrations, 11 August 1942, HPF(I) 3/29/42, NAI.
48 Reactions to the pamphlet entitled 'Congress Responsibility for Disturbances', KW IV to HPF(I) 3/79/42, NAI.
49 *People's War*, 28 February 1943.
50 *People's War*, 14 March 1943.
51 Summary of Communist Activity, Intelligence Bureau surveys for August and September 1942, HPF(I) 7/5/42, NAI.

52 Appendix A to WIS (II), 2 April 1943, L/WS/1/1433, OIOC. Similar complaints were also regularly visible in reports and memoranda prepared within the Government of India's Intelligence Bureau. See, for instance, note by S.J.L. Olver, Under Secretary, Home Department, GOI, 27 October 1943, HPF(I) 7/23/43, NAI.
53 The officials in the localities were acutely aware of the fact that the activities of CPI's cadres within their spheres of authority were informed more by the widespread economic privations among the rural poor caused by the war, rather than the internationalism which usually informed the programmes of the members of the party politbureau. Faced with a shortage of manpower, the local bureaucracies considered the Communists to be dangerous allies throughout 1942–45, and refused them the space for independent political action whenever possible. See S. Bhattacharya, 'The Colonial State And The Communist Party Of India, 1942–45: A Reappraisal', *SAR*, Vol. 15, No. 1, 1995, pp. 62–77.
54 Personal letter from P.N. Thapar, Information and Broadcasting Department, GOI, to J. Hennessy, Information Officer with the Agent General for India in the USA, 22 June 1944, L/I/1/1133, OIOC.
55 Quoted in personal letter from S.S. Bajpai, Information and Broadcasting Department, GOI to J. Hennessy, Information Officer with the Agent General for India in the USA, 7 September 1944, L/I/1/1133, OIOC.
56 Secret telegram from C.J.E. Auchinleck, Commander-in-Chief, India, to the War Office, GOBr, 30 October 1944, L/WS/1/1248, OIOC.
57 For detailed discussions of attacks made by the *Hindustan Times* and the *Amrita Bazar Patrika* against the colonial administration see HPF(I) 44/93/44, NAI, and HPF(I) 3/22/1945, NAI. Descriptions of the official reactions to the publicity blitz maintained by the pro-Congress papers against the state are available in HPF(I) 3/47/43, NAI.
58 Summary of proceedings of the legislative assembly for week ending 3 March 1945, L/I/1/842, OIOC.
59 Personal and confidential memorandum from J. Joyce, India Office, GOBr to A. Wavell, Viceroy, 17 December 1943, L/I/1/842, OIOC.
60 Departmental memorandum by S.J.L. Olver, Under Secretary, Home Department, GOI, 21 December 1943, KW to HPF(I) 48/4/44, NAI. The Information and Broadcasting Department was staffed mainly by Indians, who worked under the supervision of Frederick Puckle. See letter from B.W. Rowe, War Office, GOBr to A.F. Morley, India Office, GOBr, 12 April 1943, L/I/1/671, OIOC.
61 See, for instance, transcript of taped interview with V. Sahay, ICS, MSS EUR T 122, OIOC.
62 See, for instance, letter from R.P.N. Sahi, Deputy Commissioner, Chota Nagpur Division, GOB to E.O. Lee, Commissioner, Chota Nagpur Division, GOB, 15 May 1942, WSF 17 (xix)/1942, BSA. The frequency of reports about such problems increased dramatically in 1943, a period when the Government of India's anti-Congress publicity onslaught was supposed to be at its height. Indeed, the recurring refusal of members of the subordinate services and loyalist wartime organisations to criticise the Congress Central and Provincial Working Committee members caused much nervousness – and frustration – amongst senior civilian and military

officials in the districts. See, extracts from secret reports by District Magistrates in Bihar, Eastern United Provinces and Assam, c.1943, WSF 63/iii/43, BSA.
63 See, for instance, letter from N. Senapati, Joint Secretary, GOB to Y.A. Godbole, Chief Secretary, GOB, 24 April 1943, PPAF 49/42, BSA.
64 See letter from N. Senapati, Joint Secretary, GOB to S.J.L. Olver, Under Secretary, Home Department, GOI, 27 October 1942, PPAF 11/1942, BSA.
65 See, for instance, note by S.J.L. Olver, Under Secretary, Home Department, GOI, 27 October 1943, HPF(I) 7/23/43, NAI.
66 For instance, an intelligence report (dated 3 September 1942) from Bihar mentioned how a military party which had gone to the village Dariagawan to arrest Jagannath Singh, the local Congress leader who also happened to be the son of the local rural magnate, found that he had escaped the previous night, since the news of his forthcoming capture had been 'leaked out' by local officials. Similar incidents were also reported from the villages Chatran and Barnia. Secret military (daily) intelligence summaries, 27 August 1942 to 8 September 1942, Stanton-Ife papers, CSASA.

Chapter Five

Propaganda, Censorship and the British Indian Army: Eastern India 1942–45

A secret note penned by the British Indian army's representative in Ramgarh – a major American and Chinese base in the province of Bihar – for the local civilian administration in mid-1943 explained that the Allied war-effort against Japan was dependent on 'moral resolve, discipline and effective provisioning.'[1] Such views were, of course, by no means isolated in official circles; wartime state policies of propaganda and information, which were designed by the GHQ (India) to supply, watch and mobilise Indian and British military personnel, were intended to ensure all three needs. This chapter describes the main features and uses of the publicity and censorship schemes deployed within army detachments based in Eastern India between 1942 and 1945.[2]

I. The Provision of Food Supplies and Health Facilities

As in the case of the civilian audiences in Eastern India, the efficient provision of food and medical facilities during the disturbed economic conditions between 1942 and 1945 proved to be an extremely significant component of the state's propaganda activities within the army. Therefore, the creation of adequate supply mechanisms for military detachments in the region was given great primacy despite the difficulties faced. The challenges encountered by the authorities were complex. For instance, while barracking arrangements could, and were, tackled by the requisitioning of land and buildings for military use, the stabilisation of food supplies and medical aid proved much more complicated. The impracticability of relying wholly on local food reserves became quickly obvious, not just because of the effects of the economic dislocation and political fallout it caused, but also due to the scale of expansion of the Allied forces and the difficulties imposed by the very nature of terrain of the main battlefronts. Indeed, the deeply forested and relatively unpopulated areas bordering Burma made the local collection of food a laborious, if not impossible, process. Moreover, the disease ecology of this region began to inflict a very large number of casualties amongst Allied units, thereby affecting their battle-worthiness.

The early onset of the monsoon in 1942 postponed the prospect of a Japanese invasion, allowing the panic caused within military circles by the strategic reverses of early 1942 to subside, and the GHQ (India) to prepare more considered defensive plans, move additional troops to the front and provide them with improved facilities. An important aspect of this were the measures intended to improve the food supply situation, which was sought to be bolstered by the rapid expansion of the infrastructure capable of preparing dried rations that could be easily transported to the front-line.[3] The scale of developments is illustrated, amongst other things, by the increasing scope of the activities of the Military Food Laboratory in Kasauli. This organisation, which was only involved in arranging for the production of dried potatoes for the troops in India in 1940, was by 1943 overseeing the production of a range of dried vegetables and meat, as well as a variety of tinned food, in over sixty factories. Thus, by the end of the year, GHQ (India) was able to ensure the production and distribution of thousands of tons of dehydrated vegetables: one estimate declared that 88,271,360 pounds of tinned meat, 22,400 pounds of dehydrated meat and 60,480,000 pounds of tinned milk were provided to the front. These food stocks were bolstered with supplies collected with the assistance of the Government of India's agencies, which could take the form of fresh foods like meat, chicken, fruit, vegetables, milk and eggs purchased locally, or supplies produced in special units set up and supervised by the central Food Department. The mode of sharing responsibility is well represented by the way the burden of the Quarter Master General's 1944 indent for dried meat was distributed. Of the 3,200 tons each of *jhatka* and *halal* goat meat required, the Food Department, GOI, undertook the responsibility for providing 600 tons of *jhatka* meat and 750 tons of *halal* meat. Other modifications were, of course, introduced, especially as the improved strategic position allowed more Allied shipping lines to be opened. Increasing amounts of meat began to be imported, especially from America, and the stockpiling of such supplies was assisted by the creation of a large cold storage system in 1944. This allowed the distribution of imported frozen, instead of locally slaughtered fresh, meat to troops attached to SEAC.[4] The military authorities were able to ensure the regular movement of these supplies to selected points, usually railheads, near the front due to the colonial state's wartime policy of according absolute priority to their requirements on all forms of transport.[5]

The development of schemes intended to tackle the medical challenges thrown up in Eastern India proved more difficult, not least because of the high rates of disease that had caused a steep increase in the number of non-battle casualties, particularly in the front-line (see Table 5.1 below).

The resultant expansion of the military medical services has been described in one source as a 'continuous struggle against the handicaps imposed by shortages of medical manpower, equipment and stores.'[6] Indeed, the deficiency in personnel was so acute in 1942 that medics, surgeons and nurses escaping from the Japanese advance in Burma were regularly forced to join the military medical units active in refugee camps and the frontier regions.[7] The problem was initially sought to be tackled by drawing upon the IMS and IMD officials involved in civilian practice into military service, but this measure proved unsuccessful due to the limited numbers of such officials. The result was a series of new strategies to develop the strength of the military medical framework. For instance, the Government of India and the GHQ (India) decreed that men under forty years of age, who were fit for military service, not be recruited from the open market to fill the vacancies that had arisen from the appointments vacated by those released for military duty. They also

Table 5.1 Battle and Non-battle casualties (hospital admissions) for the British Indian Army based in the Indo-Burma Front, Burma and SEAC (excluding Ceylon), 1942–45

Year	Non-battle casualties	Battle casualties	Ratio of Battle to Non-battle casualties
1942	178,139	872	1:204
1943	531,719	3735	1:142
1944	541,575	24,680	1:22
1945	213,047	16,188	1:13

Source: B.L. Raina (ed), *Official History of the Indian Armed Forces in the Second World War 1939–45 (Medical Services): Preventive Medicine (Nutrition, Malaria Control and Prevention of Diseases)*, Kanpur, 1961, p. 435.

ordered the provincial governments to review the needs of their medical and public health services and thereby determine the maximum number of medical graduates and licentiates that these administrations could release for military service.[8]

Investigations about the usefulness of employing medical licentiates into the military was given additional attention after the Secretary of State for India's office announced that the Medical Personnel (Priority) Committee in the UK would be unable to provide medical personnel for service in the sub-continent. The result of this was the creation of a special committee to investigate the public health and medical situation in India, which arrived from Britain on 13 December 1942 and toured the sub-continent for three months. It recommended that the army make greater use of medical licentiates through the creation of a new service, the Indian Army Medical Corps, which would allow the authorities to formally accommodate their qualifications.[9] These proposals were studied for two months and then upheld by a Committee of the War Department in March 1943, leading to government orders for the formation of the IAMC with effect from 3 April 1943.[10] The establishment of this new service also assisted the expansion of the other wings of military medical service, especially the anti-malaria units. Whereas the malaria control measures before September 1939 had been largely concentrated in and around permanent cantonments, except during the periodic military tours of the North Western Frontier Provinces, the war in Eastern India forced a complete change of strategy, involving widespread spraying measures in and around troop encampment, as well as the battlefront. The resultant increase in demand of qualified manpower was dealt with by the inclusion of civilian malaria officers into the newly formed IAMC.[11]

Another major challenge to face the military medical authorities was the issue of increasing hospital capacity. Between 1942 and 1945, for instance, it was necessary to raise 117 General Hospitals, which were complemented by a series of ambulance trains capable of running on broad, metre and narrow gauge railway networks and carrying between 196 and 268 patients. Moreover, the increased scale of war by 1943 forced the military to embark on the construction of new types of hospitals and treatment centres, especially in the frontier regions. The result was the setting up of improved varieties of 'staging stations', which were capable of providing emergency surgical assistance and medical treatment to upto a hundred patients.[12] The work of these establishments was bolstered by the setting up of

'Malaria Forward Treatment Units', which could hold and treat 600 patients.[13] These special health schemes helped the GHQ (India) to successfully provide curative and preventive medical services to the Indian army detachments operating in Eastern India, even though some infrastructural frailties, especially those in the context of the nursing services, could never be completely banished during the war (see Table 5.2 below).[14]

The overall expansion of the military medical services, and its effects, was very marked: in all 1,163 medical units and 197,539 new hospital beds had been created in the region by October 1945, and this new infrastructure treated 5,000,000 military casualties.[15]

II. The Roles and Structures of Wartime Information Management

While GHQ (India) accorded great importance to arranging food and health provision networks for soldiers in the front-line, it remained aware that the development and maintenance of morale within the army in Eastern India would necessitate other varieties of intervention as well. Information management, which involved both the distribution of vetted information and the collection of intelligence regarding the soldiers' attitudes towards a variety of issues, was considered particularly significant in the context of the challenges thrown up by the Japanese entry into the Second World War.[16] The problems facing the officers involved in mobilising the Eastern Command and the Fourteenth Army were many. It proved impossible for the authorities to prevent the Indian soldiers from interacting with the

Table 5.2 Wartime shortages of nursing staff in the military medical establishment in India

Date	Requirement	Availability	Deficit
30 September 1940	211	84	127
30 September 1941	414	275	139
31 December 1942	3,258	1,549	1,709
31 December 1943	4,207	1,919	2,288
31 December 1944	4,958	2,439	2,519
31 July 1945	5,492	2,705	2,787

Source: B.L. Raina (ed), *Official History of the Indian Armed Forces in the Second World War 1939–45:Medical Services (Administration)*, Kanpur, 1953, p. 82.

local civilian populace as troops would invariably make forays into the towns or villages located near their encampments for 'entertainment' – usually described in the contemporary official documentary sources as being liquor and women – while off duty.[17] Here they would be exposed to, and in certain cases be affected by, a variety of 'unwanted influences': rumours about widespread food shortages, Axis radio broadcasts, nationalist newspapers and visible signs of extreme economic distress, all of which could stoke worries about the conditions prevailing in the soldiers' homes.[18] In addition, activists attached to the Indian National Congress, the Congress Socialist Party and the Communist Party of India made frequent attempts to gain converts amongst the army, and in certain cases even tried to browbeat Indian soldiers serving in the region.[19] A representative example of the former was a case where two Socialists – Motilal Singh and Govindeo Brahmachary – were arrested after having been found spreading anti-British views amongst Indian soldiers at their 'lemonade bar' located in the Troops' Amusement Park in Ranchi.[20] While the authorities did not experience these difficulties with regard to troops serving in the uninhabited, or sparsely populated, frontier areas in the provinces of Assam and Bengal, they had to meet other challenges, most notably from Japanese and Indian National Army propaganda transmitted over loud-speakers, dropped from the air or carried in enemy artillery shells.[21]

Strikingly, the nature of the progress of the conflict and the problems it engendered caused notable changes in the official tactics of information management. Before December 1941 any sympathy for 'pernicious persuasions', or even a diminution of commitment towards the *Raj*, within military encampments was sought to be dealt with through the implementation of strict discipline and punishment. An integral part of this system had been the official control over the mail sent by, and to, the troops; which was examined by censors, and, when deemed necessary, certain sections were 'blacked out'.[22] However, a characteristic system of censorship was developed from 1942 onwards, wherein ostensible official intervention was reduced to the bare minimum even though the examination of troops' mail continued unabated. Thus, while the mention of certain issues of strategic import – like references to the location of troop encampments and details of the movement of armed detachments – were deleted from the Indian soldier's correspondence, he was allowed, and indeed, encouraged, to state his misgivings about the contemporary political situation, wartime problems that affected his family and particular official policies. An analysis of the Indian Army's weekly intelligence summaries reveals the importance accorded in official circles to monitoring these views, using the knowledge thus harvested to produce regular reports and then making them the basis for military propaganda intended for units.[23] The importance of this was underlined by W.J. Cawthorn, the Director of Military Intelligence in India, thus:

> The effect of anti-British propaganda and attempts to suborn the troops depends largely on the amount and quality of our counter-propaganda.... Through all this period [the war] the responsibility of the British Officer in Indian battalion[s] would be of greatest importance as a counter-propaganda organization; it is suggested that special attention be paid to this aspect of his duties.[24]

The information collected by military censors also allowed the General Headquarters (India) to apprise the relevant District Soldiers' Boards and the civilian authorities about the specific problems faced by military families, which would then be promptly corrected. These remedial measures were then widely publicised in the relevant units. For instance, the apprehension caused among soldiers in January 1942 by an unsubstantiated rumour that the Government of Punjab intended to requisition – without payment – all wheat stocks above 20 *maunds*, was successfully counteracted by articles in the *Fauji Akhbar*, a newspaper distributed amongst South Asian troops, and lectures by Civil Liaison Officers and Unit Commanders, which clarified that the news had been unfounded.[25] Similarly, the fears among soldiers based in Eastern India during the famine of 1943 that their families were starving were 'allayed' by the news of the action taken by the relevant provincial governments.[26] Prompt action was also taken when a security report warned that serving men from Eastern United Provinces were anxious about news of being ousted from their holdings of land, because these had been transferred or sub-let to another person. The military authorities asked the Government of the United Provinces to investigate the matter, and assurances that the provisions of the United Provinces Tenancy Act did not apply to military personnel were advertised to great effect by the officers of the concerned units.[27]

Therefore, the system of information control developed from 1942 onwards allowed the military propaganda, created for the consumption of the *sepoy*, to remain 'in touch' with their needs throughout the conflict. Crucially, it also allowed the authorities to discard the ineffective lines of propaganda, while emphasising, or creating, more effective ones. However, the success of the policy remained rooted in the smooth transmission, rather than the suppression, of information: a fact visible in the shifting attitude within the military establishment towards censorship. Censorship no longer meant the expungtion of the troops', or their family members', criticisms about the current political or economic scenario, but began to designate the secret examination of their personal correspondence. Referring to this, a Central Intelligence Department officer mentioned that the existence of such initiatives were seldom publicised since it allowed much information of value to be collected, which would seem to suggest that the people targeted remained unaware of the censors' activities.[28]

Interestingly, other efforts were also made in this period to generate an 'openness' amongst British soldiers serving in all theatres of war, and the formation of the Army Bureau of Current Affairs in June 1941 inaugurated these initiatives.[29] But the similarities between the information policies deployed amongst British and Indian troops did not end there. Indeed, in both cases the official initiatives were informed by a combination of a difficult strategic scenario and a changed pattern of recruitment; issues that preyed, and increasingly dictated, the nature of implementation of military censorship and propaganda. As opposed to the Chief of the Imperial General Staff's, and Prime Minister Churchill's, apprehensions about the British soldier with socialist tendencies,[30] the Indian GHQ's worries centred around the inclusion of the politically conscious 'educated middle-classes': a category used in military files to refer to the urbanites, who were permeating an Indian army that was being forced to adapt to fighting a technologically modern war in ever-increasing numbers. One estimate, made as early as June 1942, declared, for instance, that these 'classes' had contributed 33 per cent of the infantry and cavalry.[31]

The military authorities' discomfiture about the new type of soldiers arose principally from a recognition of the fact that they hailed from areas lacking the comprehensive civil-military structures – the entrenched system of District Soldiers' Boards and other intricate systems of control – that had been developed in the main recruiting areas. This caused much uneasiness within the military hierarchy about the unavoidable inclusion into the Indian Army of 'non-martial classes',[32] who were considered 'other than first line' material.[33] While the changed tactics of information management allowed the military intelligence personnel to monitor attitudes in the Indian army as a whole, they were ultimately considered invaluable for determining the needs, and political predispositions, of the new army recruits.[34] In fact, the shift in information policies, and correspondingly, the ostensible lack of security in a difficult strategic situation, appeared to catch certain British military personnel by surprise. One, a Captain W.A. Barnes based in Calcutta, complained in September 1942 about 'indiscreet disclosures' made by troops in their mail and the lack of censorship of such correspondence, and declared:

> That it appeared that a report on the subject might be called for based on a careful examination of a representative batch of such [post]cards, to determine whether the leakage was serious or not, and what action should be taken in view of the fact that unit and field censors appeared to be slipping up in this regard.[35]

Nonetheless, the military intelligence community remained committed to a scheme wherein the comprehensive censorship of soldiers' mail was avoided and all official intervention downplayed; a system which, as a perusal of secret military intelligence reports show, continued even beyond the conclusion of the Second World War. The necessary structures of censorship were developed around the 'unit': regimental, divisional or battalion commanders would normally appoint their second-in-command to be the Unit Security Officer, who would, among other things, organise the examination of the soldiers' correspondence and the preparation of 'morale' reports for consumption by the GHQ (India).[36] The development of additional structures of censorship in the region was facilitated by the fact that the Indian army's interests had been allowed to dominate, and direct the development of, the official surveillance networks deployed amongst the civilian population from the onset of the war. An army official, the Director of Military Operations and Intelligence, guided censorship policy and his influence was accentuated within the central government by the deputation of two army officials as the Chief Telegraph Censor and Chief Postal Censor respectively.[37] They arranged for the establishment of postal and telegraphic censorship in the provincial capitals and the seaports of Eastern India;[38] and officials appointed by them directed operations in the localities.[39]

From 1942 onwards, the structures of civilian censorship were used by the military authorities to buttress the system of information control within army encampments. It was recognised that soldiers serving in Eastern India could, if they so wanted, transmit correspondence – letters or telegrams – from local post-offices.

Command over censorship resources in the cities, towns or the subdivisional capitals allowed military intelligence to plug this potentially damaging weakness.[40] The prominence given to this aim is represented by the fact that the available manpower resources were deployed to develop a permanent scheme of 'internal censorship' primarily in urban areas and localities with significant troop concentrations, whereas the 'continuous' screening of postal communications was avoided elsewhere.[41] Instead, ephemeral censorship structures were established only in localities considered by the army to be of strategic worth, particularly in situations where specific political or economic crises were deemed to be capable of threatening the Allied war-effort.[42]

Security within military encampments was strengthened further by monitoring the activities of newspaper or news-agency correspondents posted in operational areas. The regulations concerning their activities had declared that reporters who accompanied troops on active service could be tried under the Indian Army Act and were subject to military law. In addition, the official regulations declared 'that a license issued by the Defence Department of the Government of India to a press correspondent to accompany troops on active service only authorises that correspondent to proceed to a specified place, usually the base of operations.'[43] From December 1941, these laws translated into a system wherein correspondents attached to military detachments had their messages examined by the Unit Censorship Officer before transmission. Moreover, articles written on the basis of such information were then submitted to the military's representatives in the civilian press advisory committees prior to publication. This regulatory system was further strengthened by the legal restrictions placed on members of the armed forces regarding statements to the press. The Indian Army Rule 333 stated, for instance, that 'an officer or soldier is forbidden to publish or communicate any statement of fact or opinion which is capable of embarrassing the relations between Government and the people of India or any section thereof'; and made the writing of letters and the grant of interviews by service personnel, while on service or during leave, on the strategic or the political situation in India a punishable offence.[44] The effectiveness of this legislation was increased by the utilisation of the Defence of India Rule 116 by the provincial authorities, which allowed them to force editors of newspapers to disclose particulars in cases where service personnel had given interviews.[45]

Like in the case of censorship policy, propaganda schemes targeted at the units remained a jealously guarded preserve of the military authorities throughout the war.[46] At the outbreak of the conflict, the newspapers, bulletins and leaflets, in English and in the vernacular languages, were produced for distribution within the units by officers attached to the Directorate of Military Operations and Intelligence, GHQ (India),[47] and this arrangement remained more or less unchanged till the end of the war.[48] A similar trend was also noticeable with regard to the creation of radio and film propaganda meant for Indian troops.[49] The military authorities' control over their own publicity affairs was strengthened further by the practice of utilising the structures available within the battalions, divisions and regiments to distribute official propaganda material among serving soldiers. Lectures by commanders remained the most common mode of spreading officially prescribed views, because intelligence reviews reported them effective.[50]

The Commanding Officers and their senior subordinates also used loud-speaker systems to disseminate the daily 'news'.[51] Topics which they were expected to highlight were described in detail in pamphlets and specialised publications like *Indian Information*, the *Army in India Training Manuals* and the *War in Pictures*, which were regularly circulated.[52] The unit was also considered to be a suitable place in which to provide troops with 'vetted' printed and wireless propaganda.[53] 'Information rooms' authorised by the officers, would contain newspapers like the *Fauji Akhbar* [Soldiers' Newspaper], *Jang Ki Khabren* [News of the War] and *Duniya* [The World],[54] and house wireless sets, which would be switched on at certain times of the day.[55] These rooms would regularly be used as the venue for shows in which 'press photographs, carefully selected, [we]re exhibited under boards representative headings such as 'Air', 'Mechanisation', 'Weapons' etc.'.[56] Films screened by mobile cinemas, slide shows, and plays performed by travelling concert groups and theatre companies were also used in attempts to popularise official descriptions of the war-effort and situation.[57]

II. The Themes of Military Propaganda

While the wartime military propaganda disseminated amongst South Asian troops located in Eastern India dealt with a wide variety of themes, some of these were relics of an earlier period whereas the others resulted from specific recommendations by the DMI's office at particular junctures of the Second World War. In the former category was material aimed at strengthening regimental loyalty by extolling the 'glorious military traditions' of the 'martial classes'; as well as their bravery in the battle-field.[58] The latter commonly took the form of 'counter-propaganda', and was intended to contradict 'defeatist' suggestions made by those considered either 'external' or 'internal' enemies; redress particular fears amongst the soldiers and their families, not least, and accustom troops with new official initiatives.

Between September 1939 and December 1941 India remained relatively unaffected by the travails of war. As a result, military propaganda distributed amongst Indian troops, apart from criticising the Congress's opposition to the conflict, tended to concentrate on appreciative descriptions of India's contributions to Allied efforts in the European and African theatres of war. An apt example was the 'War time syllabus for Geography, Citizenship and General Knowledge' for serving soldiers. In this, India's economic and material contributions were consistently emphasised and geography was taught by dividing the map of India 'from the manpower point of view', the 'raw material point of view' and the 'industrial point of view'. 'Citizenship and General Knowledge' were also taught through lessons on war funds, their importance and how they were raised.[59]

The dramatic change in the strategic situation from December 1941 had a series of striking effects: well-established recruitment patterns had to be modified in order to permit the requisite rate of expansion of the Indian army and Japan's conquest of Burma in May 1942 brought the enemy close to India's borders, which, in turn, left an indelible imprint on official propaganda policies. For instance, the enforced, and hurried, inclusion of new groups of Indians into the army had a dual impact. On the one hand, it gave the authorities less time to scrutinise the political sensibilities of the entrants.[60] On the other, it was very apparent that the new recruits treated the armed forces as a well paid and stable source of employment. Indeed, one intelligence report asserted that they had joined 'not because of any patriotic motives or military tradition', but because the pay allowed them to maintain their families 'in these days of economic stress'.[61]

Hence, the Commandant of the Army School of Education declared that 'the old loyalty' would need to be replaced with a new 'sense of purpose', and added that for this the 'old form of stereotyped lecture was of little value'. He argued, as a result, that a new 'language' would be required to instil loyalty to the British war-aims,[62] and this would be centred around the 'protection' of Indian 'homes and families'.⁶³ The frequent reference to the comfortable conditions in the localities from which the Indian troops were drawn were also a result of the military authorities' assertion – on the basis of unit morale reports – that 'there was much evidence that the morale and the contentment' of the Indian soldier, especially that of the new recruits, were 'largely dependent' on the conditions back home.⁶⁴ Military propaganda would, thus, constantly highlight the 'positive action' taken by the provincial administrators in the major recruiting areas, and assure the troops that the Indian Soldiers' Board, '... exist[ed] to promote the well being and to watch the interests of serving soldiers in their civil capacity, and of ex-soldiers, and of the families of serving and ex-soldiers'. Though the prevalence of economic difficulties, when and where they existed, was never denied, it was underlined that the soldiers' families formed 'that part of the civil population' which the authorities were 'specially concerned about', that the organisations created to look after their comforts had been given comprehensive powers and that these were functioning without impediment.⁶⁵

The proximity of Japanese forces to India, and their publicists' regular radio broadcasts from South-East Asia, had an even more marked effect in determining the themes discussed in British military propaganda. Efforts were made from December 1941 onwards to underline the savagery of the Japanese by making use of 'atrocity stories', which began to dominate the lecture notes sent by the General Headquarters (India) to all Unit Commanders in the country. One set advised that officers emphasise that the entire Japanese army regarded the Indian soldier with 'unconcealed and unwarranted' contempt, which had led to '... authentic cases of prisoners being killed out of hand, and of their being used as live targets for bayonet practice'. It also asked them to warn the Indian soldier that the Japanese would treat them with 'less consideration' than they would their pack animals.⁶⁶ In addition, evidence of Japanese cruelty, in the form of published experiences of escaped prisoners, was circulated amongst troops. One such description by an escapee went thus:

> We were given only one meal a day, consisting of one small cup of rice boiled with green. The food was meagre and insufficient. In the morning we were taken out by the Japanese soldiers to repair the ... harbour, aerodrome and other military positions and also for loading and unloading goods, and were brought back to the jail in the evening. The prisoners in a barrack were given 15 minutes a week to go to the

well, fill mule troughs with water and hurriedly wash their bodies. If they could not finish this job within the specified time they were taken back to the barracks being beaten and kicked on the way. We were asked to ease ourselves in our barracks and remove the night soil personally to a trench. No soap or change of clothes was allowed. I passed the whole time in my own under-wear and shirt which I wore at the time of my arrest. The treatment of [sic] the Japanese soldiers with [sic] the Indian Prisoners was very rude and cruel.[67]

Moreover, whereas the initial British losses in South-East Asia forced the military authorities to downplay references to the strength of the British and Allied forces, propaganda material continued to discuss the inevitability of the 'ultimate' victory of the 'combination of British, Chinese, Russian and American troops'.[68] Senior officers and travelling lecturers were warned by the Military Headquarters at this juncture that they take care not to lower morale 'by the recounting of withdrawals .... [or] stress unduly the lack of certain articles of equipment.[69] The disastrous retreat from Burma was represented amongst South Asian troops as a 'brilliant delaying manoeuvre' which had allowed the Allied forces in India the time to regroup. One description of the event declared that:

> Invaluable time was gained through General Alexander's fighting retirement from Burma, in which Indian Army units played a major part. This held up the Japanese until the breaking of the monsoon, rendered any operations on a large scale impossible before the autumn, by which time sufficient forces had been concentrated to ensure the defence of India.[70]

An improvement in the Allied strategic position in Eastern India in 1943, with the introduction of significant American armed forces and defence equipment in the region, caused more attention to be accorded to anti-Japanese publicity. Military propaganda paid more attention to attacking the Axis powers' declared goals and pronouncements,[71] especially the Japanese plans for a 'Greater Asian Co-Prosperity Scheme'.[72] Interestingly, this translated into an increased emphasis on 'atrocity propaganda', which became increasingly sophisticated in content during this period. Apart from continuing to describe the behaviour of Japanese soldiers against the Chinese, increased care was now taken to mention the fate of the Indian victims in South East Asia. Consequently, descriptions of the mistreatment of policemen of Indian origin and the economic hardships faced by all 'classes' of Indians became very frequent. Radio programmes would describe the economic chaos in Malaya, Burma and the Philippines, and contrast it with the 'peace and prosperity' of Indian villages.[73] Though references to the rape of women had been made in the past, great emphasis was now given to instances where Indian women were involved.

But perhaps the issue to be given the greatest prominence during 1943–44 was the Japanese army's alleged disrespect for three major South Asian religions: Islam, Hinduism and Sikhism. This was described by references to cases where Hindus and Muslims had been pressured into eating beef and pork respectively;[74] where Indians, irrespective of religious differences, had been forced to attend *gurdwaras* on Sundays and mosques on Fridays; where Hindus and Muslims were coerced into eating from the same dishes in mosques; where Indian women had been raped inside places of worship;[75] where Hindu prisoners of war were compelled to slaughter cows and then cut up the meat for Japanese consumption, and where Sikh prisoners of war had been made to shave off their beards and cut their hair.[76]

The gradual improvement in the strategic position from mid-1943 also caused British military propaganda to adopt a more confident tone about other issues. Emphasis now began to be given to the successes of Allied armies over the Axis forces in Europe and Africa, and these were represented as being proof of what was soon to follow in the Far-East.[77] Descriptions of the strength of Allied, and British, forces were also consistently publicised in the newspaper started by the South East Asia Command – entitled *SEAC* – and the two pamphlet series started by the India Command, titled *Current Affairs* and *Winning The Peace*, in 1944.[78] For instance, articles in *SEAC* described the preparedness of the army under General Slim's command, the armour available to British forces, the newly-acquired aircraft in the Allied air-forces, and British troops making 'local friends' in Japanese-held territory.[79] This propaganda was also backed up by visual representations of Allied prowess, and films and photographs shown to service personnel portrayed 'Indian troops during realistic exercises'; the attack on an enemy tank and the surrender of its crew; troops wading through water and then attacking a hill; and the Madras Sappers practising for the 'great Burma push'; troops training for jungle warfare; attacks by Gurkhas on a village occupied by the Japanese; and Wavell watching artillery corps in Assam practising with live ammunition.[80]

To magnify the effect of propaganda highlighting the Allies' strength, material enumerating the 'hardships faced by Japanese soldiers',[81] and their low morale,[82] began to be widely distributed. Bulletins would discuss the 'myth' of the 'Japanese superman' and insist that it had been 'amply proved' that it was possible to 'outthink, outshoot and outfight' the Japanese'.[83] From mid-1943 such publicity began to be accompanied by 'confessions' made by Japanese soldiers, either during captivity or in diaries left behind on the battle-field. Such propaganda was disseminated through a series of pamphlets titled *Extracts From Japanese Diaries*, and dealt with the difficulties faced by Japanese troops and their recognition of the relative comfort of Allied troops. One issue reproduced a 'letter from a Sergeant to a Corporal', which declared that:

> Morning, noon and night we get one mess tin of sloppy rice – work every night – the whole night through [sic]. As you know Tai (commander) is perpetually fault finding. He treats the men entirely as if they were machines – not a minute or even a second's relaxation. The troops are completely cowed.[84]

Another edition of the series described the contents of 'The Diary of an Unknown Jap Soldier'. In it a Japanese soldier complained that he had:

> Found a package of enemy rations in the afternoon. It tasted very good. The enemy certainly eat well. I wish I could have a stomach full of such good food.... Received some rice from 5th Coy. [company] but no rice for tonight. No change in situation but can't fight on .0397 gals [sic] of rice per day. Enemy penetrated our situation.[85]

'Disclosures' like these dwelt at length upon the 'failing morale' of Japanese soldiers, which was re-emphasised in the texts of interviews of Japanese prisoners captured in the Arakan front.[86] Issues of the *Army in India Training Manual* used as a basis for lectures by officers, also contained sections on the topic. One edition of the publication contained 'Some Observations by Individual Jap Soldiers', which described the Japanese admiration for the Allied armies, their 'power, rapidly growing strength and firepower', and outlined the Japanese soldiers' acceptance of the 'material inferiority' of their own army.[87] Similarly, 'admissions' made allegedly in Japanese magazines, journals and radio programmes about the inferiority of their air-force and the difficulties faced in the production of aircraft production were frequently mentioned.[88] British military propaganda would also often ridicule the views of Japanese military commanders who were purported to have extolled the 'nutritive value of grass for human consumption', while bemoaning the acute food shortage within their armies and the territories held by them.[89]

British military propaganda also contradicted and belittled the claims of two other opponents: the Indian National Congress and the Indian National Army. The increasingly aggressive stance taken by the former organisation, which culminated in the launching of the 'Quit India' movement in August 1942, forced the authorities to embark on a well-defined propaganda campaign against the party. This involved consistent attempts to underline the Congress's political antagonism towards a valid cause, its 'pro-Japanese leanings', its hostility to the interests of Indian soldiers, and its lack of sympathy for the demands made by the various 'minorities'.[90] The military propaganda calculated to attack Subhas Chandra Bose and his Indian National Army, which despite its modest size was a major source of worry for the British authorities in the sub-continent,[91] revolved around a discussion of the pointlessness of joining the Imperial army; the opportunism of Subhas Chandra Bose, and the forced enlistment of prisoners of war into his new force.[92] In addition, efforts were consistently made to denounce the Indian National Army as a 'puppet army', a 'mere propaganda tool' for the Axis powers, a collection of 'stretcher bearers', and a 'group of few homeless people' who lived off crumbs offered by the Japanese.[93]

From 1943 onwards the issue of the demobilisation of the wartime Indian army also began to be given great prominence, primarily because intelligence reports from the battalions seemed to suggest that all Indian soldiers were becoming apprehensive about their occupational prospects after the conflict and wanted information on the issue.[94] A pamphlet series titled *Release and Resettlement* was inaugurated, and a hundred thousand copies of the first edition were distributed throughout India Command formations.[95] While publications such as these advertised the inevitability of the demobilisation of the wartime army, they also described the enormous potential of employing newly released soldiers in the industries and co-operatives being planned by the colonial administration. For instance, the plans enunciated by the 'Policy Committee on [the] Re-settlement and Re-employment of troops', which was set up in the last quarter of 1943 with Firoz Khan Noon at its head, were given great prominence; as were some of the re-employment strategies. This included references to the creation of 'large scale transportation companies' which would help in providing employment to the vast mass of lorry drivers in the Indian army; the initiation of vocational training courses for troops within various battalions to prepare them for new jobs after the war; the building of new canal systems within the Punjab allowing the government to settle many troops in the newly irrigated lands, and the establishment of 'co-operative savings banks' to assist ex-servicemen.[96] The White Paper prepared by the Government of India in October 1944 made similar promises, and its text was also widely publicised in all forms of military propaganda.[97] Films dealing with 'rural uplift, cottage industries and health' in the most important recruiting areas were screened; as were documentaries about post-war 'development'.[98] Even though some senior officers in the field complained that 'post-war reconstruction' was being 'over-stressed' and argued that 'more might be done towards making him [the Indian soldier] appreciate that the war must be won first, and that in the Japanese he is faced with an enemy really dangerous to his own interests and not only to those of the British connection',[99] print and wireless propaganda material targeted at soldiers persisted in discussing the issue in great detail right until the cessation of hostilities.[100]

IV. Concluding comments

Intelligence supplied by the soldiers via the postal censorship apparatus allowed GHQ (India), in collaboration with the Government of India, to rectify or pre-empt problems that might have affected imperial rule during a critical period of the Second World War. The system put into place allowed the authorities to counter the adverse effects of nationalist or Axis opposition; to generally keep up morale, and sometimes even to identify, watch and, when necessary, dismiss the unconverted, amongst troops serving in India.[101] Indeed, an examination of contemporary War Staff files suggest that the success of the scheme of information management encouraged the India and South East Asia Commands to expand the deployment of similar initiatives amongst their British and African units. While the so-called 'Padre's Hour', in the course of which British soldiers were encouraged to air their views, were continued till 1945, these official efforts at gathering information were buttressed by the preparation of regular 'morale reports' on the basis of military censorship.[102]

However, the military's information policies also had certain unintended effects. For instance, the reiteration between 1940 and

1945 of the inevitability of British withdrawal from India after the cessation of hostilities, especially in anti-Congress propaganda,[103] contributed to cases where South Asian soldiers feared that they would ultimately be left 'at the mercy' of a government dominated by the Indian National Congress.[104] Reports from the battalions declared that these apprehensions were exacerbated by the persistent economic difficulties, and indicated that this had caused a majority of the *sepoys* to fear for their future in the post-war political scenario.[105] The Indian soldiers' fears, and the intelligence structure that allowed the authorities to clock them, left a negative imprint on British attitudes too. Doubts about the *sepoy's* reliability in an increasingly politicised environment, which had emerged in rare, yet significant, bursts before December 1941,[106] became much more pronounced from 1942 onwards. A communication sent by the GHQ (India) to all commanders of Indian units after the outbreak of the 'Quit-India' movement is revealing. It asked the officers to avoid any 'suggestion of scorn for the 'unenlightened Indian' who wants independence ... since freedom and independence are probably sought after by the troops themselves.'[107]

In fact, the element of probability in such forecasts became marginal as the Second World War wore on, and the seeds of doubt which had been sown in British military minds began to take on a life of their own at a time when the 'internal security position' was expected to deteriorate rapidly after the conclusion of the war in the face of increased nationalist activism.[108] A representative example of official apprehensions about the impact of the wartime political scenario on the Indian soldiers' attitudes is an extract from a report prepared in May 1943, which asserted that:

> Proposals of changes in the political constitution of India and consequent uncertainty regarding the position of the Indian Army under any new constitution has raised, even in the minds of pre-war soldiers [as opposed to the new classes inducted into the Indian army], doubts whether the British Raj is worth saving for anything but what it pays in cash and kind. The future of the soldier's own community, and the safety of his home and family in a country which may ... be controlled by men of a community he regards as hostile, are matters which ... cause him more concern than the defeat of the Axis powers. His doubts are not diminished if his [army] include[s] Indians who look forward ... to the day when India will be independent of the British Raj.[109]

A review of documentation relating to the Indian army between January 1944 and August 1945, and significantly, the period leading upto South Asian independence and partition, reveal pronounced British doubts about the wisdom of depending on Indian troops in a period of extreme political flux. A good example of this is the tone of a secret plan prepared by the GHQ (India) soon after the end of the war. Titled 'Operation Asylum', it dealt with how the Government of India would use the Indian army to tackle a 'widespread organised armed rebellion' in the country. Notably, the opening paragraph of the section that described the aims of the project began with the warning that the success of 'all plans' could only be premised on the loyalty of the Indian forces during the disturbances.[110] Statements like these, as well as other negative appraisals about the politicisation of the Indian army, betrayed a growing wariness about their integrity, and especially that of the officer ranks, in an increasingly difficult administrative situation. One confidential report complained, for example that 'some Indian officers lecturing in the United States on military operations, after delivering their set talks ably and correctly, have expressed pro-Congress party sentiments in off-the-record conversations.'[111] The official trepidation resulting from these trends, and an awareness of the British troops' great anxiety to be repatriated from India, information about which was being collected through the medium of censorship and morale reviews, began to raise great doubts about the longevity of the *Raj*. This misgiving was, in turn, reflected in the Government of India's great nervousness about the prospect of serious civil disorder during the post-war constitutional deliberations. This theme, and the effects of the colonial state's responses to the war, is discussed in the following chapter.

Notes

1 See, correspondence between the district magistracy and local military commands, Bihar, United Provinces and Bengal, c.1943, WSF 65/1(i)/43, BSA.
2 In September 1939, India was divided into three commands – Northern, Southern and Eastern – and a 'Western Independent District'. In May 1942, this organisation was changed to three armies – North Western, Southern and Eastern – and a Central Command. There was yet another change by the middle of October 1943, when the Eastern army was divided into the Eastern Command (Directly under the India – or Central – Command) and the fourteenth army (attached to ALFSEA and SEAC). This chapter examines the structures created to target Indian and British

troops attached to the Eastern Command and the fourteenth army. B.L. Raina (ed), *Official History of the Indian Armed Forces in the Second World War 1939–45:Medical Services (Administration)*, Kanpur, 1953, p. 14.

3 B.L. Raina, whose work has relied on a range of military files and correspondence, underlines the official belief in the fact that the 'morale and efficiency of the troops depend to a considerable extent not only on a scientifically planned dietary but on the manner of its preparation and presentation. Recognition of this led to improvements in catering in the Army and ultimately to the establishment of the Army in India Catering Corps.' See, Introduction to B.L. Raina (ed), *Official History of the Indian Armed Forces in the Second World War 1939–45 (Medical Services): Preventive Medicine (Nutrition, Malaria Control and Prevention of Diseases)*, Kanpur, 1961, no pp.

4 The cold storage scheme allowed the military to deal with the distribution of 25,116 tons of meat per year. This did not involve the separate supplies of frozen meat brought in for American troops. The factories used for processing meat were located in Nowshera, Amritsar, Agra, Madras, Poona, Patna, Delhi Cantonment, Anantpur and Ranipat. B.P. Srivastava, 'Nutrition', in *ibid.*, pp. 91–97.

5 Secret War Department History – Transportation and Movements (September 1939-December 1944), 1945, L/R/5/280, OIOC.

6 See, foreword in Raina (ed), *Medical Services (Administration)*, p. vii.

7 A good, representative, example of this is provided by the way medical relief was organised in the area surrounding Dinjan in Assam. Medical work here was dealt with 'as far as possible' by the small Combined Military Hospital and the Planter's Hospital at Panitola, with additional assistance being provided by doctors and nurses from Burma, who were detained for their expertise. See, enclosure to letter from P.N. Coats, Office of the Commander-in-Chief, India, to G. Laithwaite, Private Secretary to the Viceroy of India, 12 June 1942, L/WS/1/866, OIOC.

8 At the commencement of hostilities, the actual strength of the IMS in military employ was 366 (223 British officers and 143 Indian officers). There were, at the same point of time, 265 IMS officials in civil employment. Of these, 133 belonged to the 'war reserve', 73 to the 'residuary cadre' and 59 were 'supernumerary'. The recall of the war reserve began in April 1940, and by the end of 1941 all 'war reserve' and 'supernumerary' officers had been withdrawn from civil employment. By mid-1942 a decision was taken to even call up the 'residuary' officers for war service. Similar trends were also visible with regards to the IMD. Raina (ed), *Medical Services (Administration)*, pp. 16–25.

9 The composition of the committee, which was called the Medical Personnel (Army in India) Mission, was ultimately settled in October 1942. Dr H.S. Souttar, the Chairman of the Central Medical War Committee, which represented the Medical Personnel (Priority) Committee in United Kingdom, was asked to head the committee, and Lieutenant General A. Hood and Major General E. Bradfield were made members, with Lieutenant Colonel J.T. Robinson acting as Secretary. In addition, Colonel B. Basu, of the IMS, was attached to the mission at the

recommendation of the Secretary of State for India's office. Raina (ed), *Medical Services (Administration),* p. 26. Entry into the Emergency Commissions scheme of the IMS was restricted to those in possession of medical qualifications recognised by the General Medical Council. The medical licentiates, with their 'lesser' qualifications, therefore, needed to be accommodated into a separate service. *Ibid.,* p. 27.

10 While the VEC approved the findings and report of the Medical Personnel (Army in India) Mission on 27 December 1943, the Adjutant General ordered the formation of a committee, under the Chairmanship of Brigadier F.G. Forbes, to draw up a comprehensive scheme for the setting up of an Indian Army Medical Corps, on 25 January 1943. The formation of the IAMC did not affect the IMS officers, who were merely seconded to the new service. But, the IAMC revolutionised the terms of service and prospects for IMD officers and Medical Licentiates. For more details, see Raina (ed), *Medical Services (Administration),* pp. 29–30. Separate provincial selection boards were formed in Madras, Bombay, Bengal, Bihar, Sind, UP, Punjab, CP, Assam, NWFP, Orissa, Hyderabad, Central India [Agency] and Bangalore to promote recruitment into the IAMC. War History – Recruitment to military medical services, p. 8, L/R/5/299, OIOC.

11 Raina (ed), *Preventive Medicine,* pp. 256–324. It was recognised in 1942 that an effective malaria control plan would have to ensure protection from the 'rear to the forward positions'. Thus, anti-malarial measures had to be tackled in the following contexts: in cantonment and training areas in India; along road and rail communications; in military installations along the line of control, and finally, amongst fighting troops and formations. *Ibid.,* p. 324.

12 The first 'staging station' was raised on 15 June 1943, and this was followed by the creation of four more. A total of 33 ambulance trains were raised during the war, of which 3 were disbanded before August 1945. Raina (ed), *Medical Services (Administration),* pp. 232–240.

13 Sixteen such units were planned in March 1944: four had already been raised and were in service with the fourteenth army; four were ready by the end of the month, and the other eight were mobilised by end-April. *Ibid.,* p. 233.

14 The total number of nurses at the disposal of the military authorities was totally insufficient to meet the demands of a major war. For instance, the sanctioned strength of the nursing services for the army in August 1939 was 313, and the scope of expansion was limited. There were only 6,000 trained nurses in India, of whom almost 1,500 were trained only in regional languages and were, therefore, found unsuitable for recruitment to the IMNS, as all the work – both clerical and clinical – in military hospitals was carried out in English. Another 1,000 were excluded by age, whereas 700 nurses could not be considered for military employment as they were registered in more than one province. Moreover, the army had to compete with the needs of more than 6000 civil hospitals and dispensaries in a situation where the annual increase in nurses amounted to only about 177 personnel. The result was the development of a scheme for voluntary and paid workers, which was set up in January 1944 by the

Central Command. It involved providing each military station located in urban areas with a group of local women trained in elementary nursing, who were expected to assist the regular nursing staff during emergencies. Raina (ed), *Medical Services (Administration)*, pp. 61–76.
15 Raina (ed), *Medical Services (Administration)*, p. vii.
16 See, for instance, *The Welfare Education Handbook: A Manual Designed For The Guidance Of All Officers In The Conduct Of Talks And Discussions On 'Current Affairs'*, Directorate of Welfare and Amenities, GHQ, India, 1943, Chapter 1, no pp., L/MIL/17/5/2331, OIOC.
17 The inevitable interaction between military personnel and local civilians remained uncomfortable, and the basis for several 'affrays' between them. See, for instance, letter from M.R. Sarkar, Sub-Divisional Officer, Gaibandha to the District Magistrate, Rangpur, 23 April 1944, PF 7/36/44, NAI.
18 During the famine of Bengal in 1943, which affected the neighbouring provinces as well, military intelligence reports pointed out that troops serving in the region were being exposed to widespread instances of severe starvation and that this was making them apprehensive about the conditions in their homes. See, for instance, most secret WIS(II), 20 August 1943, L/WS/1/1433, OIOC.
19 Eastern Army reports would often point to 'subversive activities' against troops. One mentioned that the 'underground Congressmen', Communist Party of India activists and members of the Revolutionary Socialist Party were addressing 'leaflet appeals' amongst Indian troops and calling upon them to revolt. It was also pointed out that these trends were primarily noticeable in the 'security soft-spots' like the recruit training establishments and non-combatant units. See most secret WIS(II) 12 March 1943, L/WS/1/1433, OIOC. Another review pointed out that the Congress cadres in Assam were 'most anxious' to 'infect service personnel' and that these efforts were 'most obvious' in units enlisting 'townsmen' and 'matriculate classes'. See most secret WIS(II) 20 August 1943, L/WS/1/1433, OIOC. Also see, H.PF (I) 3/31/42, NAI., for a selection of pamphlets distributed by Congress activists amongst troops during the 'Quit-India' movement of August 1942.
20 Secret letter from P.T. Mansfield, Chief Secretary, GOB, to the Secretary, Home Department, GOI, 10 April 1944, HPF(I) 29/6/44, NAI. Also see, most secret report on 'Subversive attempts on the loyalty of the Indian Army' by the Chiefs of Staff Committee, Indian Army, 10 May 1943, L/WS/1/707, OIOC.
21 Japanese and Indian National Army propaganda dealt with a variety of issues: apart from contradicting the British stance towards political issues it would also often advertise the high levels of pay given in their armies. See, for instance, most secret WIS(II) 23 April 1943, L/WS/1/1433, OIOC. During the battle for Kohima in 1944, the Japanese subjected the Allied forces to an 'intensive' propaganda onslaught in the form of 'gramophone' and air-dropped slogans (written in English and Hindustani). See secret WIS(II) 11 August 1944, L/WS/1/1433, OIOC. For a description of the content of short-wave broadcasts from the Japanese controlled stations in the Far-East to India see HPF(I) 51/5/44, NAI. Also see, most

secret report on 'Subversive attempts on the loyalty of the Indian Army' by the Chiefs of Staff Committee, Indian Army, 10 May 1943, L/WS/1/707, OIOC.
22 *AITM*, No. 7 (1941), L/MIL/17/5/2240, OIOC.
23 See, for instance, Monthly Intelligence Summary No. 1 of 1942, 10 January 1942, L/WS/1/317, OIOC. Also see, most secret WIS(II) 17 July 1942; most secret WIS(II) 15 February 1943; most secret WIS(II) 23 July 1943, most secret WIS(II) 10 March 1944, and secret WIS(II) 22 September, 1944, L/WS/1/1433, OIOC; note entitled 'Reactions in Indian units to Japanese propaganda' in most secret WIS(II) 31 March 1944, L/WS/1/1433, OIOC, and *The Welfare Education Handbook*, L/MIL/17/5/2331, OIOC.
24 Most secret note entitled 'The Future of the Internal Security Situation in India' by Brigadier W.J. Cawthorn, D.M.I., 31 August 1942, L/WS/1/1337, OIOC.
25 Most secret WIS(II) 27 February 1942, L/WS/1/1433, OIOC. Also see, the note entitled 'Reactions in Indian units to Japanese propaganda' in most secret WIS(II) 31 March 1944, L/WS/1/1433, OIOC.
26 The military propaganda distributed amongst troops from the Bombay Presidency serving in Eastern India constantly referred to the special concessions arranged by the provincial authorities in the districts they hailed from. Most secret WIS(II) 30 April 1943, L/WS/1/1433, OIOC. A report from Chittagong pointed out that Indian (and British troops) were so 'affected' by the 'sights around them' that they were feeding beggars with their own rations, even though they were disobeying orders while doing so. Most secret WIS(II) 20 August 1943, L/WS/1/1433, OIOC. The anxiety among the soldiers from Punjab about the food situation was that there would be a 'heavy export' of food grains from their province and would result in a local shortage. Most Secret Morale Report, August–October 1943, undated, L/WS/2/71, OIOC.
27 Most secret WIS(II) 4 August 1944, L/WS/1/1433, OIOC.
28 Recollections of G.R. Savage, CID, MSS EUR F 161/210, OIOC.
29 A. Danchev, 'The Army and the Home Front 1939–1945' in D. Chandler and I. Beckett (eds), *The Oxford History of the British Army*, Oxford, 1996, p. 304.
30 Ibid., pp. 298–306.
31 Appendix E to secret letter from Adjutant General's branch, GHQ to all branches of GHQ, 1 June 1942, L/WS/1/1335, OIOC.
32 The notion of 'martial classes', despite its apparently blimpish associations and frequently shifting definitions, remained, as a range of wartime documents clearly prove, an important category within the Indian military hierarchy. During the Second World War it was a term used to refer to particular communities like the Punjabi Muslims, Hindu Jats, Sikh Jats, the Dogras, the Pathans, particular Marathi castes and the Rajputs, from which the Indian army had drawn in the twentieth century. Rather than insinuating the presence, or indeed, the lack of military capabilities, the concept of 'martial class' was used to describe people hailing from localities with well-ordered recruitment systems and comprehensive administrative structures.

33 By November 1942, a million and a half soldiers had been recruited and many of these recruits came from these previously 'untried classes.' The main problem for the military administrators was that the so-called 'martial races' were unable to meet the increased demand in recruitment. Secret memorandum on Indian manpower from the Adjutant General's Branch, 3 November 1942, L/WS/1/968, OIOC. Madrasis' (Tamils, Telegus and Malyalis), new Marathi castes, Bengali Muslims and Assamese were taken in large numbers into the mechanised units as drivers. Secret War Department History – Expansion of the Armed Forces in India, pp. 26–33, L/R/5/273, OIOC. For a discussion of these issues in contemporary reports see, for instance, WIS(II) 20 February 1942 and 1 May 1942, L/WS/1/1433, OIOC.

34 See, for instance, most secret WIS(II) 17 July 1942; most secret WIS(II) 9 October 1942; most secret WIS(II) 15 February 1943; most secret WIS(II) 10 March 1944, and secret WIS(II) 22 September, 1944, L/WS/1/1433, OIOC.

35 Letter from W.A. Barnes to the Commanding Officer, Military Censor Station, Calcutta, 29 September 1942, Barnes Papers, CSASA.

36 Monthly Intelligence Summary No. 1 of 1942, 10 January 1942, L/WS/1/317, OIOC. Also see, *AITM*, No. 7 (1941), L/MIL/17/5/2240, OIOC., and most secret WIS(II) 23 July 1943, L/WS/1/1433, OIOC.

37 J.A. Thorne, *Confidential report on the control during war of the press, broadcasting and films; and on publicity for purposes of the war*, New Delhi, 1939 [hereafter *Thorne Report*], p. 16, L/I/1/1136, OIOC.

38 Most secret letter from War Department, GOI to Home Department, GOI, 10 February 1944, HPF(I) 20/1/44, NAI.

39 This was despite the fact that comprehensive powers of censorship were given to the local officials through Section 25 of the Emergency Powers Ordinance of 1940. For a detailed description of the legislation, see secret letter from R. Tottenham, Additional Secretary, Home Department, GOI to the Chief Secretaries of all provincial governments, 2 August 1940, PDGF 69/12, BSA.

40 The special provisions of inland censorship imposed from 1 September 1943 to the south and east of the Brahmaputra river, as well as the east of the Ganges river, at the request of the Government of Bengal and Eastern army HQ, were, for instance, clearly intended, among other things, to act as a check against the evasion of unit and field censorship. See, most secret WIS(II), 16 April 1943, L/WS/1/1433, OIOC.

41 Departmental note, Home Department, GOI, c.1943, HPF(I) 20/18/45, NAI.

42 See, for example, departmental note, Home Department, GOI, August 1942, HPF(I) 20/18/45, NAI.

43 Secret Censorship Regulations, India, Defence Department, 1939, L/MIL/17/5/4258, OIOC.

44 Most secret WIS(II), 30 October 1942, L/WS/1/1433, OIOC.

45 Ibid.

46 *Thorne Report*, L/I/1/1136, OIOC.

47 *Ibid.*

48 In November 1943 the responsibility for the production of print propaganda for Indian troops operating in Eastern India began to be

shared by the SEAC. There were, however, no attempts to involve civilian administrators in this enterprise. Secret telegram from the War Department, GOI, to the SSI, GOBr, 15 November 1943, L/I/1/1050, OIOC.
49 Secret war history of the Bureau of Public Information, 1939–45, L/R/5/295, OIOC. Also see memorandum on film publicity, p. 17, L/R/5/295, OIOC.
50 Most secret WIS(II) 2 October 1942, L/WS/1/1433, OIOC.
51 *AITM*, No. 19 (1943), L/MIL/17/5/2240, OIOC.
52 The *AITM* was issued to all arms of service at the scale of one copy for each officer. See *AITM*, No. 24 (1944), L/MIL/17/5/ 2240, OIOC.
53 *AITM*, No. 18 (1942), L/MIL/17/5/2240, OIOC.
54 Secret WIS(II) 3 August 1945, L/WS/1/1506, OIOC.
55 Most secret WIS(II) 9 April 1943, L/WS/1/1433, OIOC.
56 *AITM*, No. 19 (1943), L/MIL/17/5/2240, OIOC. Also see, letter from N. Beresford-Pierse, Welfare General in India, GHQ, New Delhi, to M. Mayne, India Office, GOBr, 7 November 1945, L/WS/2/87, OIOC.
57 Most secret, WIS(II) 22 December 1944, L/WS/1/1433, OIOC.
58 *AITM*, No. 12 (1941), L/MIL/17/5/2240, OIOC. Also see different issues of series entitled *Indian Army in Action* in L/WS/1/1319, OIOC.
59 *AITM*, No. 6 (1941), L/MIL/17/5/2240, OIOC.
60 The pre-war system of a nucleus of permanent recruiting staff and the 'ex-soldier paid recruiter' stood well the initial test of wartime expansion. However, the system proved inadequate when the 'real tapping' of new classes began from December 1941, and this forced the military to use the assistance of the local civilian authorities in the recruitment of *sepoys*. Secret War Department History: Expansion of the Armed Forces in India, p. 26, L/R/5/273, OIOC.
61 Most secret WIS(II) 30 April 1943, L/WS/1/1433, OIOC.
62 Most secret WIS(II) 23 July 1943, L/WS/1/1433, OIOC. Also see, most secret WIS(II) 21 August 1942, L/WS/1/1433, OIOC.
63 *AITM*, No. 16 (1942), L/MIL/17/5/2240, OIOC.
64 Most secret WIS(II) 30 April 1943, L/WS/1/1433, OIOC.
65 *Matters of interest to Indian soldiers and their families*, Calcutta, 1943, pp. 1–2.
66 Note on Japanese use of Indian Prisoners of War in most secret WIS(II), 30 October 1942, L/WS/1/1433, OIOC. Also see, appendix A to most secret WIS(II) 7 May 1943; appendix B to most secret WIS(II) 14 May 1943; appendix A to most secret WIS(II) 21 May 1943; appendix A to most secret WIS(II) 28 May 1943, and appendix A to most secret WIS(II) 17 September 1942, L/WS/1/1433, OIOC.
67 Most secret WIS(II) 30 October 1942, L/WS/1/1433, OIOC.
68 Secret telegram from the External Affairs Department, GOI, to the SSI, GOBr, 20 April 1942, L/WS/1/1533, OIOC.
69 *AITM*, No. 18 (1942), L/MIL/17/5/2240, OIOC.
70 *Service In India*, GHQ (India), c.1943, p. 4.
71 Most secret WIS(II) 23 July 1943, L/WS/1/1433, OIOC.
72 A good description of the Japanese theme of 'co-prosperity' went thus: 'India has now [1942] become an essential part of the Asia Co-Prosperity Scheme. With Indian co-operation Asia will not only be self-sufficient but

so rich in raw materials and so economically powerful that it can to a large extent dictate the terms of trade to the rest of the world. These advantages will be shared by the Japanese with their Indian brothers.' See note entitled 'Secret Appreciation of Indian Morale' by the Overseas Planning Committee, Ministry of Information, GOBr, c.1942, INF 1/556, PRO

73 A series called *Malaya Today* was distributed among troops, and contained descriptions of the difficult conditions under Japanese rule. Most secret WIS(II) 19 May 1944, L/WS/1/1433, OIOC.
74 Most secret WIS(II) 14 May 1943, L/WS/1/1433, OIOC.
75 Most secret WIS(II) 19 May 1944, L/WS/1/1433, OIOC.
76 Most secret WIS(II) 21 May 1943, L/WS/1/1433, OIOC.
77 See, for instance, secret WIS(II) 9 June 1944, L/WS/1/ 1433, OIOC.
78 Note on 'Wartime Education For Indian Troops', *AITM*, No. 28 (1945), L/MIL/17/5/2240, OIOC.
79 Note about SEAC paper in the Assam-Burma front, 4 April 1944, L/I/1/1050, OIOC.
80 Note on propaganda material by the Public Relations Directorate, India, 19 January 1943, L/WS/1/1533, OIOC.
81 Secret WIS(II), 9 June 1944, L/WS/1/1433, OIOC.
82 Three reasons were attributed for the low morale of Japanese soldiers in Burma: their 'mounting casualties', their 'inferior weapons', and their 'weakness in air strength'. Most secret WIS(II) 19 May 1944, L/WS/1/1433, OIOC.
83 Excerpts from a United States Marine Corps pamphlet reproduced in *AITM*, No. 21 (1943), L/MIL/17/5/2240, OIOC.
84 Appendix C to most secret WIS(II) 10 December 1943, L/WS/1/1433, OIOC.
85 Ibid.
86 Appendix E to most secret WIS(II) 21 April 1944, L/WS/1/1433, OIOC.
87 *AITM*, No. 22 (1943), L/MIL/17/5/2240, OIOC.
88 Appendix C to most secret WIS(II) 5 May 1944, L/WS/1/1433, OIOC.
89 Most secret WIS(II) 14 April 1944, L/WS/1/1433, OIOC.
90 This theme has been discussed in great detail in the previous chapter.
91 Only 8,000 Indian National Army soldiers – as opposed to 230,000 Japanese troops – were sent to the battle-front, and most of these saw relatively little action. See P. Heehs, 'India's Divided Loyalties?', *History Today*, July 1995, p. 22. However, even the most cursory glance at historically contemporary official documents, military or civilian, reveals how great a danger the 'rebel' force was seen to be by the colonial authorities in India. Indeed, the British relief about their Indian regiments' continued loyalty in operations against the Indian National Army units in Burma between 1944 and 1945 was widespread. See, for instance, most secret weekly intelligence surveys in L/WS/1/1433, OIOC.
92 See, for instance, appendix B to WIS(II) 23 July 1943; appendix B to WIS(II) 30 July 1943; appendix A to WIS(II) 6 August 1943; appendix A to WIS(II) 13 August 1943, and appendix A to WIS(II) 20 August 1943, L/WS/1/1433, OIOC.
93 Most secret WIS(II) 11 February 1944; appendix C to most secret WIS(II) 31 March 1944; secret WIS(II) 7 April 1944; most secret WIS(II) 14 April

1944; most secret WIS(II) 21 April 1944; appendix C to secret WIS(II) 12 May 1944; appendix C to most secret WIS(II) 19 May 1944; secret WIS(II) 2 June 1944; secret WIS(II) 30 June 1944; secret WIS(II) 13 October 1944, and appendix A to secret WIS(II) 24 November 1944, L/WS/1/1433, OIOC.
94 See, for instance, secret WIS(II) 6 October 1944, L/WS/1/1433, OIOC.
95 A second, revised, edition of the inaugural issue was also brought out. See letter from N. Beresford-Pierse, Welfare General in India, GHQ, New Delhi, to M. Mayne, India Office, GOBr, 7 November 1945, L/WS/2/87, OIOC.
96 Telegram from Bureau of Public Information to Information Department, India Office, 3 March 1944, L/WS/1/1335, OIOC.
97 Secret WIS(II) 27 October 1944, L/WS/1/1433, OIOC.
98 Military publications and films would advertise the inauguration of special educational facilities, like the Indian Troops Training School, established in Nowgong in November 1945, that had been arranged. See letter from N. Beresford-Pierse, Welfare General in India, GHQ, New Delhi, to M. Mayne, GOBr, London, 7 November 1945, L/WS/2/87, OIOC.
99 Most secret WIS(II) 12 November 1943, L/WS/1/1433, OIOC.
100 See, for instance, secret WIS(II) 3 August 1945, L/WS/1/1506, OIOC.
101 See, for instance, most secret WIS(II) 9 October 1942, L/WS/1/1433, OIOC.
102 Secret reports on the morale of British, Indian and Colonial troops of Allied land forces for months of August, September, October, November and December 1944, and January 1945, L/WS/2/71, OIOC.
103 See, for instance, the note entitled 'The [sic] Indian Constitutional Issue', appendix B to WIS(II) 15 December 1942, L/WS/1/1433, OIOC, and extract from most secret letter from GHQ (India) to the Military Secretary, India Office, GOBr, 20 December 1942, L/WS/1/1337, OIOC.
104 Most secret Army in India Morale Report for August-September 1943, L/WS/2/72, OIOC. Reports frequently mentioned the 'considerable anxiety' among Indian troops about post-war employment and the Government of India's demobilisation policy. See, secret report on the morale of British, Indian, and Colonial troops of Allied land forces, August–October 1944, no date, L/WS/2/71, OIOC. Also see, secret WIS(II) 6 October 1944, L/WS/1/1433, OIOC.
105 Secret WIS(II) 22 June 1945, L/WS/1/1506, OIOC. Also see, secret reports on the morale of British, Indian and Colonial troops of Allied land forces for months of August, September, October, November and December 1944, and January 1945, L/WS/2/71, OIOC.
106 One report, prepared in 1941 and dealing with the impact of the historically contemporary Sikh attitudes on the Indian army, declared, for example, that the 'atmosphere of general unrest, uncertainty and divided leadership [in the Sikh community] has had its inevitable effect on Sikhs serving in the Army.... It must inevitably take time to re-establish a more wholesome atmosphere. In the meantime, the Army cannot but regard the Sikh element in the Army with a degree of suspicion ...'. Report entitled 'A survey of the Sikh situation as it affects the army', c.1941, HPF(I) 232/1940, NAI.

107 Most secret note entitled 'The Future of the Internal Security Situation in India' by Brigadier W.J. Cawthorn, DMI, GHQ, 31 August 1942, L/WS/1/1337, OIOC.
108 See, for instance, most secret WIS(II) 9 October 1942, L/WS/1/1433, OIOC. Referring to the possibility of civil disorder after the war, one review warned, for instance, that '... it is fair to say that as the war draws to its close ... the general I.S. [internal security] position is bound to deteriorate, as interested parties begin to prepare (as they are now preparing) for the eventual struggle for power. In addition, the severe inflationary process that is going on in the country today is bound to cause serious trouble'. Extract from most secret letter from GHQ (India) to the Military Secretary, India Office, GOBr, 20 December 1942, L/WS/1/1337, OIOC.
109 Secret report entitled 'Subversive attempts on the loyalty of the Indian Army' by the Chiefs of Staff Committee, Indian Army, 10 May 1943, L/WS/1/707, OIOC.
110 Most Secret Defence HQ Outline Plan: Operation Asylum, 9 December 1945, L/WS/2/65, OIOC.
111 See, confidential report entitled 'Misconceptions about India: A Peril to Anglo-American Unity', by R. Holland, 27 May 1945, L/I/1/810, OIOC.

Conclusion

This study reveals a situation in which the 'successes' and 'failures' of the official wartime propaganda and information policies combined to weaken the colonial administrative edifice in Eastern India. The attainment of the state's goal, that is, the effective mobilisation of the war-effort, was ultimately achieved by the selective targeting of public relations and censorship schemes at specific audiences in the face of enormous logistical, manpower and resource constraints. But, it is important to reiterate here that these emergency measures, as well as their administrative uses, were always regarded as being short-term in nature by those involved in their design and implementation. And in the context of the Second World War, the Government of India and the GHQ (India) remained aware of the fact that strategic demands would force the application of policies that were expected to, and did, result in a difficult social and economic situation wherein political opposition could be fomented effectively against the Raj.

An attempt has been made throughout this monograph to highlight the great significance of studying the nature of the tensions created within the state structure by the Government of India's wartime stances. A nuanced study of bureaucratic attitudes at the various levels of the state is useful because it allows one to delve into, and assess the significance of, administrative and political trends that have not been probed at any great length before. The application of this approach in the context of wartime Eastern India reveals that the distributive policies prescribed by the central government were very often not popular amongst local officials due to the dislocation they caused. They were, nevertheless, forced to co-operate in the implementation of these schemes in certain localities due to the existence of a variety of newly introduced checks: the power given to the military authorities and the new wartime bureaucracy to oversee and report on civilian officials, as well as the threat of removal of special wartime terms of service, in very difficult economic conditions, for the continued inability to assist in the introduction of strategic priorities. The result, at least amongst the Indian element of the central services, the provincial bureaucracy and the local board structures, was the creation of stronger links with nationalist politicians in the locality, which was accentuated in the light of the increased numbers of attacks on subordinate officials in rural areas. Yet, these renewed efforts at political re-negotiation were conspicuously different from the political re-alignments that had characterised the ministry period: the wartime shifts were, perhaps necessarily, much more surreptitious and vague, with most South Asian officials trying to create links with more than one party in a period of extreme political and constitutional uncertainty. Significantly, the Government of India remained aware of these trends through a range of separate indicators, namely military intelligence and censorship reports, the persistent incapability of the local administrators to find witnesses for attacks on official personnel and the inability to apprehend the culprits, and, not least, the re-adaptation and toning down of centrally-prescribed publicity briefs during official propaganda tours in the countryside.

An examination of the reactions to, and the mode of implementation of, the wartime propaganda and information policies suggested by the Government of India also reveals other important characteristics of the late colonial state structure in South Asia. The relationship between the civilian and military authorities is a good case in point. A careful examination of the correspondence between the provincial and district administrators shows that while the local bureaucrats often disapproved of the administrative difficulties imposed by the misdemeanour of troops and their provisioning, their sense of dependence on the army for their personal safety increased markedly over the war. In fact, the change in the general bureaucratic attitude towards military assistance was really quite dramatic, shifting from an unwillingness to call out the army except during acute outbreaks of violence, to a situation where officials began to regularly request, and acquire, military escorts even for food distribution tours in rural areas. This, in turn, explains the central government's tendency to accord great importance to, and worry about, trends within the Indian army. Civilian officials who were expecting the military to take on greater administrative responsibilities during the anticipated disturbed social, economic and political post-war conditions, were instead faced with regular reports describing the politicisation of all grades of soldiers and the government's inability to maintain the force strength essential for an expanded internal security role.

A detailed assessment of the trends in the localities of Eastern India also underline other intricacies in South Asian wartime administration. For example, an analysis of secret military intelligence reveals that the distribution of official food aid set aside for the so-called non-priority sections of the civilian population were constrained by political and communal squabbles regarding the selection and management of government-controlled ration shops, which ultimately harmed the interests of the groups most in need of assistance.[1] Also, food-aid that was put aside for general distribution would often be denied to the poorest elements of the rural population, and instead be targeted by the subordinate civil services to the relatively well-off, but vocal, rural-middle classes or landed agriculturists.[2] The situation in Bengal was only stabilised by the introduction of large-scale military intervention in famine relief operations, where army officers were given the power to direct food and health measures amongst the worst affected sections of the rural poor, often in special refugee camps outside local bureaucratic control.[3]

Also, while the military attempted to strengthen their famine relief efforts by accessing the assistance of voluntary agencies, most of these new distributive networks tended, of their own accord, to be organised communally.[4] This resulted in a situation where the Muslim League catered to Muslim refugees, while the Hindu Mahasabha and active pro-Congress organisations like the Marwari Relief Association tended to distribute aid amongst Hindu famine victims. In fact, political opposition to the initiation of similar schemes by leftist or class-based organisations like the Communist Party of India, the Radical Democratic Party and the Momin Conference, or even the radical groupings within the Congress, was often caused by the tendency of these bodies to work amongst members of all communities. This, in turn, caused a party like the CPI to be reviled for collaborating with both the Congress and the League, especially as communist activism in the localities began to cater to the constituencies of, and thereby challenge, all the communally determined distributive agencies.[5]

This, of course, raises questions about the nature of wartime nationalist activism and the responses to it in Eastern India. Political parties, like the colonial authorities, were never able to completely control their members' activities in the locality. However, unlike the central government, which was keen to get at least some of its schemes carried out, the dominant groupings within local party units seemed quite willing to accommodate trends that allowed their cadres to garner political support. Thus, policies formulated by the parties' central and provincial working committees, with their specific ideological positions, were usually quietly put aside in favour of rallying agitations around local misgivings regarding shortcomings in official policy, communal disagreements and/or class tensions. However, the economic conditions during 1942 and 1945 ensured that opposition to the wartime priorities of administration – and the complete lack of governance within certain civilian sectors – remained the most common means of drawing support.

But, local political identities remained extremely fluid, with activists of the outlawed Congress operating through organisations formally linked to almost every party except possibly the Muslim League, as well as a range of ostensibly non-political associations.[6] Indeed, the indeterminate nature of the local Congress organisation – or even the local units of organisations like the Muslim League, the Hindu Mahasabha, the Forward Bloc and the Communist Party of India – was an indication of the relative insignificance of specific ideological positions in the locality during a period of extreme economic difficulty. The party organisations in the districts were often fissured, politically promiscuous and quite unencumbered of 'alliances' struck by party working committees, which was related to the tendency of members and/or activists to shift loyalties whenever it suited their interests. The predilection of supporters to accept particular schemes or participate in agitations without really ever committing to other aspects of the parties' aims, forced these organisations to continually re-shape their messages according to the audience targeted, and this impaired the development of well-defined political stances locally, except perhaps the unremitting message of anti-imperialism that tended to be linked by all parties with a range of local issues.[7]

The colonial state's responses to these trends were, thus, necessarily complex. At one level, senior civil servants – in particular the British element of the ICS and the IPS – kept insisting, usually in vain, that the pro-war alliances, like that reached by the Government of India with the CPI politbureau, be honoured in the locality.[8] The official recourse to the arrest of political activists considered was, however, complicated by a variety of factors. Apart from often not having enough staff or not being able to find witnesses against agitators and those involved in attacks against the members of the subordinate services, it also sometimes proved extremely difficult to pin-point political affiliations of the convicts and suspects. In fact, the banning of the Congress was rendered ineffective precisely by this inability to codify party members. While many of the enrolled leadership was put behind bars, the more informal party membership was left to continue agitating, and thereby representing the Congress, against the colonial administration with a range of very flexible political programmes.

These political trends intensified the progress of political re-negotiation in Eastern India, both within the structure of civilian society and the bureaucracy. One representative military report mentioned how 'considerable feeling' had been aroused in loyalist circles in Bihar due to the fact that 'relief committees' were composed of people holding 'anti-British sentiments'. The document also mentioned how the committee members were using the opportunity to spread 'subversive propaganda'; to direct 'relief money' to people holding, or sympathising with, 'revolutionary views', and also to use the funds as an incentive to join Congress ranks. As a result 'those loyal to the Government' saw little of this relief.[9] At another level, the nature of nationalist activism seemed to make Indian bureaucrats in the localities keener to develop closer links to political parties, which, interestingly, led to a situation where the political parties considered it increasingly expedient to criticise the British 'aliens' – rather than the South Asian element of the colonial administration – for all administrative ills.[10] The only organisation willing, and able, to rock this convenient shift in the language of political opposition at all levels of administration was the CPI, which continued to blame the continuation of the Raj on the class-based co-operation of Indian bureaucrats. The provincial Congress and League leadership in the region was, however, beginning to find such political messages inopportune, as the formal units attached to both parties seemed keen to encourage officials to develop links with their organisations. This finally led to a situation where the colonial bureaucracy found it expedient to boost other efforts to attack and politically isolate the CPI at all levels of administration.[11]

I

This assessment of events in Eastern India, which has been based on a wide range of archival material, should, ideally, force us to query some of the generalisations that have been made with regards to the official uses of information, the wartime state and, not least, the bases of the British withdrawal from the sub-continent in 1947. For instance, this study would need to question any tendency to represent the state's wartime propaganda measures as nothing more than an intensification of older public relations trends.[12] In fact, this work underlines the growing complexity of the state's propaganda and information policies, wherein a number of new publicity networks, the selective distribution of food, the threat of discontinuing such supplies and the secret monitoring of mail became crucially important between 1942 and 1945. At another level, an awareness of the complex goals of wartime propaganda and information strategies makes it necessary to question the recently propounded argument about the 'marks of the imminent birth in India' of a 'new constructive imperialism before partition and independence aborted it'. This 'constructive imperialism' was apparently 'prefigured in wartime government intervention in the economy and in ... official propaganda'.[13] However, such a cosy view of state intervention is problematic when one considers the selectivity of such policy, the great economic dislocation it caused within specific sectors and the degree of official dissension engendered by the schemes.[14]

Furthermore, the insights provided by this study also raise questions about the two influential studies of British intelligence in South Asia, both of which have been limited by their primary organising principles. Whereas Christopher Andrew's laudable examination of secret service organisations has been largely Eurocentric in focus,[15] Christopher Bayly has attributed inordinate manipulative powers to an interested 'native informant'.[16] This study would suggest that authorities were able to create networks through which the political sensibilities of a wide cross-section of Indian society was gauged without the assistance of the 'informant'. In fact, the wartime intelligence initiatives based on the secret examination of private correspondence were very often deployed to watch the social groups that supplied the informants. This, among other things, problematises the assumption that the British colonial state was solely dependant on political intelligence provided by agents and collaborative networks, which naturally raises questions about what has come to be categorised these days as 'colonial knowledge'. Rather than being an essentially European imposition or a jointly authored project of British officials and their chosen, and interested, Indian informants, such 'knowledge' was very often constructed on the basis of information gleaned from, among other things, the censorship of private correspondence. Therefore, one can safely infer that quite apart from being inert objects of an imposed 'knowledge', the indigenous target population contributed, albeit sometimes unknowingly, to the preparation and design of many of the official public relations projects deployed amongst them. What is striking about the wartime information gathering structure is its great intricacy, and its ability to monitor a wide variety of attitudes: those of the military personnel and bureaucrats, the 'priority' sections of the civilian population and, remarkably, even Britain's American allies.[17]

This study also permits one to problematise some of commonly prevalent assumptions associated with the colonial state's multi-faceted efforts to evolve a 'consensus' during the Second World War. While the authorities' success in averting large scale and enduring political agitations after August 1942 through advertisements, or the use of, military force cannot be questioned, it is quite another matter to claim that Eastern India was politically tranquil between 1943 and 1945.[18] Such simple view, which has an unfortunately rich ancestry, is also encouraged by a variety of recent works. For instance, studies dealing with the Quit India movement, and the period following it, have tended to over-estimate the loss of political momentum caused by the arrest of sections of the Congress leadership. The bias is also revealed in the somewhat laboured attempts to attribute the persistence of all political opposition to Raj to the presence of a Congress underground, and the unquestioning acceptance of the CPI's 'alliance' with the colonial state, where generalisations about the party stance are based on a very selective presentation of the party politbureau's statements without any reference to local party activism.[19] This study, in comparison, has stressed the fluidity of the local political situation, where activists attached to a range of parties were able to challenge the official attempts to ensure the smooth mobilisation of war. An effort has, thus, been made in this work to describe the great impact of the politically organised attacks on local administrative structures, subordinate bureaucrats and their local allies, and the complex role played by food riots in reformulating local political alliances in Eastern India.

This work also questions the widespread pre-disposition to locate the targets of the official efforts intended to develop a wartime 'consensus' *outside* the parameters of the state structure, which seems to be rooted in the rather simple belief that the central government could control its employees by the mere passage of special wartime legislation. This study shows, instead, that colonial officials, especially the Indian element, were considered a critically important target of all state-sponsored wartime propaganda and information campaigns due to their inclination to re-adapt Government of India legislation. Indeed, the messages disseminated amongst these target groups reveal a much ignored aspect of wartime government control strategies. Apart from congratulatory war publicity and economic benefits, repeated threats, in the form of warnings about the removal of special food rations for not complying with Government of India or military orders, formed an important means of keeping bureaucrats, particularly the subordinate ranks, in line with centrally-prescribed wartime policy. The use of such strategies problematises the notion of 'force', which is usually depicted in studies of colonial India as the threat of – or actually – using military/police power and meting out capital punishment.[20] This study instead suggests that the threat of removal of free or subsidised food during a period of enduring shortages was a form of force that ensured the development of a 'consensus', however transient, for the war-effort. This, in turn, challenges the neat distinction that is regularly made between consensus/hegemony and the use of violence/coercion in studies of South Asia.

Finally, the arguments presented in this work need to be related to the existing analyses of the dissolution of the Raj. There can, of course, really be little doubt that the nature of the post-war political upsurge heightened official anxieties about the longevity of Empire. Industrial and agrarian unrest apart, the radicalisation of politics across the entire spectrum of Indian politics,[21] with the concomitant increase in a range of 'private armies' with political links,[22] worried senior officials based at various levels of the administration.[23] However, it is often ignored that the official nervousness arising from the rapidly degenerating political trends in South Asia were amplified by a very specific understanding of the developments within the structure of the colonial state. Thus, it is important to recognise that whilst the farcical conclusion to the INA trials, the naval mutiny and the civilian disorders that accompanied both events raised British doubts within the state about the strength of the political opposition, these fears tended to be dominated by the nervousness engendered by longer-term trends prevalent within both the army and the bureaucracy.[24]

Fears about the political disposition of the troops in South Asia, based on wartime intelligence, caused the retention of special censorship schemes founded on the secret monitoring of soldiers' mail, and these were deployed to monitor the attitudes of both Indian and British military personnel. But, the information thus collected tended to aggravate the sense of crisis within the central government about their unreliability.[25] The problem of demobilisation had always been a complex one: the South Asian element of the army was reported to be nervous about being discharged and the prospect of returning to civilian life during politically and economically unstable times;[26] while the battle-weary British soldiers had begun to hope for a quick repatriation to Britain after the war.[27] The British element of the officer cadre had always been aware that the Indian soldiers' preparation for civilian life would involve, among other things, a more overt negotiation with, if not participation in, nationalist politics. The onset of the demobilisation proved them correct, especially as it placed troops in a situation where they were suddenly faced with the prospect of having to defend their wartime loyalty towards the Raj.[28]

The effects of the resultant official apprehensions about the army were plain to see. As early as June 1946, the Government of India, despite having the services of the bulk of its South Asian troops, began making plans, ultimately unfulfilled, to bring in five British army divisions into the sub-continent in order to prepare for a challenge from a possible Congress sponsored political movement.[29] Stafford Cripps reiterated the same sentiment a year later. In a Commons debate, he made it clear that the only way to hold on to India would be to go in for 'total repression' and that this could only be achieved by the injection of large numbers of British troops, which, keeping the situation in the United Kingdom in mind, was impossible.[30] Interestingly, the widespread official doubts in 1946 and 1947 about the reliability of serving Indian soldiers also caused the British units still present in the sub-continent to be given a vastly increased role in policing especially disruptive political agitations and communal riots,[31] and the shortage of such troops caused Nepalese Gurkha battalions to be deployed alongside them.[32] It is, therefore, surprising that the British unwillingness – and inability – to depend on the assistance of South Asian troops and the impossibility of replacing them with British soldiers has been so downplayed in the historiography dealing with independence and partition.[33]

And while the British reactions to the process of re-negotiation within the Indian element of the civilian bureaucracy were generally less dramatic, probably due to the fact that the loyalty of these officials was already considered to have been compromised by the formation of provincial ministries, there can be little doubt that they accentuated the growing feeling of loss of political control within the Raj. A good illustration of these trends is provided by Claude Auchinleck's belief, in 1946, that the situation arising from a war between Hindus and Muslims would be impossible to control due to the unreliability of the police forces, and by implication, the bureaucratic structures that controlled them.[34] This, of course, was not an isolated view, and was reiterated by a wide range of British military officers. Arthur Smith, the Chief of General Staff, India, declared that:

> The attitude of the police [during the Calcutta riots] is typical of what we must expect everywhere. All police forces are 'looking over their shoulder' with an eye to being on the right side in the future when we have 'quit India'.[35]

Auchinleck and Smith were undoubtedly affected by the tone of military intelligence reaching the GHQ, and some of these provide very interesting insights about bureaucratic attitudes at the time. A secret communication, dealing with the rioting in Calcutta on the 15, 16, and 17 of August 1946, from the Headquarters of the Eastern Command declared, for instance, that:

> Apart from a few senior officers, the police themselves were unwilling to open fire and I don't blame them.... During the whole of these riots until the army was called out and authorised to shoot, I met various police patrols and pointed out rioters and looters, but there was always some good excuse why they should not fire ... H.E. the Governor told the Commissioner of Police on the 16th ... that he would back him in any strong action taken, but I think this assurance was given too late for the information to be really absorbed by the subordinate ranks.[36]

But senior British officials also remained aware that the re-negotiation of political relations was by no means limited to the police. A good example of this is provided by the Chief Commissioner of Delhi's complaints about the tone of official film propaganda material being distributed in July 1946. He declared that:

> ... I have been very surprised to see how very pro-Congress – indeed pro-Left Wing Congress [sic] – the Indian news has now become. I know it has been handed over to some company, but nevertheless the people generally still believe that it is the Government news film.... Last night I happened to go to the Royal Cinema, and the Indian news contained quite a long account of a large meeting in Bombay of [the] Central Government Servants' Association with Jai Prakash Narain as the principal speaker invited by the Association. The President of the Association, presumably a Central Government employee in Bombay,

in his remarks introducing Jai Prakash Narain eulogised his services to the country. Apart from the utterly wrong impression which a thing like this gives to at least 90% of the audience who think that the news reel is still a Government one, what right has the Central Government Servants Association Bombay to hold a mass public meeting with Jai Prakash Narain as their principal speaker! Can anything be done to stop this sort of thing? On the other hand, the Government of India's own clerks in Lodi Colony had Jai Prakash Narain as their speaker at a meeting in their colony not very long ago, as you know.'[37]

Yet, these references and reports dealing with the unreliability of the Indian bureaucracy in South Asia, and their capacity to stoke British anxieties and shape an eagerness to withdraw from empire, has generally been ignored. The existing historiography has, instead, attributed the weakening and dissolution of the colonial state to the erosion of loyalist support.[38] Indeed, the attempts to attribute the dissolution of the Raj to the democratic instincts of India's British rulers, to a teleological upsurge of enthusiasm for an undifferentiated Congress ideology and to an incapacity to provide British recruits to the Indian administrative services have all detracted from the important role played by the weakening of formal state structures in determining decolonisation. This bias, which was initially reflected in works attempting to highlight the controlled transfer of power or in triumphalist descriptions of the Congress's ability to single-handedly force the Raj into retreat, has been strengthened in recent years by analyses that highlight the erosion of the state's informal collaborative base *after* the war.[39] But, some of these analyses seem troubled by the prospect of accepting that the formal structure of the late colonial state was predominantly South Asian in composition and that the Raj was irrevocably weakened by their decision to jump ship during a political crisis fashioned by policies and trends during a very difficult war. The reasons for this are perhaps understandable: it downplays somewhat the romantic visions of nationalism and independence; it shows up the frailty of British rule and its distance from the great bulk of the South Asian population; it does not allow one to blame the wartime excesses and tragedies simply on foreign rule and forces one to investigate the roles played in them by sections of South Asian society; and it shows up the fact that much of the colonial bureaucracy based in India was quietly welcomed into the new nationalist fraternity in 1947 for having adroitly displayed a distinct lack of ebullience in dealing with the members of the Congress central and provincial working committee while carrying out reprisals against the party cadre. The aim of this monograph, however, has been to underline just these complexities in the hope that they, and the many other unexplored and important aspects of the Second World War, might be of interest in future to researchers.

Notes

1 Most secret WIS (SEAC and II), 17 December 1943, L/WS/1/1433, OIOC. Notably, touring military officers also expressed surprise at the 'apathy' and 'non-cooperative spirit' of the better off members of the population towards the famine victims. Ibid.
2 See, for instance, correspondence between the district magistracy and local military commands, Bihar, United Provinces and Bengal, c.1943, WSF 65/1(i)/43, BSA.
3 See, for instance, chapter XVIII in B.L. Raina (ed), *Official History of the Indian Armed Forces in the Second World War 1939–45: Medical Services (Administration)*, Kanpur, 1953.
4 See, secret report on the activities of the various relief committees and legal aid committees organised by Congressmen, c.1943, HPF(I) 4/1/1944, NAI. Also see, correspondence between the district magistracy and local military commands, Bihar, United Provinces and Bengal, c.1943, WSF 65/1(i)/43, BSA. Another description of the various agencies operating in the localities of Bengal is provided in Raina (ed), *Medical Services (Administration)*, p. 411.
5 Military intelligence in the Eastern army operational area was reporting an increase in 'hunger marches' inspired by Communist and Congress groups active in the rural areas by mid-1943. These demonstrations were, of course, directed at a number of targets: the local administration, landed notables and grain merchants, *all of whom* were blamed for the food crisis. In keeping with the scale of the shortages and starvation, many of these demonstrations were aggressive in tone, and one report declared that the 'character of some is reported as such that only a very little propaganda will be required to incite the demonstrators to acts of violence.' Most secret WIS(II), 4 June 1943, L/WS/1/1433, OIOC. Also see, extracts from secret reports by District Magistrates in Bihar, Eastern United Provinces and Assam, c.1943, WSF 63/iii/43, BSA.
6 See, for example, secret report on the activities of the various relief committees and legal Aid committees organised by Congressmen, c.1943, HPF(I) 4/1/1944, NAI.
7 See, for example, pamphlet entitled 'The Freedom Struggle Front' attached to departmental note, Home Department, GOI, 11 December 1942, HPF(I) 3/8/42, NAI.
8 The differences in official attitudes towards, and expectations from the CPI at the different levels of the colonial administration is discussed in detail in S. Bhattacharya, 'The Colonial State And The Communist Party Of India, 1942–45: A Reappraisal', *SAR*, Vol. 15, No. 1, 1995, pp. 62–77.

9 Secret WIS(II) 26 January 1945, L/WS/1/1433, OIOC.
10 While these trends are apparent in a variety of official reports and correspondence, especially those prepared at the level of the district and sub-division, the tendency to absolve South Asian officials is particularly visible in the vernacular newspapers. See, for instance, issues of *Hunkar*, the mouthpiece of the Swami Sahajanand Saraswati-led *kisan sabhas*, and the Provincial Press Adviser's files in the Bihar State Archives. There were, of course, instances in Bihar where the actions of particular South Asian officials were criticised for having specific communal biases. However, even in these cases, references to their involvement in supporting the repressive policies of a foreign administration were downplayed, and they were, instead, usually accused of being lackeys of either the League or the Congress. See, for example, extracts from secret reports by District Magistrates in Bihar, Eastern United Provinces and Assam, c.1943, WSF 63/iii/43, BSA.
11 The communist activists' inclination to mobilise – or take part in – 'hunger marches', which invariably demanded the release of hoards of grain or the re-distribution of surpluses was considered disruptive both by local administrators and rural notables. Indeed, the threats from mobs demanding food were sometimes countered by the combined efforts of the police and local zamindars' guards. However, itinerant grain merchants often found it much more difficult to protect their stocks, especially due to the District Magistrates' abiding inability to offer them police escorts due to a shortage of staff. In such a situation, communist activists were seen as being threats by officials attached to the central services, the provincial bureaucracy and the members of District Local Boards, who were very often zamindars. CPI members were, therefore, frequently arrested, despite the 'alliance' between the Government of India and the party, and the guarantee of political freedom which the agreement was supposed to bestow. See, correspondence between the district magistracy and local military commands, Bihar, United Provinces and Bengal, c.1943, WSF 65/1(i)/43, BSA. The attempts to incarcerate communist activists operating in rural areas was continued in 1944 and 1945 due to a variety of reasons. The Government of India by 1944 resolved to withdraw from a rather fruitless alliance with the CPI, thereby allowing its coercive apparatus to be targeted against the communist activists at all levels of the administration. Moreover, the central governments changed priorities in this regard coincided with the release of the arrested Congress leadership and cadres, whose efforts to recreate a formal political base amongst industrial workers and in the rural areas brought the INC – and later the CSP leadership – into conflict with the CPI and the RDP See, secret note entitled 'Communist Infiltration in Indian Politics with Special Reference to Recent Civil Disorders in Bombay, Calcutta, Karachi, Madras and Lahore', by R.L. Rau, 28 February 1946, HPF(I) PR–1/103/46, NAI. Also see, secret report entitled 'A note on agrarian Situation [sic]', c.October 1946, HPF(I) 125/1946, NAI, and CSFRs from Eastern India between August 1945 and July 1947, NAI.
12 M. Israel, *Communications and power: Propaganda and the press in the Indian nationalist struggle, 1920–1947*, Cambridge, 1994.

13 C.A. Bayly, 'Returning the British to South Asian History: The Limits of Colonial Hegemony', *South Asia*, Vol. XVII, 2, 1994, p. 17.
14 Bayly has, in the aforementioned piece, referred to, among other things, an article by this historian as proof for the existence of this 'constructive imperialism', at least during the Second World War. See reference to Bhattacharya, 'The Colonial State and the Communist Party of India', in footnote 76. Ibid. While the piece did indeed mention instances of wartime economic intervention by the state, Bhattacharya referred, at the same time, to two critically important issues informing these measures: the public relations aspect of such official campaigns and the frequent administrative (British and/or Indian) fear about the outbreak of disorder. Both these points have, unfortunately, been ignored by Bayly.
15 C. Andrew, *Secret Service: The Making of the British Intelligence Community*, London, 1985.
16 C.A. Bayly 'Knowing the Country: Empire and Information in India', *MAS*, 27, 1, 1993. Also see, C.A. Bayly, *Empire & Information: Intelligence gathering and social communication in India, 1780–1870*, Cambridge, 1996.
17 Apart from targeting Indian social groups, the structures of official censorship were also used, whenever possible, to keep an eye on other 'allies', notably Americans based in India. See, secret 'American Report' by Bombay Censor Station, 15 March 1943, WO 208/816, PRO. The other side of the story, that is the attitude of the American intelligence apparatus in India towards the British Raj, is provided in a valuable new contribution. See, R.J. Aldrich, 'American Intelligence and the British Raj: The OSS, the SSU and India, 1942–1947', *Intelligence and National Security*, Spring 1998.
18 Historians like Kamtekar have claimed that 1943 was 'silent' politically, not least because 'popular momentum' had been exhausted in 1942. See, I. Kamtekar, 'The End of the Colonial State in India, 1942–47' unpublished Ph.D. thesis, University of Cambridge, 1989, p. 28. Kamtekar adds that: 'Surrounded by a basically hostile population, the colonial state nevertheless conducted a highly successful war effort, contributing men and materials to the Allied victory. While it did this, despite a terrible famine and a short-lived rebellion, India remained politically tranquil. The ingredients of internal peace were complex. The state's political strategy, including unprecedented brutality and unexpected alliances, took care of the Congress, the Communists and the Muslim League. Its army, menacingly visible to civilians, subdued thoughts of dissent. Famine and severe shortages deflected some attention away from politics. Capitalists and peasants, propitiated by their profits kept quiet; deprived of their support for the struggle, the Congress became helpless. Paradoxically, therefore, the reasons for the political silence of these years lay in the war effort itself. So did the major drawback: watching recruits flow into it, the colonial state acquired a new sense of vulnerability.' Ibid., p. 78. Such a view is, of course, overly simplistic.
19 Vinita Damodaran has, amongst others, highlighted the creation of a 'political vacuum' by the arrest of the Congress. She declares in an article dealing with the *Azad Dastas* in Bihar that 'The months following the

August outbreak of the Quit India movement were a period of great trial for the Congress leaders, most of whom were put behind bars. By September 1942 the British had completely repressed the mass movement, the Congress organization had been banned, and all legitimate political activity had come to a standstill. However, elements of the mass movement still remained active, despite the best efforts of the British to stamp them out, in the form of disparate terrorist organizations and dacoit gangs that had sprung up all over Bihar by 1943.... They roamed the countryside, some with political affiliations, some with none, but all with the support of the village populations. In the context of economic crisis they filled what was otherwise a political vacuum between 1942 and 1944.' See, V. Damodaran, 'Azad Dastas and Dacoit Gangs: The Congress and Underground Activity in Bihar, 1942–44', *MAS*, 26, 3, 1992, pp. 417–418. However, such an assessment of the political situation completely ignores the fact that activists attached to other political formations, like the CPI, the RDP and the *kisan sabhas* organised by Swami Sahajanand Saraswati, continually criticised the Raj between 1942 and 1945 in their attempts to mobilise support for themselves. Damodaran's ability to ignore these trends is particularly surprising considering that a variety of files in the Bihar State Archives – notably those in the Political Department (Special Section) series, the Provincial Press Advisory series and the War series – and the Bihar Chief Secretary's Fortnightly Reports dealing with the period between 1942 and 1945 continually refer to the persistence of, and the challenges posed by, such activism. Interestingly, these political manoeuvrings are clearly distinguished from activities of role of dacoit gangs, and the diverse CSP and Congress underground organisations. Interestingly, Swami Sahajanand re-appears, albeit fleetingly, in Damodaran's analysis of the post-war period. See, for instance, V. Damodaran, *Broken Promises: Popular Protest, Indian Nationalism and the Congress Party in Bihar 1935–1946*, Delhi, 1992, p. 363. This approach is in keeping with the long-lasting, but flawed, historiographical tradition of equating the so-called 'pro-war' stances of Sahajanand, the RDP and the CPI with their supposed inability to castigate, openly or otherwise, the Raj on the basis of an array of local difficulties and administrative deficiencies. Moreover, the archival material available in Bihar would also suggest that the disagreements between the communist and pro-Sahajanand *kisan sabhas* were often rooted in their attempts to mobilise competing sections of the peasantry and that their mobilisation was successful enough to rattle both the CSP and INC Indeed, the hostility of their local party units against the organisations attached to the CPI and the RDP, between 1945 and 1947, can be effectively located in just these trends. It is also well worth remembering in this context that it is useful for historians to remain aware of the Congress Working Committee's efforts to advertise its vetted briefs as the only true basis for anti-imperialism while assessing the complexities of the post-war nationalist political debates.

20 A good example of the wartime administration's decision to widely advertise its intention to use capital punishment as a deterrent against political agitators is provided in the period after the 'Quit India'

movement. See, for instance, express letter from F. Puckle, Secretary, Information and Broadcasting Department, GOI to the Chief Secretary, GOB, 20 August 1942, PPAF 49/42, BSA. For the wording of the official threats, see press note on the imposition of the death penalty for involvement in cases of 'sabotage' within India by L.J.D. Wakely, Deputy Secretary, Home Department, GOI, 16 January 1943, HPF(I) 3/9/43, NAI.

21 This was, of course, affected by trends within the structures of all the major political parties. Elements within the Muslim League in Bengal, particularly local activists like Abdul Hashem, had, for instance, effectively forced a radicalisation of the party's agrarian programme. Similarly, the Congress's diverse left-wing and the CSP, which was back in favour with an INC working committee busily seeking allies for their attacks on the CPI, were agressively trying to re-develop formal support bases both in the industrial and agricultural sector. The Hindu Mahasabha's self-conscious assertion of a 'Hindu Nationalist' image – in response to the colonial authorities' rebuff towards its advances during constitutional negotiations, the sidelining of S.P. Mookerjea's failed pro-Congress strategies, the formal return of Savarkar – boosted its communal activism at all levels of administration. A report dealing with the United Provinces declared, for example, that the 'most striking feature of the communal situation in this province during the last few weeks has been the emergence of orthodox Hinduism as potent factor. The Hindu Mahasabha, which had very little following or political background, as a purely religious body, have come into the open, and are rallying Hindus all over the country to fight Islam. At their meetings speakers have also been critical of the Congress Interim Government – for their failure to protect the Hindus of East Bengal and for their support to the Muslims. The effect of the call to religion can be seen in Benares, where the circulation of the two local Congress newspapers has greatly diminished, while that of the single orthodox Hindu local daily has much increased.' Secret extract from a fortnightly appreciation of the political situation in the UP by the CID, October 1946, L/PO/10/24, OIOC. And unfortunately, the Communist politbureau's support for the formation of Pakistan only encouraged the communal debates being encouraged by the Mahasabha, the League and elements within the Congress. However, it should not be forgotten that CPI activists in the districts of Eastern India continued in their attempts to tap into local class tensions in order to mobilise support. Notably, their efforts to draw the poorer sections of the Muslim peasantry into the local CPI units, and away from the Congress and the League, often caused them to downplay, or even to weaken, the Muslim self-determination thesis. One official report about the agrarian unrest in Bihar complained how the contemporary political situation was 'rendered still more difficult because of the present communal tension but both the CSP and the CPI hope that by intensifying the Kisan agitation they would be diverting the attention of the goonda element in the population into another channel. By this, they also hope to combat communalism. The zamindars have already shown that both the Muslims and the Hindus are prepared to work on a common platform to resist any attempt on the part of either the Government or Kisans in taking away their patrimony.' Secret

report entitled 'A note on agrarian Situation [sic]', c.October 1946, HPF(I) 125/1946, NAI. Indeed, the tensions created within the CPI structure by the politbureau's presentation of a pro-Pakistan thesis deserves more careful research.

22 There was, over time, an increasing fear within the Government of India and GHQ (India) about the formation of private armies, which were linked to one party or another. In 1947, for instance, it was estimated that there were about twelve such forces, which contained a total of 413,000 volunteers. See, extract from minutes of Governor's Conference (second day), 16 April 1947, L/P&J/ 8/679, Coll 117/C/81/A, OIOC. For another description of the armed 'wings' of the RSS, the Hindu Mahasabha, the Akali Dal and the Muslim League (the Khaksars and the Muslim National Guards), see WO 216/468, PRO.

23 As the material presented above suggests, the resulting official – especially British – nervousness resulting about the post-war political situation was linked to a variety of trends. For instance, there was great official unease in the immediate post-war period about the visible rise in support for Congress-led agitations. For a good example of this, see secret WIS(II), 14 September 1945, L/WS/1/1506, OIOC. The scale of violence in the agitations held during the INA trials worried both the civilian and military authorities, especially when it appeared that all the parties were 'combining' against the administration, and also daring to attack army targets. One report described how, 'All traffic is being halted and attacked, both British and American. About 17 military vehicles have been burnt. All main thoroughfares are being blocked by barricades and mobs'. See, copy of a secret report from Assistant Director, Military Intelligence, General Staff Branch, New Delhi, 12 February 1946, HPF(I) 5/22/46, NAI. There were also widespread worries about the fact that there was much hostility towards Europeans in the city. Another report declared that 'there have been assaults on Anglo-Indian and European women, and attacks on European clubs and residences. Members of the mobs have used lighted torches to set fire to cars and in attempts to set fire to European establishments. Generally there is a bitter racial feeling and attempts are being made to boycott everything European, to disaffect servants and to prevent the sale of food to Europeans. Today the butchers refused to sell meat to Europeans.' See, CIO Calcutta's secret telephone report no. 3, 13 February 1946, HPF(I) 5/22/46, NAI. Such reports were by no means isolated. In fact, the analysis prepared after the agitation was brought under control makes even more interesting reading: although there was much relief about the fact that Congress leadership in the province had opposed the agitations, and that they had been involved in efforts to get the mobs to disperse, albeit without much success, there was great uneasiness about the communist involvement in the disturbances. It concluded by stating that 'One significant fact emerges from a study of these disturbances, namely that any small collection of individuals – they might be irresponsible students – has the power to upset completely and immediately the equilibrium of Calcutta and to cause a reign of mob-violence.... Anti-Government propaganda has been so continued, persistent and unrebutted that the average man in the street really believes

all that political leaders say. As a result there is no respect for Government institutions and the tendency is growing for them to be treated with open disrespect.... If a difference of opinion arises between the authorities responsible for discipline, public sympathy, regardless of the facts of each case, is always given to the latter who are treated as national heroes for actions for which they should rightly be caned. This absence of a correcting influence in Indian life is gradually leading to a point where no authority is respected and if matters do not improve, chaos and disorder are the inevitable outcome of all organized activities.' Extract from secret report entitled 'Political Aspects of Calcutta Disturbances of February 1946', by the Commissioner of Police, Calcutta, 3 April 1946, HPF(I) 5/22/46, NAI. In addition, officials remained worried about the Hindu Mahasabha's capacity to foment communal trouble, which, in a period of high level of political flux, was considered particularly unwelcome. This is reflected, for example, in the Intelligence Bureau's fears about the sudden increase in membership of the Hindustan National Guards – often also referred to as the Hindu Rashtra Dal – and the Ram Sena, both of which were linked to the Mahasabha. Top secret report on the All India Hindu Mahasabha, c.1946, L/WS/1/746, OIOC. And, the prevalence of such assessments in the post-war period had caused Claude Auchinleck to envisage the possibility of a religious war between the Hindus and Muslims. See note by C.J.E. Auchinleck, Commander-in-Chief, India, to D. Monteath, Under Secretary of State for India, GOBr, c.1946, L/WS/1/1008, OIOC. The fears about the effects Mahasabha – and other communally determined – political activism were palpable in a province like the United Provinces. One commentator cautioned that the province 'faces communal anarchy unless very strong action and immediate action is taken to restrain the activities of volunteer bodies, relief committees.' See, secret extract from a fortnightly appreciation of the political situation in the UP by the CID, October 1946, L/PO/10/24, OIOC. Also, military intelligence provided by the Eastern Command seemed to believe that the Hindu mobs during the Calcutta riots of 15, 16 and 17 August 1946 were organised by the Mahasabha. One report declared that 'From secret information obtained.... I believe that the Hindu side of the fracas was organised by the Hindu Mahasabha who misguided the upcountry Hindus, such as gwallahs, rickshaw pullers, parn berri wallhahs, tea shop wallhahs and other rif raf, by telling them that they had to fight for their existence or be exterminated [sic].' See, secret and personal letter from HQ Eastern Command to Brigadier T.Y. Boyce, Director of Intelligence, GHQ (India), 24 August 1946, WO 216/662, PRO. There can really be little doubt that the Mahasabha's – and the RSS's – ability to stoke communal trouble rattled the British representatives involved in partition deliberations, which seemed to contribute to their eagerness to leave what was considered a dangerously unstable empire. Indeed, by April 1947 older plans of creating food dumps, in order to prepare for a possible 'prolonged siege', were being re-assessed. See, note by A.E. Porter, GOI, 19 April 1947, HPF(I) 21/3/47, NAI.

24 See, for instance, departmental memorandum titled 'The Indian National Army Agitation', c.November 1945, Home Department, GOI, HPF(I)

21/6/45, NAI, and a memorandum titled 'Calcutta Disturbances in Retrospect' by Central Intelligence Officer, IB, Home Department, GOI, 28 November 1945, HPF(I) 21/16/45, NAI.

25 Indeed, one work has recognised the important point that the question of loyalty of Indian troops cannot merely be tied to their reactions towards the Congress, and that it was often informed by deep-seated fears about the future uncertainty. See, N. Narain, 'Co-option and Control: The role of the colonial army in India 1918–1947', unpublished Ph.D. thesis, University of Cambridge, 1992, p. 70. This work has also pointed out that 'War, by seriously weakening both central and provincial administrations, enhanced their military dependency. But Internal Security plans were now troubled by the likelihood of large scale disloyalty by Indian troops, their probable capitulation to communalism, and subsequent and subsequent unavailability for dealing with such riots, the rapid demobilisation and war weariness of British troops, and the alarming emergence of an anti-military trend in mob-violence.' Ibid., p. 81.

26 A unit censorship report explained that the end of the Second World War represented to the *sepoy* the inevitable return to a not very easy civilian life, wherein 'the Indian soldiers face the realities of the rationing of cloth, kerosine [sic], food-grains and sugar.' WIS(SEAC&II), 15 September 1945, L/WS/1/1506, OIOC. The GHQ (India), in co-operation with the Government of India, did try to make the burden of demobilisation lighter by creating special links between the army re-settlement directorate and the provincial employment exchanges. See, HPF(I) 21/36/46, NAI.

27 For references to the war-wariness amongst British soldiers in the last phase of the war, see secret reports on the morale of British, Indian and Colonial troops of Allied land forces for months of August, September, October, November and December 1944, and January 1945, L/WS/2/71, OIOC. Also see, most secret letter from Lord Munster to SSI, GOBr, c.November 1944, and confidential letter from S.R. Kaiwar, Deputy Secretary, Defence Department, GOI, to the Under Secretary of State for India, GOBr, 14 August 1945, in L/WS/2/80, OIOC.

28 Most provinces agreed to reserve between 50 to 70 percent of the post-war permanent jobs in the police for ex-soldiers. See, Home Department memorandum by Lt Col H.A. Gordon, 2 February 1946, PF 207/46, NAI. However, the creation of such positions and getting them filled, most of which were in services in the provincial list, proved quite another matter. Therefore, it led to a situation where relatively few of the demobilised soldiers found work immediately. A report from Punjab, for instance, mentioned that even by end-1946, less than 20 per cent of ex-soldiers registered with employment exchanges had been found work. See, fortnightly report, Government of Punjab, 14 December 1946, L/PJ/5/249, OIOC. Moreover, one needs to keep in mind that the vast range of technical service personnel who were released from the army hailed from provinces other than Punjab, and were based often in urban centres without access to farming land.

29 S. Sarkar, *Modern India*, Delhi, 1983, p. 435. The Government of India's stance is perhaps best explained by the fact that it was expecting trouble to erupt after the elections of 1946. Of the various possibilities it was

preparing itself for, the most striking was the anticipated effect of a Congress victory, which was described thus: 'A demand by Congress for immediate transfer to itself of power. If this demand is refused Congress may instigate a well organized revolt. This might amount to anything from disorders on the 1942 model to full-scale war, *depending on the attitude of the Indian Army* [emphasis mine].' See, top secret note on the political situation in India, 19 December 1945, WO 208/822, PRO.

30 V.P. Menon, *Transfer of Power in India*, Bombay, 1950, p. 346. Indeed, it was government policy to vigorously reduce British army commitments world-wide between 1946 and 1949. See, A. Farrar-Hockley, 'The Post-War Army 1945–1963', in D. Chandler and I. Beckett (eds), *The Oxford History of the British Army*, Oxford, 1996, pp. 317–319.

31 The feeling that it was important to raise the proportion of British troops in any military force involved in internal security was being articulated in official circles even before the Second World War ended. For example, see secret letter from Secretary, GOP, to the Secretary, Home Department, GOI, 12 February 1945, PF No. 174/32/46 (c), NAI. However, the tendency to deploy British troops to deal with – or supervise military action against – serious cases of civilian disorder became so pronounced from 1946 onwards that it is only possible to refer to a few representative samples here. For example, the Eastern Command HQ decided to deploy two British battalions to tackle the serious disturbances in Calcutta related to the INA trials. See, copy of a secret report from Assistant Director, Military Intelligence, General Staff Branch, New Delhi, 12 February 1946, HPF(I) 5/22/46, NAI. Another excellent example of the deep British suspicion about the integrity of Indian troops in 1947 is provided by the high-level debates regarding a charter for British troops in India in July that year. The discussion regarding paragraph 4(a) of this document, which declared that 'British Troops in India will NOT [sic] be used in any operational role other than the protection of British lives. They will therefore NOT [sic] be used to intervene if he is satisfied this is essential to protect British lives', is particularly interesting. General Arthur Smith, the Chief of General Staff, New Delhi, said that this needed explanation, which he did by providing the following imaginary situation: 'We will say that Calcutta has gone all rioty. The Police have proved unreliable, communal fighting is widespread and British lives in the affected area are threatened. The Commander-in-Chief (on the recommendation of the local commander) may consider that the only way to safeguard British lives is to help stop the communal rioting. In other words, it will not be possible (as you may well imagine) for British troops merely to go and rescue British folk, and the only way they can protect them is by helping to quell the communal outbreak. This may be an extreme case, but is not an impossibility, and I suggest we should be prepared for it. I hope, therefore, that my explanation of the wording of para 4(a) may be helpful.' See, top secret and personal letter from General A. Smith, Chief of General Staff, New Delhi, to General G. Scoones, Secretary, Military Department, India Office, GOBr, 1 July 1947, WO 216/668, PRO. These fears about the unreliability of Indian troops, especially the officer ranks, were, of course, informed by reports from senior British officers based in

India. See note by T.W. Rees, Commanding Officer, 4th Division, India, 30 June 1947, attached to secret minute dated 9 July 1947, WO 216/668, PRO.

32 One battalion of Gurkha troops was, for instance, called out to assist the two battalions of British infantry to tackle the disturbances in Calcutta connected to the INA trials. See, CIO Calcutta's secret telephone report no. 3, 13 February 1946, HPF(I) 5/22/46, NAI. For a wholesome discussion on the complications that begun to arise with the use of Nepalese Gurkha battalions for internal security purposes in an increasingly unstable political situation, see WO 216/828, PRO.

33 A self-professed study of the colonial state has declared that: 'On the whole, imperial authority was considered to remain adequate for a confrontation with the nationalists. Consequently direct challenges, like the urban riots and the mutiny, were squarely faced and promptly extinguished. This was possible because at no point did the state have qualms about the immediate obedience of the army: if it was commanded to take care of a Congress movement, it was expected to click its heels and strike hard.' Kamtekar, 'The End of the Colonial State', p. 111. My attempt has been to query just such simplistic assumptions, which in the case of Kamtekar's thesis is, one assumes, drawn from the secondary sources he has relied on. His work is rather thin on primary research – he has, for instance, ignored a whole corpus of rich archival material dealing with the British War Office and its interactions with the Government of India, available in the Public Record Office, and records in provincial repositories – and quite lumbered by notions of state autonomy. Both tendencies can be problematic, especially when one attempts to study a complex period like the 1940s. The best examples of this are probably provided by the aforementioned quote itself, but are also visible in Kamtekar's generalisations regarding the administrative challenges posed by 'urban riots'. It is important to remember that government representatives located at the various levels of administration had quite differing notions about who their nationalist opponents were throughout the war, and that official definitions of the protagonist changed dramatically with the Congress's decision to join the interim government in 1947. So, while the disruptive potential of the Congress was feared before the elections of 1946, those in 'authority' after the formation of the interim government – that is the representatives of the British government, the Congress and the League – began to fear the capacity of the Communists, the Mahasabha, the RSS and various *Kisan Sabhas* to create trouble. The riots that worried administrators were by no means only urban in nature. Indeed, rural outbreaks of violence caused great official apprehension, especially as they tended to peter out not due to effective official intervention but the 'defeat' of the zamindari, usually the forcible removal and redistribution of grain. At another level, Kamtekar's decision to ignore the complex character of official responses to 'urban riots' seems analytically predetermined. After all, these outbreaks caused a situation where the Congress central/provincial leadership was often forced to accompany British military personnel into the streets in order to issue appeals to maintain the peace, usually with notably little success. The

Congress leadership remained equally keen to put an end to the trouble engendered by the mutiny by RIN ratings in Bombay, as well as the disturbances following it. Moreover, one should not really forget that the naval ratings in Calcutta struck work in sympathy with mutinies in Western India, and even though the issue was resolved without violence, senior military officers did consider the event a mutiny despite publicly downplaying it. But, it needs to be pointed out here that one work does declare that 'One of the factors influencing the timing of independence was a condition of nervousness on the part of the Raj, regarding the state of military loyalty.' See, Narain, 'Co-option and Control', p. 283. However, Narain does not investigate the issue in any great detail, and she certainly does not seem aware of the great role played by the structures and tone of military intelligence in shaping the official nervousness about Indian troops between 1945 and 1947.

34 See, note by C.J.E. Auchinleck, Commander-in-Chief, India, to D. Monteath, Under Secretary of State for India, GoBr, c.1946, L/WS/1/1008, OIOC.
35 Confidential letter from General A. Smith, Chief of General Staff, India, to Lieutenant General F.E.W. Simpson, Vice Chief of the Imperial General Staff, War Office, GOBr, 28 August 1946, WO 216/662, PRO.
36 See secret and personal letter from HQ Eastern Command to Brigadier T.Y. Boyce, DMI, GHQ (India), 24 August 1946, WO 216/662, PRO.
37 See, personal letter from W. Christie, Chief Commissioner, Delhi, to A. Waugh, Home Member, GOI, 29 July 1946, HPF(I) 107/46, NAI.
38 A good description of the trends within the zamindari in the United Provinces, and the political formations deployed by them, is provided in P. Reeves, *Landlords And Governments in Uttar Pradesh: A study of their relations under Zamindari abolition*, Bombay, 1991. Descriptions of the erosion of loyalist support have, of course, taken a variety of forms. Of particular interest, in the context of this study, has been the reference to the loss of intelligence provided by the state's informal allies. For instance, one study tells us that, while referring to the situation in 1947, that: 'The intelligence system had in the meantime disintegrated. A couple of years earlier the system had been efficient, informing the state of the aims, fears and plans of political parties. News from agents and informants was distilled by police inspectors who produced a daily diary, a precis of which was sent to the chief secretary and the governor. The situation now changed. Many of the usual sources disappeared, either in panic or as victims of riot and arson, and as the personnel split and scattered, suspicion and hatred permeated the ranks. The results were calamitous. The disintegration of the intelligence system meant that the state no longer knew what the various parties were doing or planning, and this at a time of considerable disorder when it really needed such information.' Kamtekar, 'The End of the Colonial State', p. 140. A similar argument has also been put forward by Chris Bayly. See, Bayly 'Knowing the Country: Empire and Information in India'. A refreshing and well researched difference in opinion is provided by Swarna Aiyar, who has pointed out that intelligence gathering – which she calls 'a crucial aspect to the maintenance of state power' – remained in efficient working order right up to the first week of August 1947. See, S. Aiyar, 'Violence and the

State in the Partition of Punjab: 1947–48' unpublished Ph.D. thesis, University of Cambridge, 1994, p. 14.

39 Judith Brown is one of the very few historians to recognise the capacity of Indians within the structure of the state to weaken the Raj. However, Brown, like the other scholars dealing with the transfer of power, seems to locate the strains in the period after the war, when she declares that: 'By 1946 the British knew their network of Indian allies in the services was a fast weakening ... instrument of their rule. The strains of war, the prospect of transferred power, and the communal conflict had eroded efficiency and morale, and now threatened ultimately loyalty to the raj itself. Wavell was in no doubt that he was ... presiding over an imperial edifice which must be dismantled or collapse.' J.M. Brown, *Modern India: The Origins of an Asian Democracy*, Delhi, 1984, p. 316.

Bibliography

A. Manuscript Sources

Archives for Contemporary History, Jawaharlal Nehru University, New Delhi, India.

Miscellaneous papers relating to the Communist Party of India, 1939–45.

Bihar State Record Office, Patna, India.

Political Department (Special Section) Files
Provincial Press Advisory Department Files
War Department Files

Centre of South Asian Studies Archives, Cambridge, UK

Abraham papers
Ansorge papers
Baker papers
Barnes papers
Bayley papers
Bell papers
Biggie papers
Bose papers
Gimson papers
Hyde papers
MacDonald (T.) papers
Maclean papers
Martin papers
McCall papers
Srewart (A.) papers
Stanton-Ife papers
Stephens papers
Stuart papers

Churchill Archives Centre, Cambridge, UK

Grigg papers
Slim papers

House of Lords Record Office, London, UK

Sorensen papers

National Archives of India, New Delhi, India.

Nanavati papers
Proceedings of the Education, Health and Lands Department, Government of India.
Proceedings of the Home Political (Internal) Department, Government of India
Proceedings of the Home Public Department, Government of India
Proceedings of the Home Police Department, Government of India
Proceedings of the Medical Department.
Proceedings of the Public Health Depatment, Government of India
Proscribed Literature Collection

Nehru Memorial Museum and Library, New Delhi, India.

AICC Collections
CID Collections
Hindu Mahasabha Collections
Peasant Movements Collections
M.N Roy Collections
Quit India Movement Collections
Selections from Uttar Pradesh State Archives

Ministry of Defence (India), Historical Section, New Delhi, India.

Demobilisation Files

Oriental and India Office Collections, British Library, London, UK

Bengal Governor's Secretariat papers (R/3/2 series)
Information Department papers (L/I series)
Military Department papers (L/MIL series)
Political and Secret Department papers (L/PS series)
Private Office papers (L/PO series)
Proscribed Literature Collection (PIB series)
Public and Judicial Department papers (L/PJ series)

Record Department papers (L/R series)
War Staff Department papers (L/WS series)

Burmah Oil Company Collection	MSS Eur F. 156
Datta Collection	MSS Eur F. 178
Dorman-Smith Collection	MSS Eur E. 215
Indian Civil Service (District Officers) Collection	MSS Eur F. 180
Indian Police Collection	MSS Eur F. 161
Indian Tea Association Collection	MSS Eur F. 174
Irrawaddy Flotilla Company Collection	MSS Eur E. 375
Lakher Pioneer Mission Collection	MSS Eur D. 914 and F. 138
Linlithgow Collection	MSS Eur F. 125
MacDonald (I.H.) Collection	MSS Eur E. 360
McCall Collection	MSS Eur E. 361
Oral Archives Collection	MSS Eur R/ MSS Eur T
Pearce Collection	MSS Eur D. 947
Tyson Collection	MSS Eur E. 341
Wallace Collection	MSS Eur E. 338

Public Record Office, Surrey, UK

War Office Series
Information Series
Foreign Office Series

Thomas Duff Archives, Dundee University, UK

Thomas Duff & Co. Manager's Reports for Directors, 1940–44

Uttar Pradesh State Archives, Lucknow, India.

Medical Department Collections.
Political Department Collections.

B. Printed Sources

Government Publications

A Summary of Important Matters concerning the Defence Services in India, 1939–40, Delhi (no date).
Congress Responsibility for the Disturbances 1942–43, Delhi, 1943.
Correspondence with Mr. Gandhi, August 1942-April 1944, Delhi, 1944.
Matters of interest to Indian Soldiers and their families, Calcutta, 1943.
Report on the Disturbances 1942–43, Supplementary Secret Evidence, New Delhi, 1944.
Secret District Calendar of Events of the Civil Disobedience Movement, July–December 1942, Patna, 1943.

Statistical Appendices to Annual Reports of the Public Health Commissioner with the Government of India for the period 1940–44, Simla, 1947.
The Famine Enquiry Commission, Final Report, Madras, 1945.

Newspapers (Selected issues, 1939–45)

Calcutta Municipal Gazette
Civil and Military Gazette
Dehat
Forward Bloc
Harijan
Hunkar
People's War
Searchlight
The Hindustan Times
The Statesman
The Times of India

C. Secondary Sources

Printed Books

Adhikari, G. (ed), *Pakistan And National Unity*, Bombay, 1942.
Agarwal, S., *Press: Public Opinion and Government of India*, Jaipur, 1970.
Agarwal, S.N.,*The Gandhian Plan of Economic Development for India*, Bombay, 1944.
Allen, L., *Burma: The Longest War, 1941–45*, London, 1984.
Amery, L.S., *The Forward View*, London, 1935.
Andrew, C., *Secret Service: The Making of the British Intelligence Community*, London, 1985.
Arnold, D., *Police Power and Colonial Rule: Madras, 1859–1947*, Delhi, 1986.
Baird, J.W., *The Mythical World of Nazi Propaganda 1939–45*, Minneapolis, 1974.
Banerjee, B.N. et al, *People's Plan for Economic Development of India*, Delhi, 1944.
Barker, A.J.,*The March on Delhi*, London, 1963.
Barrier, N.G., *Banned: Controversial Literature and Political Control in British India 1907–1947*, Columbia, 1974.
Bayly, C.A., *Empire & Information: Intelligence gathering and social communication in India, 1780–1870*, Cambridge, 1996.
Bhargava, M.L., *Role of the Press in the Freedom Movement*, New Delhi, 1987.
Bharucha, P.C., *The North African Campaign, 1940–1943*, New Delhi, 1956.
Bhattacharya, S. and Thapar, R. (eds), *Situating Indian History*, Delhi, 1986.
Bhuyan, A.C., *The Quit India Movement, the Second World War and Indian Nationalism*, Delhi, 1975.
Brass, P. (ed), *Indian National Congress and Indian Society, 1885–1985: Ideology, Social Structure and Political Dominance*, Delhi, 1987.

Briggs, A., *The History of Broadcasting in the United Kingdom, Vol. 3: The War of Words*, London, 1970.
Brivati, B. and Jones, H. (eds),*What Difference Did the War Make?*, London, 1993.
Brown, J.M., *Modern India: The Origins of an Asian Democracy*, Delhi, 1984.
Burden, H.T., *The Nuremberg Rallies 1932-39*, London, 1967.
Burleigh, M. and Wippermann, W., *The Racial State: Germany 1933-1945*, Cambridge, 1992.
Casey, R.G., *An Australian In India*, London, 1947.
Chakrabarty, B., *Local Politics and Indian Nationalism: Midnapur, 1919-1944*, Delhi, 1997.
Chandra, B. et al, *India's Struggle for Independence, 1857-1947*, Delhi, 1979.
Chatterjee, P., *Nationalist Thought and the Colonial World: A Derivative Discourse?*, Delhi, 1986.
Chatterji, J., *Bengal Divided: Hindu Communalism and Partition, 1932-47*, Cambridge, 1994.
Chettur, S.K., *The Steel Frame And I: Life In The I.C.S*, London, 1962.
Chowdhury, N.N., *Subhas Chandra Bose and Socialism*, Calcutta, 1965.
Clews, J.C., *Communist Propaganda Techniques*, London, 1964.
Cohen, S., *The Indian Army: Its Contribution to the Development of a Nation*, Berkeley, 1971.
Constantine, S., *The Making of British Colonial Development Policy, 1914-40*, London, 1984.
Damodaran, V., *Broken Promises: Popular Protest, Indian Nationalism and the Congress Party in Bihar, 1935-1946*, New Delhi, 1992.
Darling, M.L., *The Punjab Peasant in Prosperity and Debt*, Oxford, 1925.
Das, A.N., *Agrarian Unrest and Socio-economic change in Bihar, 1900-1980*, New Delhi, 1983.
Das, S., *Communal Riots in Bengal, 1905-1947*, New Delhi, 1993.
Deb, J.M., *Blood and Tears*, Bombay, 1945.
Dewey, C., *Anglo-Indian Attitudes: The mind of the Indian Civil Service*, london, 1993.
Donald, J. and Hall, S. (eds), *Politics and Ideology: A Reader*, Milton Keynes, 1986.
Druhe, D.N., *Soviet Russia and Indian Communism, 1917-47*, New York, 1959.
Dutta, A., *Assam in the Freedom Movement*, Calcutta, 1991.
Ellul, J., *Propaganda: The Formation of Men's Attitudes*, New York, 1973.
Engels, D. and Marks, S. (eds),*Contesting Colonial Hegemony: State and Society in Africa and India*, London, 1994.
French, P., *Libery or Death: India's Journey to Independence and Division*, London, 1997.
Gallagher, J., Johnson, G. and Seal (eds), A., *Locality, Province and Nation: Essays on Indian Politics, 1870-1940*, Cambridge, 1973.
Gamson, W.A., *Talking Politics*, Cambridge, 1992.
Ganpuley, N.G., *Netaji in Germany*, Bombay, 1959.
Gellner, E., *Nations and Nationalism*, Oxford, 1983.

Ghose, B.C., *The Development of Tea Industry in the district of Jalpaiguri, 1869–1968*, Calcutta, 1970.
Ghosh, K.K., *The Indian National Army: The Second Front of the Indian Independence Movement*, Meerut, 1969.
Gombrich, E.H., *Myth and Reality in German Wartime Broadcasts*, London, 1970.
Gopal, M., *Freedom Movement and the Press: The Role of Hindi Newspapers*, New Delhi, 1980.
Graml, H. et al, *The German Resistance to Hitler*, London, 1970.
Greenough, P.R., *Prosperity and Misery in Modern Bengal: The Famine of 1943–44*, New York, 1982.
Gupta, P.S., *Imperialism and the British Labour Movement, 1914–1964*, London, 1975.
——, *Radio and the Raj 1921–47*, Calcutta, 1995.
Gupta, R., *The Bihar Peasantry and the Kisan Sabhas*, Delhi, 1982.
Hale, J., *Radio Power: Propaganda and International Broadcasting*, London, 1975.
Hasan, M., *Nationalism and Communalism in Indian Politics*, New Delhi, 1979.
Hayashida, T., *Netaji Subhas Chandra Bose*, Bombay, 1970.
Haynes, D.E., *Rhetoric and Ritual in Colonial India: The shaping of a Public Culture in Surat City, 1852–1928*, Berkeley, 1991.
Henningham, S., *Peasant Movements in Colonial India; North Bihar 1917–1942*, Canberra, 1982.
Hinz, B., *Art in the Third Reich*, Oxford, 1980.
Hobsbawm, E. and Ranger, T. (eds),*The Invention of Tradition*, Cambridge, 1993.
Hoffmann, P., *German Resistance to Hitler*, Cambridge, 1988.
Howe, S., *Anticolonialism in British Politics: The Left and the End of Empire, 1918–1964*, Oxford, 1993.
Hunt, R and Harrison, J., *The District Officer in India, 1930–1947*, London, 1980.
Hutchins, F.G., *Spontaneous Revolution: The Quit India Movement*, Delhi, 1971.
Israel, M., *Communications and power: Propaganda and the press in the Indian nationalist struggle, 1920–1947*, Cambridge, 1994.
Jalal, A., *The Sole Spokesman: Jinnah, the Muslim League and the Demand for Pakistan*, Cambridge, 1985.
Jha, S., *Political Elites in Bihar*, Delhi, 1972.
Josh, B., *Communist Movement in Punjab, 1926–47*, Delhi, 1979.
——, *The Colonial State, the Left and the National Movement, Volume II: 1934–41*, New Delhi, 1992.
Joshi, P.C., *Release The Patriots: To Rally The People For The Defence of The Motherland*, Bombay, 1942.
——,*Omnibus Reply to Congress Working Committee's Charges*, Bombay, 1945.
Kaura, U.*Muslims and Indian Nationalism: The Emergence of the Demand for India's Partition*, New Delhi, 1977.
Kaushik, K., *Russian Revolution (1917) and Indian Nationalism: Studies of Lajpat Rai, Subhas Chandra Bose and Ram Manohar Lohia*, Delhi, 1984.

Kershaw, I., *The Nazi Dictatorship. Problems and Perspectives of Interpretation*, London, 1985.
Kiernan, V.G., *European Empires From Conquest To Collapse, 1815–1960*, Leicester, 1982.
Kimball, W.F. (ed), *Churchill and Roosevelt: The Complete Correspondence* (3 volumes), Princeton, 1984.
Kirby, S.W.,*The Decisive Battles*, London, 1961.
Knight, H., *Food Administration in India, 1939–1947*, Stanford, 1954
Kumar, R., *Essays in the Social History of Modern India*, Delhi, 1983.
Kumar, U.K., *Political Prisoners in India*, Delhi, 1998.
Lebra, J., *Jungle Alliance: Japan and the Indian National Army*, Singapore, 1971.
Li, L., *The Japanese Army in North China, 1937–1941: Problems of Political and Economic Control*, Oxford, 1975.
Liu, A.P.L., *Communications and National Integration in Communist China*, Berkeley, 1971.
Longer, V., *Red Coats to Olive Green: A History of the Indian Army, 1860–1974*, Bombay, 1974.
Low, D.A. (ed),*Congress and the Raj*, London, 1977.
Lucas-Phillips, C.E., *Springboard to Victory*, London, 1966.
Mackenzie, J.M., *Propaganda and Empire: The Manipulation of British Public Opinion, 1880–1960*, Manchester, 1984.
Majumdar, R.C., *History of the Freedom Movement, Volume 3*, Calcutta, 1963.
Mansergh, N. (ed), *India: The Transfer of Power (12 Volumes)*, London, 1970–1983.
Martin, J.L., *International Propaganda: Its Legal and Diplomatic Control*, Minneapolis, 1958.
Mason, P., *A Shaft of Sunlight*, London, 1978.
Mazumdar, A., *Indian Press and Freedom Struggle, 1937–42*, Calcutta, 1993.
McKay, A., *Tibet and the British Raj: The Frontier Cadres 1904–1947*, Richmond, 1997.
McLaine, I., *Ministry of Morale: Home Front Morale and the Ministry of Information in World War II*, London, 1979.
Meran, B.*Non-fiction film: A Critical History*, London, 1974.
Merson, A., *Communist Resistance in Nazi Germany*, London, 1987.
Misra, B.B., *The Indian Political Parties*, Delhi, 1976.
Mitchell, R.H., *Thought Control in Pre-War Japan*, London, 1976.
Moitra, M., *A History of Indian Journalism*, Calcutta, 1969.
Moon, P., (ed), *Wavell: The Viceroy's Journal*, London, 1973.
Moore, R.J., *Escape From Empire: The Attlee Government and the Indian Problem*, Oxford, 1983.
Mukherjee, H. (ed), *US: A People's Symposium*, Calcutta, 1943.
Mukherjee, S., *The Story of the Calcutta Theatres: 1753–1980*, Calcutta, 1982.
Nag, B., *Netaji Speaks: A Collection of Speeches and Writings*, Calcutta, 1973.
Natrajan, J., *History of Indian Journalism*, Delhi, 1955.
——, *A History of the Press in India*, Bombay, 1962.

Noronha, R.P., *A Tale Told By An Idiot*, New Delhi, 1976.
Orwell, G., *The War Broadcasts*, London, 1987.
——, *The War Commentaries*, London, 1987.
Overstreet, G.D. and Windmiller, M., *Communism in India*, Bombay, 1960.
Page, D., *Prelude to Partition*, Oxford, 1982.
Pandey, G. (ed), *The Indian Nation in 1942*, Calcutta, 1989.
Panjabi, K.L., *The Civil Servant in India*, Bombay, 1965.
Pati, B., *Resisting Domination: Peasants, Tribals and the National Movement in Orissa 1920–1950*, New Delhi, 1993.
—— (ed), *Turbulent Times: India 1940–44*, Mumbai,1998.
Patra, K.M., *Orissa State Legislature And Freedom Struggle 1912–47*, New Delhi, 1979.
Pe, T., *What Happened in Burma: the Frank Revelations of a young Burmese Revolutionary Leader who has recently escaped from Burma to India*, Allahabad, 1943.
Potter, D.C., *India's Political Administrators, 1919–1983*, Oxford, 1983.
Pronay, N. and Thorpe, F., *British Official Films in the Second World War*, Oxford, 1980.
Raina, B.L. (ed), *Official History of the Indian Armed Forces in the Second World War 1939–45:Medical Services (Administration)*, Kanpur, 1953.
——, *Official History of the Indian Armed Forces in the Second World War 1939–45 (Medical Services): Preventive Medicine (Nutrition, Malaria Control and Prevention of Diseases)*, Kanpur, 1961.
Rau, M.C., *Journalism and Politics*, New Delhi, 1984.
Reeves, P., *Landlords and Governments in Uttar Pradesh: A study of their relations under Zamindari abolition*, Bombay, 1991.
Robb, P., *The Evolution of British Policy towards Indian Politics, 1880–1920: Essays on Colonial Attitudes, Imperial Strategies and Bihar*, New Delhi, 1992.
Robins, L., *Policing the Raj*, London, 1985.
Roy, M.N et al, *India And War*, Lucknow, 1942.
——, *I.N.A and the August Revolution*, Calcutta, 1946.
Sareen, T.R., *Select Documents on the Indian National Army*, Delhi, 1988.
Sarkar, S., *'Popular Movements' and 'Middle Class' Leadership in Late Colonial India, Perspectives and Problems of a 'History from Below'*, Calcutta, 1983.
——, *Modern India, 1885–1947*, Delhi, 1983.
——, *Marxian Approaches to the History of Indian Nationalism*, Calcutta, 1990.
Sen, A.K., *Poverty and Famines: An essay on Entitlement and Deprivation*, Oxford, 1981.
Sen, B., *Rural Bengal in Ruins*, Bombay, 1945.
Sen, S., *Muslim Politics in Bengal, 1937–47*, New Delhi, 1976.
Sen, S.P., *The Indian Press*, Calcutta, 1967.
Sharma, S.R. (ed), *Netaji: His Life and Work*, Agra, 1948.
Singh, A.I., *The Origins of Partition of India, 1936–1947*, Delhi, 1987.
Singh, D., *The Rebel President: A Biographical Study of Subhas Chandra Bose*, Lahore, 1941.
——, *Netaji Speaks to the Nation, 1928–1945*, Lahore, 1946.

Skocpol, T., *States and Social Revolutions: A Comparative Analysis of France, Russia and China*, Cambridge, 1979.
Swann, P., *The British Documentary Film Movement, 1926–1946*, Cambridge, 1989.
Swinson, A., *The Battle of Kohima*, New York, 1971.
Tallents, S.G., *The Projection of England*, London, 1932.
Tatsuo, H., *Netaji Subhas Chandra Bose*, Bombay, 1970.
Taylor, P.M., *The Projection of Britain: British overseas publicity and propaganda*, Cambridge, 1981.
Taylor, R., *Film Propaganda: Soviet Russia and Nazi Germany*, London, 1979.
Thaker, J., *Flaming Sword*, Bombay, 1942.
Thorne, C., *Allies of a Kind*, London, 1978.
Tomlinson, B.R., *The Indian National Congress and the Raj, 1929–42: The Penultimate Phase*, London, 1976.
Vasudev, A., *Liberty and License in the Indian Cinema*, Delhi, 1978.
Venkatramani, M.S. and Shrivastava, B.K, *Quit India: The American Response to the 1942 Struggle*, New Delhi, 1979.
Voigt, J.H., *India in the Second World War*, New Delhi, 1987.
Welch, D., *Nazi Propaganda: The Power and the Limitations*, London, 1983.
——, *The Third Reich: Politics and Propaganda*, London, 1995.
West, W.J., *Truth Betrayed*, London, 1987.
Woodruff, P., *The Men who ruled India, Vol. 2: The Guardians*, London, 1965.
Wykes, A., *The Nuremberg Rallies*, New York, 1970.
Zaidi, Z.H. (ed), *M.A Jinnah – Ispahani Correspondence*, Karachi, 1976.
Zeman, Z.A.B., *Nazi Propaganda*, Oxford, 1973.

Published Articles

Aldrich, R.J., 'American Intelligence and the British Raj: The OSS, the SSU and India, 1942–1947', *Intelligence and National Security*, Spring 1998.
Anderson, D.M., 'Policing the Settler State: colonial hegemony in Kenya, 1900–1952', in D. Engels and S. Marks (eds),*Contesting Colonial Hegemony: State and Society in Africa and India*, London, 1994.
Arnold, D., 'Quit India in Madras: Hiatus or Climacteric?', in G. Pandey (ed), *The Indian Nation in 1942*, Calcutta, 1989.
——, 'Public Health and Public Power: medicine and hegemony in colonial India', in D. Engels and S. Marks (eds), *Contesting Colonial Hegemony: State and Society in Africa and India*, London, 1994.
——, 'Colonial medicine in transition: Medical research in India, 1910–47', *SAR*, 14, 1, 1994.
Bayly, C.A., 'The Pre-History of 'Communalism'? Religious Conflict in India, 1700–1860', *MAS*, 19, 2, 1985.
——, 'Knowing the Country: Empire and Information in India', *MAS*, 27, 1, 1993.
——, 'Returning the British to South Asian History: The Limits of Colonial Hegemony', *South Asia*, 17, 2, 1994.

Bhattacharya, S., 'The Colonial State And The Communist Party of India, 1942–45: A Reappraisal', *SAR*, 15, 1, 1995.

——, 'Wartime policies of State Censorship and the Civilian Population: Eastern India, 1939–45', *SAR*, 17, 2, 1997.

——, 'Re-devising Jennerian Vaccines?: European technologies, Indian innovation and the control of smallpox in South Asia, 1850–1950', *Social Scientist*, Vol. 26, 11–12, Nov.–Dec. 1998.

——, '"A Grear Destiny": The British colonial state and the advertisement of post-war reconstruction in India, 1942–45', *SAR*, 19, 1, 1999. Jointly authored with B. Zachariah.

Bose, S., 'Starvation amidst Plenty: The Making of Famine in Bengal, Honan and Tonkin, 1943–46', *MAS*, 24, 4, 1990.

Chakrabarty, B., 'The Communal Award of 1932 and its Implications in Bengal', *MAS*, 23, 3, 1989.

——, 'Jawaharlal Nehru and Planning 1938–41: India at the Crossroads', *MAS*, 26, 2, 1992.

——, 'Political Mobilization in the Localities: The 1942 Quit India Movement in Midnapur', *MAS*, 26, 4, 1992.

Chander, S., 'Congress-Raj Conflict and the Rise of the Muslim League in the Ministry Period, 1937–39', *MAS*, 21, 2, 1987.

Chatterjee, P., 'Was there a Hegemonic Project of the Colonial State?', in D. Engels and S. Marks (eds), *Contesting Colonial Hegemony: State and Society in Africa and India*, London, 1994.

Chowdhry, P., 'Social Support Base and Electoral Politics: The Congress in Colonial Southeast Punjab', *MAS*, 25,4, 1991.

Cohn, B.S., 'Representing Authority in Victorian India', in E. Hobsbawn and T. Ranger (eds), *The Invention of Tradition*, Cambridge, 1993.

Damodaran, V., 'Azad Dastas and Dacoit Gangs: The Congress and Underground Activity in Bihar, 1942–44', *MAS*, 26,3, 1992.

Dyson, T. and A. Maharatna, 'Excess mortality during the Bengal famine: A re-evaluation', *IESHR*, 28, 3, 1991.

Engels, D., 'Modes of Knowledge, Modes of Power: universities in 19th-century India', in D. Engels and S. Marks (eds), *Contesting Colonial Hegemony: State and Society in Africa and India*, London, 1994.

Epstein, S., 'District Officers in Decline: The Erosion of British authority in the Bombay countryside, 1919 to 1947', *MAS*, 16, 3, 1982.

Ewing, A., 'The Indian Civil Service 1919–1924: Service Department and the Response in London and in Delhi', *MAS*, 18, 1, 1984.

Figlio, K., 'Oral History and the Unconscious', *History Workshop*, Issue 26, 1988.

Fisher, M.H., 'The Office of Akhbar Nawis: The Transition from Mughal to British Forms', *MAS*, 27, 1, 1993.

Forbes, G., 'Managing Midwifery in India', in *Contesting Colonial Hegemony: State and Society in Africa and India*, London, 1994.

Gervase Clarence-Smith, W., 'The Organization of 'Consent' in British West Africa, 1820s to 1960s', in D. Engels and S. Marks (eds), *Contesting Colonial Hegemony: State and Society in Africa and India*, London, 1994.

Ghose, A.K., 'Food Supply and Starvation: A Study of Famines with reference to the Indian Sub-Continent', *Oxford Economic Papers*, Volume 34, Number 2, July 1982.

Goswami, O., 'The Bengal Famine of 1943: re-examining the data', *IESHR*, 27, 4, 1990.
Greenough, P.R., 'Indian Famines and Peasant Victims: the Case of Bengal in 1943–44', *MAS*, 14, 2, 1980.
——, 'Political Mobilization and the Underground Literature of the Quit India Movement, 1942–44', *MAS*, 17,3, 1983.
Hasan, Z., 'The Congress in a District, 1930–46: Problems of Political Mobilization', *IESHR*, 23, 1, 1986.
Heehs, P., 'Foreign Influences on Bengali Revolutionary Terrorism, 1902–1908', *MAS*, 28, 3, 1994.
Henningham, S., 'Bureaucracy and Control in India's Great Landed Estates: The Raj Darbhanga of Bihar, 1878 to 1950', *MAS*, 17, 1, 1983.
Heskett, J., 'Art and Design in Nazi Germany', *History Workshop*, Issue 6, 1978.
Hobsbawm, E., 'Mass-Producing Traditions: Europe, 1870–1914', in E. Hobsbawn and T. Ranger (eds), *The Invention of Tradition*, Cambridge, 1993.
Horn, D., 'Youth Resistance in the Third Reich: A Social Portrait', *Journal of Social History*, 1973.
Hunt, L., 'The Rhetoric of Revolution in France', *History Workshop*, Issue 15, 1983.
Jalal, A., 'Inheriting the Raj: Jinnah and the Governor Generalship Issue', *MAS*, 19, 1, 1985.
Kamat, M.N., The War Years and the Sholapur Cotton Textile Industry, *Social Scientist*, Vol. 26, 11–12, Nov.–Dec. 1998.
Kumar, A., 'Visions of Cultural Transformation: The IPTA in Bengal, 1940–44', in B. Pati (ed), *Turbulent Times: India 1940–44*, Mumbai,1998.
Kumar, R., 'From Swaraj to Purna Swaraj: Nationalist Politics in the City of Bombay, 1920–1932', in D.A Low (ed), *Congress and the Raj*, London, 1977.
Lyons, M., 'The Power to Heal: African auxiliaries in colonial Belgian Congo and Uganda', in D. Engels and S. Marks (eds), *Contesting Colonial Hegemony: State and Society in Africa and India*, London, 1994.
Maharatna, A., 'Malaria ecology, relief provision and regional variation in mortality during the Bengal famine of 1943–44', *SAR*, 13, 1, 1993.
Masselos, J., 'Bombay, August 1942: Re-readings in a Nationalist Text', in B. Pati (ed), *Turbulent Times: India 1940–44*, Mumbai,1998.
McKay, A.C., 'The Cinderella of the Foreign Service: The Role of the British Trade Agents in Tibet 1910–1920', *SAR*, 12, 2, 1992.
——, 'The Other 'Great Game': Politics and Sport in Tibet, 1904–47', *History of Sport*, 11, 3, December 1994.
Menon, V., 'The Indian National Congress and Mass Mobilisation: A Study of the U.P. 1937–39', *Studies in History*, Vol. II,.2, 1980.
Mitra, C., 'Popular Uprising in 1942: The Case of Ballia', in G. Pandey (ed), *The Indian Nation in 1942*, Calcutta, 1989.
Mohapatra, P.P., 'Class conflict and agrarian regimes in Chotanagpur, 1860–1950', *IESHR*, 28, 1, 1981.
Moore, R.J., 'Jinnah and the Pakistan Demand', *MAS*, 17, 4, 1983.
Morris-Jones, W.H., 'The Transfer of Power, 1947: A View from the Sidelines', *MAS*, 16, 1, 1982.

Omvedt, G., 'The Satara Prati Sarkar', in G. Pandey (ed), *The Indian Nation in 1942*, Calcutta, 1989.
Pandey, D., 'Congress-Muslim League Relations 1937–39: The Parting of the Ways', *MAS*, 12,4, 1978.
Pandey, G., 'Mobilization in a Mass Movement: Congress 'Propaganda' in the United Provinces (India), 1930–34', *MAS*, 9, 2, 1975.
Pati, B., 'Storm over Malkangiri: A Note on Laxman Naiko's Revolt, 1942', in G. Pandey (ed), *The Indian Nation in 1942*, Calcutta, 1989.
——, 'The Climax of Popular Protest: The Quit India Movement in Orissa', in B. Pati (ed), *Turbulent Times: India 1940–44*, Mumbai,1998.
——, 'Siting the Body: Perspectives on Health and Medicine in Colonial Orissa', *Social Scientist*, Vol. 26, Nos. 11–12, Nov.–Dec. 1998 (July 1999).
Portelli, A., 'The Peculiarities of Oral History', *History Workshop*, Issue 12, 1981.
Pronay, N., 'British Newsreels in the 1930s, 1: Audiences and Producers', *History*, 56 (1971)
——, 'British Newsreels in the 1930s, 2: Their Policies and Impact', *History*, 57 (1972).
Ranger, T., 'The Invention of Traditions in Colonial Africa', in E. Hobsbawn and T. Ranger (eds), *The Invention of Tradition*, Cambridge, 1993.
Rathbone, R., 'Law, Lawyers and Politics in Ghana in the 1940s', in D. Engels and S. Marks (eds), *Contesting Colonial Hegemony: State and Society in Africa and India*, London, 1994.
Ray, R., 'Man, Woman and the Novel: The Rise of a New Consciousness in Bengal (1858–1947)', *IEHSR*, 14,1, 1980.
Ray, R., 'The Changing Fortunes of the Bengali Gentry under Colonial Rule-Pal Chaudhuris of Mahesganj, 1800–1950', *MAS*, 21, 3, 1987.
Raychaudhuri, T., 'Dominance, Hegemony and the Colonial State: the Indian and African experiences', in D. Engels and S. Marks (eds), *Contesting Colonial Hegemony: State and Society in Africa and India*, London, 1994.
Reeves, N., 'The Power of Film Propaganda – myth or reality?', *Historical Journal of Film, Radio and Television*, Vol. 13, No. 2, 1993.
Sanyal, H., 'The Quit India Movement in Medinipur District', in G. Pandey (ed), *The Indian Nation in 1942*, Calcutta, 1989.
Sarkar, S., 'Hegemony and Historical Practice', in D. Engels and S. Marks (eds), *Contesting Colonial Hegemony: State and Society in Africa and India*, London, 1994.
Seal, A., 'Imperialism and Nationalism in India', *MAS*, 7, 3, 1973.
Selth, A., 'Race and Resistance in Burma, 1942–45', *MAS*, 20, 3, 1986.
Shaikh, F., 'Muslims and Political Representation in Colonial India: The Making of Pakistan', *MAS*, 20, 3, 1986.
Sheel, A., 'The Peasantry and Nationalism in Late Colonial India', *Studies in History*, 2, 2 (n.s.), 1986.
Smyth, R., 'Britain's African Colonies and British Propaganda during the Second World War', *JICH*, 14, 1985.
Southard, B., 'Colonial Politics and Women's Rights: Woman Suffrage Campaigns in Bengal, British India in the 1920s', *MAS*, 27, 2, 1993.
Srimanjiri, 'Denial, Dissent and Hunger: War-time Bengal, 1942–44, in B. Pati (ed), *Turbulent Times: India 1940–44*, Mumbai,1998.

Talbot, I., 'The Role of the Crowd in the Muslim League Struggle for Pakistan', *JICH*, 21, 2.
——, 'Planning for Pakistan: The Planning Committee of the All-India Muslim League 1943–46', *MAS*, 28, 4, 1994.
Tan, T.Y., 'Maintaining the Military Districts: Civil-Military Integration and District Soldiers' Boards in the Punjab, 1919–1939', *MAS*, 28, 4, 1994.
Tilly, L.A., 'People's History and Social Science History', *International Journal of Oral History*, Vol. 7, No. 4, Fall 1983.
Tinker, H., 'Burma's Struggle for Independence: The Transfer of Power Thesis Re-Examined', *MAS*, 20, 3, 1986.
Tomlinson, B.R., 'Indo-British Relations in the Post-Colonial Era: The Sterling Balances Negotiations 1947–49', *JICH*, 13, 1985.
Vaughan, M., 'Health and Hegemony: representation of disease and the creation of the colonial subject in Nyasaland', in D. Engels and S. Marks (eds), *Contesting Colonial Hegemony: State and Society in Africa and India*, London, 1994.
Zachariah, B., 'Imperial Economic Policy for India, 1942–44: Confusion and Readjustment', in B. Pati (ed), *Turbulent Times: India 1940–44*, Mumbai,1998.

Unpublished Theses

Aiyar, S. 'Violence and the State in the Partition of Punjab: 1947–48', unpublished Ph.D. thesis, University of Cambridge, 1994.
Charrier, P. 'India, Britain and the Colombo Plan', Unpublished Ph.D. thesis, University of Cambridge, 1995.
Chatterji, J. 'Communal Politics and the Partition of Bengal, 1932–1947', Unpublished Ph.D. thesis, University of Cambridge, 1990.
Kamtekar, I. 'The End of the Colonial State in India, 1942–47', Unpublished Ph.D. thesis, University of Cambridge, 1989.
Kudaisya, G. 'State Power and the Erosion of Colonial Authority in Uttar Pradesh, India, 1930–42', Unpublished Ph.D. thesis, University of Cambridge, 1992.
Narain, N. 'Co-option and Control: The Role of the Colonial Army in India, 1918–1947', Unpublished Ph.D. thesis, University of Cambridge, 1993
Tan, T.Y. 'The Military and the State in Colonial India, 1900–1939', Unpublished Ph.D. thesis, University of Cambridge, 1992.
Zachariah, B. 'Controlling The Economy, Planning The Nation: The Origins of Economic Planning in India, 1930–1947', Unpublished M.Phil. thesis, University of Cambridge.

Personally conducted interviews

Interview with I. Banerjee at Cambridge on 11 November 1993.
Interview with N.C. Banerjee at New Delhi, 21 October 1993.
Interview with D. Powell at Saffron Walden on 6 July 1994.

Index

A.C. Cossor Ltd. 66–67, 69
aboriginal tribes 20
aerodromes/airports 19
affrays 24–25, 132
African troops 23, 190
All Bengal Food and Famine Relief Committee 35
All India Congress Committee 7, 17, 154, 164, 167
Allahabad Legal Aid Committee 35
Allied army/personnel 1, 27–28, 41, 75, 84, 186
Allied Forces [United States of America] Ordinance of 1942 25
All-India Newspaper Editors' Conference 128, 131–132, 135
All-India Radio 65–66, 68–69, 76–78, 124, 127, 160
Aman Sabhas 7
ambulance trains 176
America 25, 28, 67, 174, 192
American army/forces 19, 23–27, 44
Amrita Bazar Patrika 31, 33,
anti-malaria operations 86, 93, 176
Army Bureau of Current Affairs 180
Army in India Training Manuals 183
Army School of Education 184
ARP publicity 76
Assam Access Road 19
Associated Press of India 130
atrocities 32, 132–133, 139, 158, 161, 185–186
Auchinleck, Claude 210

Axis broadcasts 178
Axis forces 1, 136–137, 186

Banerjee, K.K. 137
Bangkok 29, 124
Barnes, W.A. 181
Bay of Bengal 19
Bell, J.M.G. 78
Ben, Mira 21
Bengal famine 2, 31–32, 88, 204
Bose, Subhas Chandra 189
British Broadcasting Corporation 67, 78, 124, 127
British Movietone News 73
British/Indian army 23–24, 38, 168, 183, 190, 204, 209–210
Bureau of Public Information 80, 95
Burma 1, 17–18, 28, 173, 186–187
Burma rice 28

Calcutta 19, 21, 88
Calcutta Committee 76, 82
Central Board of Information 7, 72, 74
Central Bureau of Public Information 161
Central Government Servants' Association 211
Central Intelligence Department 127, 180
Chief Broadcasting Censor 124
Chief Postal Censor 128, 181
Chief Press Adviser 26, 135
Chief Telegraph Censor 181

INDEX

China 1, 24, 124, 186
Chinese army 23–24, 44
Chungking 124
Churchill, Winston 134, 180
civil defence 22, 42, 80, 82
Civil Disobedience 7, 151–152
Civil Liaison Officers 71
civilian anti-malaria officers 89
civilian malaria hospitals 176
collective fines 139
Commercial Distributing Committee 82
Communist Party of India 28, 32–33, 83, 92, 137, 140, 161, 165, 168, 204–206, 208
Communist Party of India activists 28, 32, 92, 138, 166, 168, 204–206, 208
Communist Party of India politbureau 23, 34, 205
Congress ministries 7, 17, 35–37
Congress Responsibility for the Disturbances, 1942–43 159
Congress Samachar 27
Congress Socialist Party 33, 161
Congress underground 17, 27–28, 30–31, 34, 43, 168, 208
Controller of Broadcasting 124
Criminal Law Amendment Act 126
Criminal Procedure Code 137
Cripp's Mission 94, 154, 162
Current Affairs 187

Das Gupta, Satish 21
Dawn 27
dearness allowances 85
Defence Exhibition Train 79
Defence of India Rules 40, 92, 125, 128, 132, 136, 182
Dehat 77
demobilisation 189
denial/scorched earth policy 21–23, 28, 152
Digboi 21
Director of Military Operations and Intelligence 122, 183
Directorate of Civil Supplies 83
District Agricultural Supervisors 81
District Local Boards 6, 95
District Press Advisers 125
District Soldier's Boards 6, 179
District War Committees 80, 81
documentaries 73
Duniya 183

Eastern Army Command 38, 44, 71, 81, 177
Emergency Commissioning Scheme 89
Emergency Powers Ordnance of 1940 126
engineering department 19
epidemics 30, 32
Eram incident 43
Essential Services (Maintenance) Ordinance of 1941 41
evacuees 21, 41
Excess Profit Tax 40, 92
Extracts From Japanese Diaries 188

famine/famine conditions 29, 31, 88–90, 204
Fauji Akhbar 183
Fazlul Huq 22, 23, 139
Film Advisory Board 74
Film Publicity Board 72
First World War 6
food debate 32
food department 30
food riots 96
food shortages 29, 88, 96, 203–204
Forward Bloc 161, 205
free trade 29–31, 44, 88

Gandhi, M.K. 17–18, 21, 23, 26, 34, 137, 151, 153, 155, 160–161, 164, 167
Ganguly, Khitish Chandra 36
General Headquarters (India) 4, 81, 84, 89, 91, 174–175, 179, 181, 183, 185, 202, 211
Government of India Act of 1935 123
grain shops 84
grainshops 84
Greater Asian Co-Prosperity Scheme 186
Grow More Food campaign 80–81
Gurkhas 187, 210

239

Harijan 165
Hayley, T.T.S. 78
Herbert, John 22–23, 133
Hindu 132
Hindu Mahasabha 137, 165
Hindustan Relief Fund 31
Hindustan Times 31, 33, 166
Holland 124
Hong Kong 29

India Office 68
Indian Army Medical Corps 90, 176
Indian Army Rules 182
Indian Federation of Labour 138
Indian Information 183
Indian Information 76
Indian Jute Mills Association 82
Indian Legislative Assembly 27, 32, 158, 166
Indian Medical Department 89, 175
Indian Medical Service 87, 89, 175
Indian Movietone News 73
Indian Nation 167
Indian National Army 2, 178, 189, 209
Indian National Congress 17, 20, 24, 30, 33, 36, 129, 140, 150–152, 160, 165, 191, 205–206
Indian News Parade 95
Indian Penal Code 126
Indian Tea Association 82
Information Films of India 73
internal censorship 182

Jang Ki Khabren 183
Japanese army/invasion 1, 17, 19, 22, 41, 43, 92, 124, 132, 151, 178, 188

Khadi Pratisthan 21
Khan, Liaquat Ali 167
Khan, Yamin 167
Krishak Praja Party 36

labour 39, 40, 41, 84, 85, 92, 133, 141
labour battalions 20, 40, 86–87, 92, 141

Lend Lease 40, 70
Linlithgow, Marquess of 17, 163
Luxembourg 124

Madras Sappers 187
Maharaja of Parlakhimedi 32
Malaria Forward Treatment Units 177
Malaria Institute of India 87
Malaya 187
Marwari Relief Association 204
Maxwell, Reginald 7, 153, 162
medical facilities 85–87, 89, 173
medical graduates 89
medical licentiates 90
Medical Personnel (Priority) Committee 176
Military Food Laboratory 174
military hospitals 176–178
military medical services 175–177
military nursing services 177
mines/mining concerns 40, 86
Momin Conference 35, 204
Mookerjee, Shyama Prasad 139–140
Mountbatten, Lord 168
Muslim League 27, 165–166, 204–206

Narain, Jai Prakash 211–212
National Defence Council 160
National Herald 129
National Relief Committee 35
National War Front 81, 160–161, 166–167
National Weeks 33
Natrajan, J. 157
naval mutiny 209
Nazimuddin 28
Nehru, Jawaharlal 155
Non-Cooperation Movement of 1920–21 7
Noon Firoz Khan Noon 189

Olver, S.J.L. 162
Operation Asylum 192
Orissa Relief Committee 35

Padre's Hour 190
Paper Control Oders of 1942 130

INDEX

Patna Daily News 78
People's Volunteer Brigades 22
People's War 32, 140, 165–166
Permanent Economic Adviser to the Government of India 87–88
Philippines 187
police 24, 42, 168
Policy Committee on [the] Re-settlement and Re-employment of troops 189
Port Committees 41, 85
ports 19
Prasad, Rajendra 21
Press and Registration of Books Act of 1867 125
Priorities Committees 85
propaganda vans 75
Provincial Congress Committees 22, 152, 156
provincial elections of 1937 7
Provincial Labour Supply Committees 87
Provincial Press Advisory Committees 129, 133
Public Information Bureau 76
public protests 27, 94
Public Relations Committees 161
Publicity Planning and Co-ordination Board 80
Puckle, Frederick 68, 151, 154, 156–157
Punjab 6

Quit India Movement 1, 17–18, 30, 33, 35, 43, 77, 131, 132, 139, 158–159, 164, 167, 189, 208

Radical Democratic Party 83, 137, 138, 204
Radio Relay Services 71
railways 19, 41
Rajagopalachari, C.R. 154
Ramgarh 173
Rangoon 29, 42, 129
rationing 83, 88, 173, 204
refugees 31, 88–89, 133, 204
Reginald Maxwell 7
Regional Transport Controllers 85
Release and Resettlement 189

requisitioning 20, 23, 96, 173
Reuters 131
road communications 19
Rowlands, Archibald 68
Royal Indian Air Force 19
rumours 37
Rushbrook Williams 67

Sahajanand Saraswati 34
Sahay, Vishnu 167
Saigon 124
Sansar 134
satyagraha of 1940 18
Singapore 17–18, 29
Slim, William 187
Smith, Arthur 211
Some Facts About The Disturbances, 1942–43 161
South East Asia Command 4, 38, 71, 175, 187, 190
starvation deaths 31–32
subsidies 6
Sufferer's Relief Committee 35

Talking Points 77, 82
Tea Districts Emigrant Labour Act 86
The Statesman 31
Times of India 82
Tottenham, Richard 151, 156–157, 162–163
Twentieth Century Fox 73

Ujhar Sahajya Office 21
Unit Security Officer 181
United Planters Association 82
United Press of India 130
United Provinces Tenancy Act 179

Viceroy's Executive Council 155–156
Vichy France 124
Village Broadcasting Plan 69
Village Publicity Scheme 74–75
Vishwa Bandhu 165
Voice of America 68

War in Pictures 183
war industries/works 39, 40, 85

War Risks (Factories) Insurance Ordinance 40
War Risks (Goods) Insurance Ordinance 39
War Transport Board 85
Wardha Resolutions 154, 159

Wavell, Archibald 32, 88, 161, 163, 168, 187
Williams, Rushbrook 67
Winning The Peace 187
women medical practitioners 89